D1545939

JOAN OF ARC

Other books by John Holland Smith

The Great Schism

Constantine the Great

Francis of Assisi

Nine Days to Eternity

There is no Peace

The Relic

Joan of Arc

*John
Holland Smith*

SIDGWICK & JACKSON
LONDON

First published in Great Britain in 1973
by Sidgwick and Jackson Limited
Copyright © 1973 by John Holland Smith

ISBN 0 283 97943 7

Printed in Great Britain by
Morrison and Gibb Ltd., London and Edinburgh
for Sidgwick and Jackson Limited
1 Tavistock Chambers, Bloomsbury Way
London WC1A 2SG

Contents

Illustrations

We are most grateful to Photographie Bulloz for permission to reproduce plates 4, 5, 6, 7, 8, 9, 10, 11, 12, 13 and 16; to Alexander Dru for plates 2 and 15; to the National Portrait Gallery for plate 1; to Giraudon for plates 14 and 17; and to Segalat & Cie for the plates on pages 87 and 119.

'For Wannie and Clarrie'

1

Joan's France

Joan of Domrémy, who called herself *La Pucelle de Dieu*, 'God's Virgin', and is now often called the Maid of Orléans, was neither a witch queen nor a protestant leader. She never fought for women's rights, she was only briefly a heroine and her devotees found it a hard task to prove that she was really a saint. She was not, as writers more romantic than realistic have claimed, a queen's bastard in disguise, nor did she, as they have also claimed, survive the fire laid for her at Rouen. The truth about her is at one and the same time more straightforward and more strange. She was, as she said, an unlettered country girl with a message for her king. She meddled in the machinery of state till its heavy cogs caught and crushed her. Both before and after her death, what she symbolized was greater than what she was. What makes her unforgettable is the inevitability of her destruction as well as the unforeseeable measure of her success.

It is remarkable how little is known about God's Virgin Joan apart from what she herself revealed. French sources say little about her and English less. Most of the towns of the Loire Valley and several elsewhere in France are crowded with her statues, portraits and alleged relics, but none of the likenesses is authentic and few if any of the relics are genuine. The only surviving personal links with her are her signatures on three letters that she dictated, one in November 1429 to the citizens of Rouen and two in March 1430 to the people of Rheims—if those signatures are genuine. Handwriting experts say that between the earlier and later examples the writer seems to have learned self-confidence in handling a pen and probably in other aspects of life as well. Joan herself said that when she left home in 1427–8 she 'knew neither A nor B'. Her three signatures support that statement. Their writer had learned to form the letters of her name—she spelled it Jehanne—relatively late in life. Moreover, it was superficial knowledge, for under duress she forgot the trick of doing it, or so it seems, for the documents of her trial record that in 1431 she signed her name with a cross[1].

The story of how this illiterate child came for a brief period to be the chief councillor to Charles of Viennois, the Dauphin of France, is one of the most fascinating in European history. Unfortunately, it is nowhere clearly related by anyone familiar with the events at first hand, but has to be pieced together from a number of sources. The main documents in the case are seven copies of the papers relating to Joan's trial, one in French and six in Latin.[2] The other sources include the brief letters she dictated, other hostile letters written about her, some references in contemporary and later chronicles, and the evidence collected in the process of her rehabilitation, twenty years and more after her death.

In this book Joan shall, as far as possible, speak for herself through the record of the replies she gave to her interrogators. Unhappily, that record is incomplete and possibly has been deliberately falsified in places. There are discrepancies between the various versions and each contains some material excluded from the others. The lawyer responsible to the court for making the original transcript later claimed that the court president, Bishop Pierre Cauchon of Beauvais, forced him to alter some of the accused's answers and omit others altogether. Where the falsifications are is not always obvious. Worse still, the records do not include a copy of the original statement by the accused on which the weeks-long interrogation was based, so that the story is not consecutively told and there are significant gaps where the questioners were not interested in the material. Nevertheless, this is Joan's story, and she must be allowed to speak for herself, even when what she says is difficult to follow. This book will therefore be found to consist largely of quotations from Joan's own evidence at her trial, put back into chronological order, and filled out with necessary back-ground material.

There is no record of Joan's birth in the form of an entry in a parish register or on a birth certificate. She told her judges what little she knew about herself in the opening stages of her trial: 'in the place where she was born she was called Jhennette, and in France Jhenne . . . She was born in a village they called Dompremy de Grus, Grus being the principle church. Her father was Jacques Tarc and her mother Ysabeau . . . she was nineteen or thereabouts' (that is, in 1431, so that she believed she had been born about 1412) . . . 'her mother had taught her the *Pater noster, Ave Maria* and *Credo*, and no one apart from her mother had taught her the faith', or anything else[3].

Legend says that her father Jacques was the keeper of the cattle-pound at Domrémy and so a person of some local prominence entrusted with the task of organizing local defences against enemies; but in fact he was a man of so little account in the wider scheme of things that when Joan's story came to be written down no one was quite sure what his name was and it appears in the documents as Jacques Tart, Tarc, Darc, Dare, and Day. The quasi-aristocratic form now familiar, d'Arc, seems to have been invented in 1576 when it was first attached to Joan by a poet from Orléans.

Joan had three brothers, Jacquemin, who was left unmoved by her glory, and Jean and Pierre who amounted to anything only through their association with her. She also had a sister, Catherine, who died young. A great many stories have been told about her childhood, but they enshrine very few hard facts from the years before 1425 when she was thirteen and heard her voices for the first time.

When Joan was born at Domrémy, it was in many ways a typical 'French' community, using the word French in its modern, wide geographical sense; when Joan used the word it meant 'belonging to the Valois king'—which Domrémy in 1412–25 was by no means certain that it did. Like all the area in which it lay its ownership was disputed. The River Meuse ran through the village and the river was the boundary between the Provostry of Montéclaire-Andelot which was subject to the Counts of Champagne and loyal to the Valois, and the County of Bar in Lorraine which was allied to Burgundy.

Throughout Joan's short life there were in France three views on every subject, all claiming to be authoritative: the Valois, the Burgundian and the English. (There ought also to have been a fourth, the Christian and Papal, but after forty years of schism, with two and sometimes three popes claiming the allegiance of Christendom, the church was in disarray and all too often churchmen followed their lay lords rather than their own Christian consciences.)

Domrémy itself was divided. The houses on the west bank of the river were French (in Joan's sense of the word), those on the east Burgundian. Where the loyalties of the people inhabiting those houses lay, most kept prudently to themselves. What united them was hatred for soldiers. Soldiers meant destruction. Most feared of all were the *écorcheurs*, the skinners, armed bandits and unemployed mercenaries hunting through France in savage packs, harrying the roads and the country places, avoiding only the garrisoned cities, burning and stealing, raping and destroying everywhere else. If the peasant economy had been burdened with no other troubles, the evil of the skinners would have been enough to keep it depressed. But the skinners were only one of the burdens weighing upon France and in 'frontier' villages like Domrémy trade was often at a standstill. Fortunately the land, although not specially attractive to look at, is rich, and can be made to produce food at almost any season, so that on the Meuse the danger of actual starvation was more remote than in harsher lands. But life was narrow and poor. Domrémy seems to have been incapable of supporting even a village priest—else surely it would not have been left to Joan's mother to teach her religion? During her childhood, Joan left the village only twice: 'She said she had left her father's house to go away for fear of the Burgundians: she had gone to Neufchatel, to a woman named La Rousse, and had stayed there for a fortnight', so the trial-report records; 'in her house, she had been occupied with household affairs, and had not gone into the fields to watch over the sheep or other animals'.[4] 'Asked if she took the beasts to the fields, she replied that . . . since she had grown up, and had reached years of discretion, she had not herded them, but had once helped lead them to the Castle named the Island, for fear of soldiers; but as to whether in her infancy she had herded cattle or not,

she could not recall'.[5] Her only training, it seems, was to be a
housewife: 'Asked if she had learned any art or craft: replied,
Yes; her mother had taught her to sew'.[6]

Joan's enemies were the Burgundians first, and later, the
English: those who disturbed the peace, and made it unsafe
for girls to go out even to herd cattle within their home
parishes. Asked at her trial if she had hated Burgundians as a
child, she replied yes—but added that she had only ever met
one Burgundian in those days 'and she wished heartily that he
could have his head cut off, if God so pleased'.[7]

Neither Joan nor anyone else gives a concise, detailed
picture of the life she and thousands like her led in early
fifteenth-century France. But the few sentences quoted are
enough to catch the imagination: life was like the countryside itself, barely undulating, dull, where all strangers
were foreigners and potential enemies, and all new ideas
suspect.

How had provincial France declined into this miserable
condition?

Its deep economic causes are so obscure that even now they
are only dimly understood and are still a matter for argument
among scholars. Superficially, we might say that aristocracy as a
system was failing throughout Europe, though it had a long
time to live yet, bolstered, to some degree, by plutocracy, the
rule of the rich and successful. Under the aristocratic system
that had developed from feudalism the land was divided too
many ways, among too many lords, for efficiency. The primi-
tive economic system made too many demands for those thrust
into possessions and into positions of power by accidents of
birth to be able to sustain them. The units were too small—
and the ambitions of those who ruled them too wide.

In a very real sense, the wars that racked France were family
quarrels. The Hundred Years War itself was precipitated by
the aristocratic system of inheritance: its most obvious and
immediate cause was a decision in 1328 by the Parlement of
Paris on the death of Charles IV of France that his successor
should be his cousin Philip, Count of Valois, his eldest surviving
male kinsman, rather than Edward III of England, the husband
of his sister Isabelle (cf. the genealogical table, p. 224).

However, it was not merely greed, or ambition—or to put

*Isabelle married Edward II of England!

the best light on it, concern for the proper interpretation of the laws of inheritance—that kept the war alive so long. For the first time in western European history nationalism in something like the modern sense was also an important factor. For some time before the fighting began, the French and English alike had been increasingly aware of the national differences dividing them, and forgetful of the historical, legal and religious similarities binding them. As early as the fourteenth century the kings of England had begun to think of themselves not so much as the continental overlords of certain off-shore islands won for them by William of Normandy, but rather as English-based sovereigns with extensive personal holdings on the continental mainland. Not unnaturally, their English subjects were more comfortable with this outlook, though as their continental subjects became aware of it they grew increasingly uneasy. The change occurred on the psychological level long before it was reflected in law and policy. Most of the grand lords, both 'French' and 'English', of the early fifteenth century were closely related to one another, and fought their wars inside the family as it were. Nevertheless the development was a real one. One of its most subtle but significant results was that it became the patriotic pleasure (as well as the feudal duty) of English men to support their king's aims in Europe, and the English as a people—the *godons*, God-damns, as Joan called them in the slang of the time—became identifiable as a national enemy to those in France loyal to the Valois: 'a rapacious people, a sacrilegious people'[8] as Robert Blondell said, above all, a people different from 'us'. To the English what had been a matter of the duty owed to the Plantagenet Lords of Normandy, Acquitaine and England now became a question of national pride in the defence and greedy extension of 'national' rights (identified with royal rights) on the continent. If the Hundred Years War began, and was largely continued, as a family quarrel over a dead man's personal estate, it ended as an international struggle, a conflict between nations, a modern war which the English ultimately lost partly as a result of their 'foreignness' on the continent. Joan of Domrémy had a good deal to do with their recognition there as foreigners.

By the time that Joan was born, the world had already

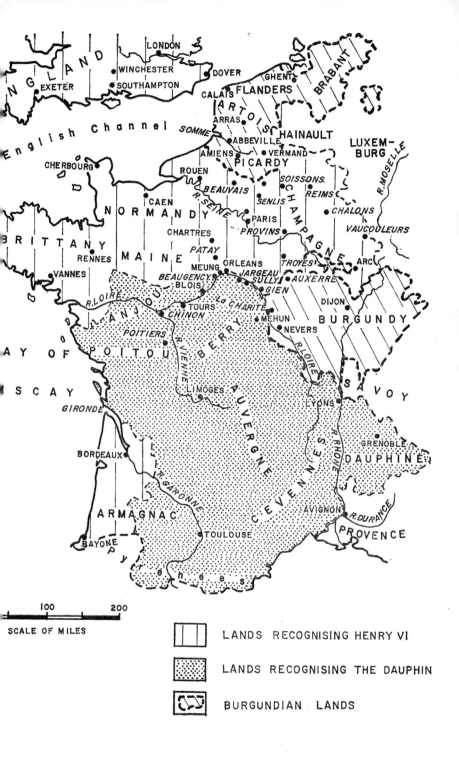

ENGLAND

LONDON
WINCHESTER
EXETER
SOUTHAMPTON
DOVER

English Channel

CHERBOURG

CALAIS
GHENT
FLANDERS
BRABANT
ARTOIS
ARRAS
SOMME
ABBEVILLE
AMIENS
VERMAND
HAINAULT
LUXEM-
BURG
PICARDY
R.MOSELLE

ROUEN
BEAUVAIS
SOISSONS
REIMS
SENLIS
CHALONS
VAUCOULEURS

CAEN
NORMANDY
R. SEINE
PARIS
CHAMPAGNE

CHARTRES
PROVINS
BRITTANY
MAINE
PATAY
RENNES
MEUNG
ORLEANS
TROYES
ARC
VANNES
BEAUGENCY
JARGEAU
AUXERRE
R. LOIRE
BLOIS
SULLY
ANJOU
TOURS
La Charité
GIEN
DIJON
CHINON
MEHUN
BURGUNDY
POITIERS
BERRY
NEVERS
BAY OF
POITOU
R. VIENNE
R. LOIRE
SAVOY

ISCAY
LIMOGES
AUVERGNE
LYONS

GIRONDE
GRENOBLE
BORDEAUX
CEVENNES
R. RHONE
DAUPHINE

R. GARONNE
ARMAGNAC
AVIGNON
R. DURANCE
BAYONE
TOULOUSE
PROVENCE
Pyrenees

100   200
SCALE OF MILES

| | LANDS RECOGNISING HENRY VI

| | LANDS RECOGNISING THE DAUPHIN

| | BURGUNDIAN LANDS

changed greatly from that in which Edward III had been
refused the French crown. All the leading contenders in the
early years of the struggle were long since dead. In 1412 the
king of France was Charles VI, who had been crowned in
1380 at the age of twelve, and at seventeen had been married
to another Isabella, the daughter of Stephen of Bavaria-
Ingolstadt.

In Valois France Isabella of Bavaria was known as Queen
Venus. Her sexuality and prodigality were notorious. During
the twenty-one years 1386–1407 she gave birth to twelve
children. All France wondered, often loudly, how many of
them Charles had fathered. Several of them did not survive
infancy; those living in 1412, later important in French history,
were the seventh, Michelle, married in 1419 to Philip the Good
of Burgundy, the eighth, Louis the Dauphin, betrothed to
Philip's sister Marguerite, the ninth, Jean, the tenth, Catherine,
the future wife of Henry V of England, and the eleventh,
Charles, later to be Joan's 'good Christian' king, Charles VII of
France.

The epic tragedy that was French history from 1404 to 1430
might well have been averted if in 1392 King Charles VI had
not become undisguisably insane, exhibiting continually
worsening symptoms of manic-depression, a disease that had
also affected his mother. Sometimes he was inordinately
exhilarated, but also suspicious and short-tempered: in these
moods he would slash with his sword at anyone who displeased
him. In his depressed phases, he would lie alone in a dim room
refusing food and help, growing dirtier, weaker, and ever
more apathetic while the endless round of feasts alternating
with murderous quarrels that were such a feature of Valois life
continued around him. As his illness became known, it aroused
a great deal of sympathy for him among his people—and
awakened the ambitions of the great lords, his cousins and
nephews. In July 1393, when he made the pilgrimage to Puy
in search of a cure, he was attended by a vast concourse of
children, praying for his recovery: 'there was such a multitude
on the road to this pilgrimage', an Italian merchant wrote,
'that it was a thing impossible'. The general sympathy
for the king was not, however, shared by his Queen Venus.
Whether to be safe from him (as she declared) or be happily

alone with her lover (as rumour said), by 1402 she no longer lived with him and had taken the royal children to a separate palace in another part of Paris.

It was there that her son Charles was born on 21 February 1403, in circumstances such that the fear that he might be illegitimate haunted him throughout the early part of his life. If he was a bastard, his father was the mad king's brother, Louis, the Duke of Orléans—a circumstance which may well have been added fuel to his self-disgust (cf. table on p. 223).

Louis, a prince of the blood, was already married to (and estranged from) Valentina Visconti of Milan, by whom he had a son, also named Charles. In addition, his mistress, the noble Yolande d'Enghien, had borne him another son, whom he had acknowledged and whom his wife had taken into her own household: this child was Jean, later Count of Dunois, the famous 'Bastard of Orléans' (as he signed himself) whose loyalty to his legitimate half-brother was to lead many years later to his playing an important rôle in Joan's life.

The story of the struggle for power around the pathetic but seemingly immortal wreck of a man that was Charles VI is unusually well documented.[9] It is a distressing tale of murder and intrigue, lying, lust and treachery. The key to it was the hatred of John the Fearless, the son of Philip the Bold of Burgundy, for his brilliant uncle, the queen's lover, Louis of Orléans, of which hatred the world was left in no doubt when, on becoming the Duke of Burgundy at his father's death, John denounced Louis for the theft of the whole proceeds of a tax raised to fight Henry IV of England. From then on the quarrel was relentlessly pursued, with disastrous results for all France. Financial collapse at Paris and debasement of the coinage followed John's refusal to allow collection in Burgundy or Flanders of a new tax ordered in 1405 'to resist the undertakings of Henry of Lancaster so-called King of England'. Only months later, Orléans was murdered by Burgundians and civil war began, a war which Bernard of Armagnac, Orléans' friend, said he was fighting to avenge him, but which was really fought by 'Armagnacs' and 'Burgundians' alike in pursuit of power and the wealth that might have gone with it if they had not wrecked the finances of France with their quarrels. Power-mad, they seemed unable to stop destroying themselves and their world. During one period of Burgundian supremacy at Paris in 1413 the day-to-day administration of the city was actually in the hands of the public executioner—seemingly, the only functionary still at work. Even the capture of Harfleur by Henry V in September 1415 could not bring them to their senses. How disorganized economics and values were is illustrated by the fact that although Charles of Orléans, Bernard of Armagnac's son-in-law, was one of France's great champions when he was made prisoner at Agincourt, no one could—or would—find the ransom demanded for him, and he was destined to remain a prisoner in the Tower of London for a quarter of a century.

His loss was an insurmountable blow to his party. It was followed by another when, two months after Agincourt, Louis the Dauphin died, to be briefly succeeded as heir-apparent by his younger brother Jean of Touraine. For nearly a year, while Bernard of Armagnac spent his energies and the dwindling resources of the kingdom vainly trying to recapture Harfleur, the future lay in the balance. Then, in October 1416, John the Fearless showed the world that his enmity for his royal cousins was stronger than his national feelings by signing at Calais an agreement with Henry V under which he recognized Henry as lawful heir to France, promising him 'aid in all ways and secret forms possible to him'. But winter was at hand. There was no more serious fighting that year.

Early in spring 1417 yet another blow fell on the Valois. Jean the Dauphin died. The new heir-apparent, the mad king's sole surviving son—if the king's son he was—was Charles, then aged only fourteen. He was proclaimed Dauphin in April, and made lieutenant-general of France in June—but the real power was exercised by the Duke of Armagnac. Bernard, however, was growing increasingly unpopular, largely because losing battles had proved very expensive, and plans for the defence of what was left to the Valois had made it necessary once more to debase the coinage, after levying four new taxes on the city of Paris in a single year. The enmity of the university, the bankers, and the city guilds soon proved fatal to his cause. While the English took town after town in Normandy, and the Burgundians laid siege to Paris itself, his enemy John the Fearless struck a deadly blow at the credibility of his government by setting up an alternative Council of Regency at Troyes, headed by Queen Isabella 'she having the government and administration of the kingdom by reason of our Lord the King being otherwise engaged', by his fits of madness.

Inevitably, the Burgundians occupied Paris. Inevitably, there was yet another sickening massacre there. Bernard of Armagnac, made a prisoner together with the mad king, survived until June 1419 when the Dauphin Charles attempted and failed to retake the capital and rescue his father. Then he was dragged from prison and murdered. Six weeks later, Queen Isabella re-entered Paris in triumph, John the Fearless riding beside her carriage. A fortnight after, Henry V was able to lay an ultimately successful siege to Rouen. France was destroying herself.

By mid-1419, when Henry had returned to London to beg subsidies from the city merchants to allow him to continue his campaign, all Normandy apart from the grim fortress of Mont Saint-Michel was once again in English hands, and it was obvious that if Valois France was to survive, peace would have to be made between the Dauphin, his mother, and his cousin John the Fearless. A meeting between the Dauphin and the duke was arranged at Pouilly on the Loire, then another at Montereau. What happened there, on the bridge where the cousins met, has never been adequately explained. But when the meeting ended, John the Fearless was dead of a single blow on the forehead with a mace, and the Dauphin, aged sixteen, was apparently the strong man of France. He was also all but universally condemned.

The dead duke's son, Philip, called 'the Good', naturally encouraged the popular fury. When the Council of Regency decided to send a delegation to Arras to make peace with Henry V, it was Philip and not Charles who represented the mad king. The queen's purpose was clearly to exclude Charles from the succession. To seal the agreement between England and France, Charles's sister Catherine was betrothed to Henry V, while at the same time Philip the Good was married to Catherine's elder sister Michelle. The Treaty of Troyes was explicit in its total exclusion of Charles from the succession: 'immediately upon our passing', his father was made to say, 'and from that time forward, the crown and kingdom of

France, with all the rights and appurtenances thereof, shall dwell in, and remain forever with, our son Henry and his heirs'.

It would be easy to feel for the Dauphin Charles at this moment in his life if only he were a more sympathetic character. But he had no more loyalty towards his family than they felt towards him. A typical Valois in his pride and ambition, he looked surly—and was found unlikable by everyone who knew him except those few he made his favourites: first, the former Provost of Paris, who had rescued him from the Burgundians, and had probably organized the murder of John the Fearless for him; then, the Archbishop of Rheims, Regnauld of Chartres, an Armagnac by conviction and association, who could not hope to return to his see-city unless Charles was victorious; and later, treacherous, self-seeking men, like Arthur of Richemont and Georges de la Trémouille, whom we shall meet often in Joan's story.

He established his government-in-exile wherever he could, and clung with some determination to the Valois holdings south of the Loire, financed by an aid from Languedoc. His forces defeated the Duke of Clarence's army at Baugé, and laid siege to Chartres, but he was too poor to pay enough men to take the city. When he married Marie of Anjou, the daughter of the King of Naples, he was reduced to selling the tapestries from the walls to pay for the ceremony.

The wedding of Henry V to Catherine of Valois took place on 2 June 1420, and on 7 December 1421 an heir to the united kingdoms of France and England was born to them, the future Henry VI. Nine months later, once more in France, proposing to take up the war where he had left it—but this time, as the French king's son-in-law and champion against his rebel son— Henry fell sick and died of dysentery. Two months later, on 21 October, King Charles VI also died. So at less than a year old Prince Henry was proclaimed King of England in London in September and King of France in Paris before Christmas, the regent in both kingdoms, in accordance with his father's will, being John of Lancaster, the Duke of Bedford. No one in either kingdom publicly demurred, except Charles the Dauphin, now a proscribed rebel, who named himself King of France at Méhun-sur-Yèvre a week after his father's death, but probably did not believe in his claim himself, let alone seriously consider the possibility that he might one day make it good. French historians have speculated that he would not even have made the gesture if it had not been for the promptings of his mother-in-law, Yolande, who, determined that her daughter Marie should not forfeit possible glory through her husband's pusillanimity, enlisted Regnauld of Chartres's help in badgering Charles into speaking up for himself. Yolande's determination can no doubt be explained by her own unfulfilled ambition. She was the widow of the Duke of Anjou, entitled, she believed, to call herself Yolande of Sicily, the rightful Queen of Naples and Sicily, kept from her inheritance by the machinations of evil men.

Looking back on the years 1422–8 through the eyes of Joan La Pucelle and her followers, it is easy to be dazzled by her particular vision of French history and blinded to the truth. Not all France was behind Charles 'the so-called Dauphin of Viennois' as the Council of Regency stigmatized him. He had general support in central France and the Loire valley (in Berry, Orléanais, Touraine, Anjou and Poitou) and also in much of the south (Dauphiné, Provence, Auvergne, Languedoc, La Rochelle, and parts of Saintonge), but little backing elsewhere except among individuals. Similarly not all France felt itself oppressed by the murderous Bedford, the regent for an alien king whose treacherous French allies were keeping the rightful sovereign out of his inheritance. There was a great confusion of feeling and many were willing to acquiesce in the union of the crowns as promising peace and hope for the future. King Henry VI and II was Catherine of Valois's son as well as Henry of England's. To French supporters of the united kingdom, the Angloys-Francoys as they were sometimes called, the war in France in which Bedford engaged English and Burgundian troops after 1422 was not a war against France but a war for France against an obstinate, misguided and unworthy young man repudiated by his parents as their heir.

What defeated Bedford's attempts to unite the kingdoms were the unsteadiness of the alliance with Burgundy in the early years of the experiment, the symbolic impact of Joan of Arc after 1428, and the harsh realities of the financial situation throughout the period.

Charles of Viennois's ministers always dreamed of ending what they regarded as the unnatural alliance between England and Burgundy and reattaching Burgundy to 'France'. They failed for years to do so because 'Burgundy' was Philip the Good and 'France' Charles of Viennois by whom the murder of Philip's father had been procured. Philip was a good hater, throughout life a hard, embittered man.

In 1422–3 he almost added the English to his list of unforgivable persons, and so withdrew into total isolation. That year there was a great scandal when Jacqueline of Hainault, Holland and Zeeland deserted the fifteen-year-old Duke of Brabant to whom she had been married for political and financial reasons into which mutual attraction did not enter, fled to England and there fell in love, or said she did, with Henry of Gloucester, the Protector of the country while Bedford the Regent was in France. There was no hope of Jacqueline's being granted an annulment by the pope recently elected with English and Dutch help to end the Great Schism, Martin V of Rome, so the couple appealed for a dispensation to the Spanish antipope, Benedict XIII; valuing Gloucester's recognition of him, he granted their request. Together with the lady and her lands in the Low Countries, Gloucester also acquired enemies upon his marriage to her, chief among them Brabant and his neighbour and protector Philip of Burgundy, who also held title to Flanders. Nothing the English court could do would persuade Philip that the marriage was not a direct insult to him and part of a dark plot to rob him—a conviction fed by Gloucester's insulting him and threatening to invade Hainault. Although after a time he allowed himself to be outwardly pacified, he never quite trusted Englishmen again. It was a situation which Charles of Viennois might well have used to his own advantage, if he had not been himself the man most hated by Philip the Good.

The problems of finance however posed a much graver and more lasting threat to Bedford's plans for union. Charles of Viennois is often represented as poor—and indeed he was. But the regions of France loyal to him were infinitely rich in comparison with the north, where the wars, both English and Civil, had largely been fought, and where brigands (the wearers of that reinforced leather jacket called the *brigantine*), and those unemployed and unemployable mercenaries known locally as 'the skinners' were as great a threat to ordinary life as organized enemy troops. Paris itself was in an unbelievably shattered condition. 'When the dog-killer slew any dogs', a contemporary writer records,[10] 'the poor followed him into the fields to obtain the flesh or the intestines for food . . . they ate what the pigs scorned . . . I do not believe from the time of Clovis, the first Christian King, France has been so desolate and divided as it is today'.

In conditions such as this, hopes for the united kingdom were bound to run aground. Bedford did what he could. It is on record that in Normandy alone ten thousand brigands were hanged in a single year to help the local population. The coinage was improved. A new faculty of French law was opened at Caen. The taxes on individual towns were remitted to help local economies. But Bedford himself was an arrogant, hard man, surrounded by arrogant, hard men who could be vicious when their best efforts were misunderstood and grew puzzled and angry when their soldierly gifts and training proved unadaptable to diplomacy and economics.

What weakened Charles of Viennois was not so much that his country was war-ravaged as that most of his troops were mercenaries, hated by his people, outlawed by all civilized authorities, and expensive to maintain. They were led by men whom the rest of the world saw as little better than robber chieftains, Archibald, Earl of Douglas (whom Charles named Duke of Touraine, thereby insulting many in France) and John Stuart, Earl of Buchan (whom he named as his Constable). Final confirmation that he was unfit to rule was given to many when he accepted the help of Arthur, the Duke of Richmond, and made him a favourite at his court.

Richemont, as he was called in France, was probably not more ambitious, self-seeking and treacherous than many another in his day. It is perhaps the fact that he was quite shameless in his schemes for self-help that makes him so unattractive a character.

He was the fourth son of John IV, Duke of Brittany and Joan of Navarre, whose second husband was Henry Boling-broke, so that Arthur was stepson and stepbrother to successive English kings, and 'step-uncle' to Henry VI. When he was aged six, in 1399, Bolingbroke, becoming Henry IV, named him Duke of Richmond, but he lived most of his early life in France. In the civil war of 1410-14, he fought with the Armagnacs as the intimate friend of Louis of Anjou. He was wounded at Agincourt, and made a prisoner. By 1420, he had so far swung round to the English side that he was used as an English ambassador to his brother, by now John V of Brittany, and persuaded him to sign the Treaty of Troyes. In 1423, he married Philip the Good's sister, Marguerite of Burgundy, and was linked by marriage to the Duke of Bedford when the regent married Philip's other sister Anne. Bedford, Burgundy and Brittany had formed a triple alliance in April of that year, binding them together to complete the destruction of Charles of Valois. Richemont asked them for a command, and when it was refused him, denounced them all and fled to Poitiers, where he quickly became the intimate friend and somewhat inept adviser of the former Dauphin, rising quickly in his service through winning the confidence of Yolande of Aragon.

Overwhelmingly stronger in the field and with their belief in the rightness of their cause reinforced by such events as Richemont's defection, the forces of the triple alliance under Bedford went at first from victory to victory. In the south of France, John I, Count of Foix, declared for Henry VI. In Normandy and the north and east almost all opposition ceased. In Champagne, Etienne de Vignolles, called la Hire, surrendered Vitry to Pierre Cauchon, the Bishop of Beauvais: the one was later to fight with Joan, the other to try and condemn her. Bedford himself led the army at the battle of Verneuil (17 August 1424) which completed and confirmed the reconquest of Normandy and destroyed Charles's Scottish contingents. After this disastrous setback, Yolande of Aragon decided that if anything was to be saved for her daughter, she must save it. She began an intrigue designed to detach John of Brittany from the triple alliance and as part of the plot successfully engineered the replacement of the Earl of Buchan (a losing general at Verneuil) by Richemont as her son-in-law's Constable. On 7 October the fabric of Anglo-French unity in the north was rent by the defection of John V, who allied himself to Charles and signed a treaty with him at Saumur. Wriggling himself more firmly into his seat of power, Richemont had two of Charles's closest friends murdered and sat back to await the glory that he felt was bound to come. But he made two terrible mistakes: he trusted his brother John's resolution, and he introduced into the court (now removed to Bourges) a favourite of his own, a scarcely if at all more savoury character than himself, the noble Georges de la Trémouille.

Nobody, apart from Yolande of Aragon and her son-in-law, ever seems long to have maintained a good opinion of de la Trémouille. And that not merely because he was later the enemy of Joan the Maid. He belonged to a Poitou family which had been ennobled by King Philip Augustus, the hero of the third crusade. His father was a favourite of Philip the Bold of Burgundy, and through him in 1407 Georges had been appointed chamberlain to John the Fearless, a position he appears to have held until John the Fearless was murdered, doubling with it, after 1413, the post of 'Grand Master and Restorer of Waters and Forests' in France. His name was constantly coupled with that of Louis the Dauphin in pro-fligacy and debauchery. In 1415, he fought at Agincourt and was captured but unlike many better men was soon ransomed and went home to his castle at Sully on the Loire. In November 1416 he became Count of Boulogne and Duke of Auvergne by marriage to Joan, the widow of the Duke of Berry, who had herself inherited those titles. He treated his wife so badly that in 1418 she petitioned the Council of Regency to have the marriage-settlement she had made revoked, and her cousin named as her heiress. John the Fearless supported her petition, and refused permission to de la Trémouille even to call himself Count of Boulogne, an empty title, as the town was in English hands. Now the sworn but secret enemy of Burgundy, he nevertheless continued to haunt the court, for he had made a friend of Queen Isabella. In 1418 he was one of the mediators named by the queen in the conversations intended to lead to a reconciliation between the Dauphin Charles and John the Fearless—conversations which ended with John's assassination. When Charles fled to Berry after the murder, Georges de la Trémouille went with him, the last link between him and his mother.

Among those who fled from the wrath of the Burgundians at Paris was the Bishop of Clermont. He made his way to

Orléans, where Charles then was, seeking his protection, but at Orléans de la Trémouille had him kidnapped and carried off to his own castle at Sully, a few miles up-river. He complained against the bishop that there had been irregularities in his administration of the Duke of Berry's estate—in which de la Trémouille, as the widow's husband, although estranged, believed he had an interest. And he swore not to release his prisoner until there had been a proper cash settlement. However the bishop was not friendless. Charles laid siege to Sully. De la Trémouille surrendered, handed over his prisoner, and forthwith declared himself a convert to the Armagnacs, though a secret one, because he was still the queen's legate and hoped to win some advantage from it.

His activities between 1419 and 1424 are very obscure. All that is certain is that by the time he joined Richemont in the overt service of Charles of Viennois he had somehow made himself one of the richest men in France. His enemies accused him of extortion, murder, blackmail and highway robbery, and he never troubled to repudiate their charges. He won himself instant favour from Charles and his mother-in-law by lending sums to the family that seemed vast to a prince who the previous year had been reduced to borrowing the price of a dinner from his cook. His pocket seemed bottomless, so the prince smiled on him, repaying his loans with titles empty of meaning while the lands to which they referred were outside the Dauphin's control. But as he coveted titles, everyone was happy. However, the newfound contentment in the Valois court did not last for long.

In January 1426 the Duke of Bedford declared war on John of Brittany in his king's name and ordered an immediate invasion of his treacherous ally's territory. With Charles's agreement, Richemont hurried to his brother's help, but on 8 March at Saint Jacques, a little south of Avranches, he was so completely outgeneralled by the English commanders that his retreat from the field became a rout. John V drew the obvious conclusions from that day's fighting, apologized to Bedford for his defection from the alliance set up at Troyes, and by midsummer was readopted as a loyal subject of the King of England. Richemont fought hard to salvage his reputation with the court at Bourges, but Charles—or, rather, Yolande of

Aragon—could not afford defeat, and Richemont's star began to wane.

Meanwhile, an English army under the Earls of Suffolk and Warwick laid siege to Montargis, one of Charles's few remaining strongholds north-east of the Loire valley, Lord Talbot attacked and eventually took Laval in Maine and Georges de la Trémouille, pursuing plans of his own intended to undermine the triple alliance and further enrich himself, began an intrigue aimed at reconciling Charles and Philip the Good. However, all that he achieved was his own arrest by Burgundian troops at La Charité-sur-Loire, a complication from which it cost him 14,000 gold écus to extricate himself. He seems to have had no difficulty in finding the money, although everyone else in France was apparently desperate for cash. His return to Charles's court was a triumph. His prince heaped new honours upon him. But made reckless by favour shown him, he committed the folly of quarrelling with the first favourite of the time being, the Lord of Giac, insulting him in Charles's presence. Refusing to make a sufficient apology, he was exiled from the court. However, he was not beaten yet.

Meanwhile, the Anglo-Burgundian advance had slowed, and the Earl of Salisbury was sent back to England with a commission to raise reinforcements to tighten the ring around Montargis. Instead of making good use of this respite, the court at Bourges continued to behave quite irresponsibly. By January 1427, de la Trémouille had renewed his friendship with Richemont, and through him was once again in contact with Charles. That month, he persuaded 'his king' and his king's friend de Giac to visit him at Issoudun, and while they were there, he had de Giac drowned. Instead of recoiling from him in horror at this treachery, Charles suddenly rediscovered what a wonderful fellow he was—and so started a disastrous quarrel between him and Richemont.

In the middle of all this, he suddenly remarried (his wife had died in 1423). His new bride was naturally very rich. She was Catherine de l'Ile Bourchard, de Giac's widow. Soon, de la Trémouille was named lieutenant-general to his prince and governor of Auxerre, while Richemont was summarily dismissed.[11]

Lord Salisbury returned to France in January 1428 with reinforcements of 450 men-at-arms and 2,200 archers. Instead of going to the support of Suffolk and Warwick at Montargis, he led them to lay siege first to Angers, then to Orléans, occupying the Loire towns to the east and west of the city— Meung, Beaugency and Jargeau—before, on 12 October, taking up an aggressive position immediately opposite the city and setting his engineers to build siege-towers there. The governor of Orléans, Jean 'the Bastard of Orléans' representing his brother, the Duke Charles, still imprisoned in London, prepared for a long, hard struggle.

While these English manoeuvres were threatening the very existence of the Bourges government, Richemont and de la Trémouille pursued their personal quarrel bitterly. In early 1428 instead of fighting the English, de la Trémouille fought the former Constable, aided by the Count of Foix and the Duke of Alençon. In the end, their forces succeeded in driving Richemont into hiding, while Salisbury's English troops took de la Trémouille's castle in September, so reinforcing the threat to the whole Loire valley.

De la Trémouille was, however, equal to any setback on so trivial a scale. While he had been working with Charles, his brother Jean, the Lord of Jonvelle, had been consistently loyal to Philip the Good and now his loyalty had its reward. He was able to act as an intermediary between Georges and the Anglo-Burgundians and on his own petition was appointed warden of Sully, so that he was able to protect his brother's possessions during the occupation. Thus during the siege of Orléans, as a contemporary chronicler wrote, 'the men of Sully vittelled the English as much as they could' while their lord was acting as lieutenant-general to the French.

As Charles's principal adviser, de la Trémouille was in fact pursuing a definite policy at this time though he himself must often have lost sight of it in the midst of the petty squabbles and dangerous intrigues that made up day-to-day life at Bourges. His primary aim was to separate Burgundy from England, so isolating the English in France and ultimately uniting all Frenchmen against them. This was the policy that was finally to drive the English from the continent, but while de la Trémouille lived it failed to achieve its object for a

number of reasons, not least of them the fact that no Burgundian except his brother could trust him. One of the chief
causes of its failure, however, was that Joan the Maid hated
Burgundians and when she challenged Georges de la Trémouille
as chief adviser to Charles, contact between 'the King of
Bourges' and the Burgundians became for a while all but
impossible.

2

Voices

Joan's story began three years before she became a threat to Georges de la Trémouille, when she heard a voice and saw a light, and then met her saints Michael, Catherine and Margaret.

The year was 1425, not politically a very active one: during it Salisbury captured the Castle of Mayenne, Arthur of Richmond was made Constable of France, John of Brittany tried to defect from the triple alliance, the English burned Revigny in the County of Bar, and all the cattle from around Domrémy were rustled by Burgundians.

Joan was thirteen and living at her father's house from where by her own account she never stirred to go on a journey except when driven away by the enemy.

She described the beginning of the revelations to her in these words: 'From the age of thirteen I had revelations from our Lord by a voice which taught me how to behave.[1] The first time I was very much afraid. I first heard the voice at midday in summer, on a fast-day. The voice came from the right-hand side, from the direction of the church'.

In the early days, there seems to have been only one voice, but later Joan identified three personalities as visiting her, though she was never explicit as to how she recognized them. Her first visitant was St Michael the Archangel, the captain-general of the armies of heaven, whom mediaeval icono-graphers usually depicted winged, wearing body armour and carrying a sword in one hand with either a shield or scales (for the weighing of souls) in the other. There was probably a representation of his heroic figure in the church at Domrémy. He was reckoned one of the guardians and patrons of France and was thought to be especially active at the beginning of the fifteenth century when the gallant defence of Mont Saint Michel symbolized so much to those to whom Englishmen were foreign aggressors. Joan's account of his coming to her is fragmentary and disjointed. The record may be incomplete but it reads rather as though she let scraps of information fall without concern for their continuity. A literal translation of what she said in the original indirect form of the court report reads:

'Asked who had appeared first: replied, she did not know them immediately . . . If they had advice they offered it freely—and this is in the record of Poitiers [the record of her first interrogation, of which more will be said later].

'Item: she said also that she had received advice from St Michael.

'Asked who had come first: replied, I did not speak of St Michael's voice, but I was speaking of great comfort.

'Asked what was the first voice which had come to her at the age of thirteen: replied, that it was St Michael who had appeared before her eyes and he was not alone but was accompanied by the angels of heaven.

'Asked if she saw St Michael and the angels physically and formally [the question was a trap: the angels were said not to be corporeal—but Joan did not realize that]: replied, I saw them with my physical eyes, as well as I see you.

'Added, when they left her, she cried and heartily wished that they had taken her away [with them].

'Asked what St Michael was like: replied, I shall not answer that yet. I have not permission to tell you.

'Asked what St Michael said the first time he appeared: replied, I shall not answer that yet.'

(In the Latin version, the argument continues for several more lines, but the questions elicited no more than a curt, 'Believe me [or not] as you like.'[2])

At the fifth interrogation, Joan was asked in what form St Michael had appeared, and she replied that she had 'not seen his crown, and knew nothing about his clothes'. Asked im-

mediately if he was naked, she retorted, 'Do you think our
lord Jesus had nothing to dress him in?', and asked if he had
hair: 'Why should he have cut it off?'[3]

The other two saints whom she said came regularly to her
were both 'female' (St Michael was always depicted as mascu-
line, although mediaeval theology claimed that angels were
sexless). They were St Catherine of Alexandria and St Margaret
of Antioch, both great Christian heroines, who had defied the
authorities and suffered death for it. It is said that statues of
them stood in the church at Domrémy. They spoke to Joan
occasionally at Domrémy, but in later times, when she was 'in
France', were with her almost continually, except, it seems,
when she was actually being interrogated.[4] She said that they
were crowned (as martyrs were usually depicted), 'with
beautiful crowns, very rich and precious. She knew very well
who they were', she said on 27 February, 'and knew them very
clearly from one another', but she never explained how she
had first identified them. Pressed on this point, she said, 'she
knew who they were, because they had identified themselves',
but asked if they were identically dressed, she retorted, 'I shall
tell you nothing about that now. I have no permission to
reveal it'. On 1 March, however, she said of them jointly that
they always appeared to her in the same form, their hair and
faces were 'quite normal' and 'their voices beautiful, sweet and
gentle—and they spoke the French dialect (*ydioma Francie*)'.
Apart from this, and the fact that she believed that they came
to her at the direct command of God himself, she would say
nothing about them as individuals, and generally spoke of
them as 'her (my) voices' or 'St Catherine' or 'St Margaret' or
even 'St Catherine and St Margaret', as though it was of no
consequence to her which of them had spoken—as indeed it
was not if, as she consistently claimed, they were the messengers of a God whom both she and they were devoted to obeying. The identity of the carrier of a message is relatively
immaterial in comparison with the identity of its originator,
as long as the messenger's honesty is beyond question. It was,
however, precisely this last point which worried Joan's
interrogators and intrigues us still today.

The fact that Joan's revelations first came to her at the age
of thirteen is bound to lead to the speculation that they were

somehow related to the onset of her adolescence. Her judges
did not miss this point, but probed it with such questions as
whether St Michael was clothed or naked when he appeared,
or what part of her the saints touched when they woke her in
the night to tell her things. Joan's adolescence was in fact
unusual. According to her squire, Jean d'Aulon, she never
menstruated, and there is no evidence that she ever formed any
attachment to a man. Both Yolande of Aragon, and Anne of
Burgundy, the Duchess of Bedford, examined her at different
times and swore that she was physically virgin. One man did
in fact ask her father if he might marry her; she talks of her
rejection of him with a brusque offhandedness that is un-
intentionally touching. Her interrogators had obviously
received a garbled report of the circumstances. Introducing
the subject, one of them, Jean de la Fontaine, suddenly asked
her if 'she had promised our Lord to keep her virginity'. She
replied, 'It should be enough to have promised those sent by
him, St Catherine, that is, and St Margaret.'

So what had moved her, he asked, to solicit marriage from a
man at Toul? 'I did not ask him,' she replied. 'It was he who
asked for me. In this, I swear before the Judge that I am speaking the truth . . . And another thing: I made no promises to
him.' Obviously, her parents had pressed her to accept (the
proposal had come before she had left home), and her rejection
of their pleas worried her, for later the same day she herself
returned to the point, saying that 'her father and mother had
taken great care to guard her well, and held her in great
subjection: and she had obeyed them in everything, except the
Toul matter, the business of her marriage'.[5] She believed
that God had wanted her to vow her virginity to him,[6] and
there is some evidence to suggest that she chose to risk
execution rather than accept the possibility of being raped in
prison.

However, one of the judges, Jean Beaupère, had other ideas
about the possible origin of Joan's voices. Perhaps alerted to
the thought by her reference to having first heard something
unusual on a fast-day, he asked many questions over several
sessions of the enquiry designed to explore the possibility that
semi-starvation made Joan hallucinate, perhaps in sexually-
orientated ways. (Joan herself never seems to have guessed

what he was hinting at: if she had, she would doubtless have denied it vehemently. To her, the voices were from God, and there was an end of the matter.) At the second session, his first question to her was when had she stopped eating and drinking —obviously, her guards had mentioned her fasting in their report. She replied, 'Since yesterday, at midday.'

He then asked when she had last heard the voices, and she replied, 'I heard them yesterday and today.'

'When did you hear them yesterday?'

'I heard them three times: once in the morning, once at the hour of vespers, and again at the hour of the *ave Maria*.'

'What were you doing yesterday morning, when you had the visions?'

'I was asleep, and the voice woke me.'

'Did it wake you by speaking, or by touching you on the arm or elsewhere?'

'The voice woke me without touching me.'

'Is the voice still in your room now?'

'No, as far as I know. But it is here in the castle.'

'Did you give thanks to your voice? Did you kneel to it?' (Did you, in other words, treat it as divine?)

'I did thank it. I sat up in bed. I joined my hands, and prayed, asking it to help me, and give me advice in this business. It told me to ask help from our Lord.'

Neither the starvation-theory nor the sex-theory of the voices drew much support from this exchange. Nor again did it offer any evidence that Joan was a witch: her voice did not behave in the least like a familiar spirit, for such spirits commonly touched witches intimately and offered them advice.

This line was so unrewarding, in fact, that a little later, the Bishop of Beauvais, who was directing the enquiry, interrupted to ask with some asperity if she thought God would be angry if she were to speak the truth.[7] Later on, however, she admitted that she had touched her saints—an admission which must have raised hopes of further startling disclosures, though none in fact came: they were, she said, warm to the touch (though devils were usually said to be cold), and when she put her arms around them, it was 'lower down', round the knees or below, rather than 'higher up'—as a suppliant, not as a lover. The evidence was all very confusing to those proceeding against her by mediaeval rules, for to Joan her voices were normal human beings (St Michael the angel was a very gallant gentleman—*un preudhomme*), though now living in heaven, except when they were with her. Although she could be infuriatingly reticent on points that she believed she ought not to discuss, her voices manifestly fitted into none of the generally recognized categories of diabolical manifestations. Nevertheless, if Joan's voices had not come from God, they *must* have come from the devil (in mediaeval theory), and so proved to her interrogators' satisfaction that from the age of thirteen she had been a witch. Only corroborative evidence was needed. They set out to find it and naturally did so.

Fascinated and horrified by the open manifestation of evil the revelations represented to them, they constantly returned to them during the weeks of Joan's interrogation. For some of them, indeed, the evil seems to have had a horrid fascination, especially it would seem to Jean Beaupère, a lawyer and theologian of the University of Paris whose master at the University, the former chancellor Gerson, had written an authoritative book on witchcraft entitled *On trying the Spirits*, the text-book for all those involved in cases like Joan's.

Joan increased the suspicion about herself by refusing to give a full and frank account of her revelations. There were several reasons for this. In the first place, she knew her judges believed them evil and was unwilling to expose to hostile probing things sacred to her. Secondly, she had real difficulty in explaining precisely what she had seen and heard; such difficulty is often felt by those who have had mystical experiences, whether spontaneous and genuine or drug-induced. Thirdly, and most importantly, Joan was convinced that her manifestations themselves had forbidden her to talk about their message in detail except to her king Charles of Viennois. There were heated arguments between her and her judges on the subject and over the oath, because she would not promise to tell the whole truth. 'I do not know what you are planning to ask me,' she told Beaupère at the opening of the second session of interrogation. 'It may be you will ask me about things I shall certainly not tell you,' and the next day she said to him, 'You will ask me some things about which I shall tell you the truth: others, not,' adding after a pause, 'if you

really knew about me you would wish me out of your hands:
I have done nothing without revelations.'

Throughout her life, Joan was convinced that her voices
came from God. Though no one else could hear them, they
proved that she was 'the Virgin from God' or as they themselves called her after Orléans 'the Daughter of God'—
titles which in themselves seemed presumptuous to her
ecclesiastical judges because she used them as titles and not
merely as descriptions. Step by step, the voices convinced
Joan—or Joan convinced herself by those projections of her
own thoughts and wishes which she objectivized and called
revelations and voices—that she was not just another daughter
of Eve and therefore of God, but *the* Daughter of God, *the*
Virgin from God, *La* Pucelle. Obviously, before her voices
could drive her out of her parents' home into the great world
they had to build her up in her own mind till she felt strong
enough, sure enough of herself, to face the difficulties that
would inevitably confront her there. They had first to make her
believe in them and trust them implicitly, and then make her
believe in and trust herself.

Joan may have been untaught and unsophisticated, but she
was not credulous or stupid. Obviously one's own private
revelations are always more credible to one than those made
to anyone else. But when Joan met another visionary claiming
to be like herself, she saw through her pretensions to the truth
about her very quickly indeed. Let Joan tell the story herself,
as she told it to her judges at the sixth session of her interrogation:

Asked if she knew Catherine de la Rochelle, or had met
her, she replied, Yes: at Jargeau, and at Montfaucon-in-
Berry.

Asked if she had shown to her a woman dressed in white
whom, she said, had appeared to her on many occasions:
replied, No.

Asked what [Catherine] had told her: replied, Catherine
had told her that a woman came, a white woman, dressed in
cloth-of-gold, telling her to go to the loyal towns, and that
the king would give her heralds and trumpets to make
proclamations. She would be given a golden treasure, which

she would first have, and then lose, but she would unfailingly know those who had taken it, and those who had hidden it. And she would know how to find it again. And the treasure would be for the payment of Joan's soldiers.

To which she, Joan, had replied that [Catherine] should go back to her husband, look after him and feed her children. But so as to be sure of the truth, she had talked to St Catherine and St Margaret, who had told her that the said Catherine was simply mad, quite out of her mind.

But then [Catherine] had written to her king about what she had said and intended to do. And when she [Joan] had come to him, she had told him that Catherine's true story was one of foolishness and madness; Brother Richard (a priest who seems to have been particularly credulous and superstitious, in a style more typical of the times than Joan's own hardheaded approach) had several times talked about trying it—but she herself had not wanted to, so both Brother Richard and Catherine were displeased with her.

Asked if she had talked over with Catherine the possibility of going to La Charité, she replied, Catherine had discussed it with her, but it had been too cold, and she had not gone.

She then added that she had told Catherine, who had wanted her to go to the Duke of Burgundy to make peace that it seemed to her they would never make peace, except at the point of a lance.

She further added that she had asked the said Catherine if the woman appeared every night, and if she did if she might spend the night with her. And she did sleep there, and watched till midnight, and did not see anything, and went to sleep. And when morning came, she had asked: did she come? And [Catherine] replied that she had come while she was sleeping, and she had not been able to wake her. Then she [Joan] had asked if she would come the next day, and Catherine had answered Yes. So she had slept through the day in order to be able to watch through the night. And the following night, she had slept with Catherine and kept watch all night. But she had not seen anything. And she had often asked, Is she coming soon? And Catherine had replied, Yes: soon.

The interesting point about this story is that Joan obviously wanted to be able to believe Catherine, but could not bring herself to do so, even when encouraged by Brother Richard. Her story of the pale woman dressed in cloth-of-gold, and the treasure that would be lost and found again, was obviously typical enough to tempt belief—the sort of story on which country children were brought up, and which (to judge by the number of witches and soothsayers condemned through the years) ecclesiastical judges had no difficulty in believing; but Joan did not believe it, partly, at any rate, because she herself did not see the woman in cloth-of-gold. She was not a credulous person by nature. It is not hard to believe her, therefore, when she makes it appear that her own revelations found it difficult to win her trust.

When they first came to her she 'tried the spirits' in so far as she was able. She clearly thought it significant that when she first 'heard' and 'saw' the manifestations, they came to her in broad daylight and 'from the direction of the church'. This told her that they were things of the light and the church, and not 'works of darkness' however frightening they might seem. Even so, she did not trust them immediately. It was only after she had heard them on three separate occasions that she believed they were angelic; the voices 'taught her how to behave' and she knew they came from God 'because of the salvation that they brought her'.[8] Gerson and his pupils would have approved—if this 'trial of the spirits' had been conducted by competent authorities. In fact, however, Joan did not take her problems to a priest: 'she had never been constrained by her voices to conceal them' she told the tribunal[9] but 'she had been afraid to reveal them, for fear of the Burgundians, lest they had prevented her journey, and specially she had been afraid of her father, that he might stop her making her journey'. This statement is less than satisfactory; in fact, as an answer to the question, which had been 'had she ever spoken of her voices to her parish priest or any other clergyman?' it was sheer nonsense. By her own account it was two years or more after her voices first spoke to her before they told her to go to her king. Neither her father nor 'the Burgundians' would have stepped in to stop a visit she did not know she was to make. No: Joan concealed her voices because she was afraid of losing them, of having them in some way or another taken from her—in other words, because she believed that others would think them wrong, though she herself was convinced there was nothing evil about them. Even at the beginning, when she was suspicious of them, she did not want to be 'cured' of them, either with a whipping or by a combination of medicine and prayer. She said they gave her great comfort and that she cried at first when they went away, wishing that they would take her with them. She had conjured them up out of her own mind, they were her only real friends, and she longed to escape with them from the real world into a fantasy realm. She built that dream-world out of what little she knew of the Christian religion (by her own account, her knowledge was very small) and her voices promised her that in the end they would take her to it, for they promised her 'salvation'.

When her first fears of the voices had lessened, she had to learn to identify them, personalize them, and grow into an easy relationship with them. She named them—or they named themselves—Michael, Margaret and Catherine. The tribunal realized that it was significant that all three were acknowledged heroes; Jehan de la Fontaine even asked her if St Denis, France's champion, had never appeared to her and was told, 'Not to my knowledge'. As a child, she may never have heard of him, though later in life she offered him a suit of armour 'from devotion for so fighting men are wont to do when they are wounded—and she herself had been wounded before Paris, so she offered it to St Denis, whose name was France's battle-cry'.[10] But the point was not pursued in depth, interesting though it is.

At what stage the voices began to educate Joan politically is not clear. Throughout her childhood she had been aware of Burgundians as 'the enemy' and when she was asked if her voices had taught her then to hate Burgundians she replied that 'since she had learned that her voices were for the king of France she had not cared for Burgundians' but did not give a clear answer—perhaps because she could not remember—to the question as to when she herself had decided to 'persecute Burgundians'. All she was certain about was that as a child she had 'firmly desired that the king should have his kingdom'.

Time and again in her replies to questions Joan seemed to identify the interests of God with those of Charles of Viennois, so that her nationalism is of a very intense and personal kind, almost jingoistic in flavour. Her revelations were sent to her, she claimed time and again, not for her own sake, but so that she could convey their message to her king. Because she firmly desired that the king should have his kingdom and her voices were 'for the king of France' she hated Burgundians. From first to last she consistently refused to tell the court what the voices had promised her in detail, but the two promises she did disclose—all in one breath, as though they were part of one and the same promise—were 'that the king should have his kingdom again whether his enemies liked it or not' and 'the saints would lead her to paradise'[11]: the one assertion was treasonable and the other blasphemous in the eyes of those trying her. No Angloys-Francoys could contemplate Charles as king of all France. No mediaeval theologian would accept that anyone could be sure of his own salvation; to assume it was presumption, a mortal sin. From her view that she was (or would be) saved without reference to the church that binds and looses Joan has been held to be essentially a protestant— although, of course, the word itself would have meant nothing to her.

Together with trust in them, Joan's voices endowed her with self-confidence and trust in herself going far beyond the ordinary. It took months of imprisonment, weeks of interrogation, and the threat of torture and excommunication to shake her belief in the Joan the voices created. The certitude they gave her of her own rightness—she was never much concerned with other people's wrongness: they were wrong if they did not agree with her, and their opinions could be discounted—was bound to look like pride and presumption to her judges. What mediaeval bishop could accept calmly that a female prisoner should be so unmoved by his authority that she should threaten him? Yet Joan threatened Cauchon, who tried her, and on Wednesday, 14 March, when she was asked 'why she had said that My Lord of Beauvais would put himself in danger by trying her' she replied, 'Because it is a fact: I said to the Lord of Beauvais: You say that you are my judge. I am not sure that you are. Be careful that you do not judge badly—you would put yourself in great danger. Be warned. Our Lord will punish you. I am doing my duty by telling you of it.'

In her room, on Saturday, 24 March, after a hard session of interrogation, her voices commanded her always to answer the court boldly. Throughout her trial she did her best to live up to their injunctions in this respect not only because it suited her temperament but also because she felt bound to obey them.

Her assertion that she knew she would be saved and go to heaven with her voices was one of the beliefs that condemned her. Shortly after she was asked why she had warned—or threatened—Cauchon about mistrying her, she was asked if since her voices had assured her that she would finally reach 'the kingdom of paradise' she held it for certain that she would be saved, and not be damned in hell, and she replied that 'she believed firmly what her voices told her, that she would be saved—as truly as though she were there already'.

'And when they told her that was an answer of great moment,' the compilation of evidence continues, 'she replied that "she held it a great treasure".'

'Asked if, after this revelation she believed that she could not do a mortal sin, she replied, "I know nothing of that. For all that, I look to our Lord" '—a perfectly good 'protestant' answer, but in mediaeval thinking, it was her religious duty to inform herself about such subjects as mortal sin and salvation, not by trusting voices that she herself had decided came direct from God, but by reference to the authorities of the church. It was a point on which she and her judges were never to agree. Under threat of torture, at the end of the proceedings against her, Joan tried to make herself see their point of view, as we shall show—but it threw her into a deadly conflict with herself. As she said, 'she believed as firmly in the words and deeds of the St Michael who had appeared to her as she did that our Lord Jesus Christ had undergone death and suffering for us and what had moved her to believe it was the good advice, comfort and sound teaching that he had made and given to her.'[12]

Once as firmly convinced as this that her voices intended her no evil but promised her ultimate good, Joan was ready to do anything they wanted her to do. Thus, when she was taxed with wearing male clothing, she said, 'because she did it at our Lord's command, and in his service, she did not think that she had done ill: whatever it pleased him to command, he would always be right',[13] and in the first two conflicts that arose between her accepted duties and her inclinations (or her 'voices')—over her marriage, and her leaving home—it was inevitably her voices that had their way.

When Joan refused to marry the man from Toul, she was preserving her virginity for God. When she left home so that the king might have his realm, she was going to paradise the long way round. Strange as it may seem to say so, there was a sense in which Joan was escaping from life in this world by throwing herself headlong into it.

Apparently Joan was restless and showed an unfortunate inclination to run after the soldiers for some time before she actually left home. In later years, many stories grew up and were widely believed about how piously and quietly she spent her days there, but Joan's own brief references to them, though less well provided with indications of dates and times, ring truer than the tales her worshippers told.

Late in her trial, obviously basing their questions 'on information received', the judges at Rouen suddenly asked Joan for the first time about her father's dreams. If the trial record is to be trusted, she realized immediately what they were talking about, and replied that 'while she was still with her father and mother, her mother had often told her that her father had said that he had dreamed that she, his daughter Joan, had gone away with the soldiers, and her mother and father had [consequently] taken great care to guard her well, and held her in great subjection: and she had obeyed them in everything except the Toul affair, the matter of her marriage.'

But then she added, 'She had heard her mother say that her father had said to her brothers: if I could imagine anything like this that I have dreamed about her [really happening], I would have asked you to drown her, and if you had not done it, I would have done it myself. And they had nearly gone out of their minds when she had left to go to Vaucouleurs.'

The grammar of these sentences is difficult, but obviously the second paragraph refers to a time after she had at least once 'gone away with the soldiers' to Vaucouleurs, the nearest

Valois stronghold to Domrémy, held for Charles by Robert de
Baudricourt. Joan's father had not merely had a premonitory
dream or dreams about his daughter, but had been torn by
vivid fears and imaginings, based at least partly on his
daughter's behaviour—fears that may have shown themselves
in dreams, and that came all too true for his peace of mind. He
was afraid that she was planning to run away with the soldiers.
He kept a close watch on her, and warned her mother to do so,
but because 'she obeyed them in everything' they let their
attention wander, and she ran away. 'They nearly went out of
their minds' when they heard that she was at Vaucouleurs: her
father told her brothers he would rather have drowned her
than that she should have become a camp-follower.

It would seem that Joan went three times to Captain de
Baudricourt before she persuaded him that she had something
of importance to convey to him. She herself admitted that he
'repulsed her twice'. As the story emerged at her rehabilitation
in 1452, some time late in 1427 or early in 1428, when the armies
of Charles of Valois looked to be floundering on the edge of a
collapse into chaos, Joan ran away to her mother's cousin's
husband, Durand Laxart or Lassois, who lived in one of two
tiny villages both called Burey, about midway between
Domrémy and Vaucouleurs, and begged him to take her to
de Baudricourt, so that she could 'save France'. How long it
took her to persuade Laxart to see her safely to the castle is not
known, nor whether this was her first or second trip to the
castle. At the castle, according to Laxart himself, Robert de
Baudricourt 'told him several times to take her back to her
father's house after thoroughly boxing her ears'—and this he
did, whereupon, presumably, her father said that he would
rather have drowned her than that this should have happened.[14]

Another witness of what happened at the castle, Bertrand de
Poulegny, who later became one of Joan's squires and body-
guards, gave the commission for her rehabilitation a very
circumstantial account of her confrontation with the captain:

She said that she had come to him on her Lord's behalf to
be sent to the Dauphin so that he would be all right, and
that he should not make war on his enemies at that moment,
because the Lord would send him help before mid-Lent;

Joan said that the Dauphin's kingdom belonged not to him but to her Lord and that her Lord intended that the dauphin should be the king, and would restore his kingdom to his control, saying that in spite of the dauphin's enemies he would be king, and that she herself would take him to be anointed.

Poulegny's evidence was believed at the time, but it should be treated with caution, if only because it was collected so long after the events it purports to describe. (It is for this reason—and because all the witnesses to the commission must have been anxious to stand well with the victorious French authorities and so tempted to tell them what they wanted to hear—that the least possible use is made in this book of material collected specifically for Joan's rehabilitation.) Poulegny seems in fact to be summarizing all Joan's message to de Baudricourt and his master, the Dauphin, rather than recalling details of a specific interview. However that may be, whatever form of words Joan couched her message in at her first meetings with de Baudricourt, she obviously made a poor impression with her promises from heaven. De Baudricourt sent her home in disgrace, as a naughty child. It was apparently the best part of a year before she dared to try and see him again—a year during which Vaucouleurs sustained a terrible siege, and de Baudricourt clothed himself in glory.

In later times two stories were told about how Joan spent the intervening months. They were the pious French and the ribald English, and they were irreconcilable.

The French view was that she lived at home, and prayed, and listened to her voices, till God made it clear to her that the moment had come at last when Robert de Baudricourt and Charles of Valois would listen to her. The Angloys-Francoys and English opinion was that she went to the bad, and all but the very worst of her father's fears for her were fulfilled. This version of her story has the advantage of explaining how Joan acquired some of the skills she later demonstrated, skills such as riding across rough country that she cannot have learned while sewing and praying at home, closely guarded by her parents lest she should run away with the soldiers. In its most scurrilous form—a form probably already current around the

English camp while Joan was still alive, but perhaps even further coarsened later by abrasive hatred—Grafton preserves it in these words:

there came . . . to Chynon a mayde of the age of XX yeres, and in mannes apparell, named Ione, born in Burgoyne, in a towne called Dromy besyde Vancolour, which was a grete space a Chamberlain in a common hostry, and was a rompe of such boldnesse that she could course horses, and ride them to water, and do thinges that other yonge maydens both abhorred and were ashamed to do: yet as some say, whether it were because of her foule face, that no man would desire it either because she had made a vowe to live chaste, she kept her maydenhed, and preserved her virginitie .[15]

3

Knight of France

In January 1429 Joan again made the short but potentially perilous journey to Vaucouleurs and finally persuaded Robert de Baudricourt that she must be given an escort and taken to Charles the Dauphin, who was wintering at his castle of Chinon on the Loire.

What made de Baudricourt change his mind about Joan? Her intensity and fixity of purpose must have had something to do with it. So also must the utter desperateness of the situation. If Joan could do anything at all to help, even if it were no more than to show Charles that it mattered to some of his people whether he fought on or not, de Baudricourt's France needed her.

Charles's position that January was all but hopeless. De Baudricourt himself still held Vaucouleurs, but he had already sustained one brief siege and could not be sure of surviving another were the castle to be massively attacked. There was no other Valois fortress still holding out north-east of the Loire except Montargis. All that held Anglo-Burgundian forces from breaking into the southern half of France was the beseiged town of Orléans, governed by Roland de Goncourt and defended by forces under the command of Jean the Bastard of Orléans.[1]

Protected on the north, east and west by moats and walls, and on the south by the river itself, Orléans was one of the strongest towns in all France, but at the very beginning of the siege the English had managed to seize the southern suburb

of Portereau over the river, together with the fortified monastery of Les Augustins nearby, so bringing under direct threat
the inmost defences of Orléans bridge, the twin towers of the
'bastille of Tourelles'. On 23 October 1429, twelve days after
the siege had begun, Les Tourelles was captured by storm and
an English battery established there, forcing the French to cut
the bridge to save the city. The attack had flagged after that,
however, for on the evening of that day the Earl of Salisbury
had been mortally wounded by a shell splinter and command
had devolved upon the Earl of Suffolk. Content merely to
blockade the city throughout the winter, he had sent most of
his forces into winter quarters in the Loire towns of Beaugency,
Jargeau and Meung, but had kept his engineers busy building
a ring of forts around Orléans, connected together by trenches
and walls. For several months, the defences of the city were
scarcely tested though the morale of those inside the walls was
certainly severely tried. Rations grew scarce as the English
blockade grew daily more effective. There were four new
English forts south of the river by the new year, and seven
more were begun north of it immediately after Christmas.
Some supplies still won through from the east, but the whole
of France was short of food that winter. In objective terms,
English besiegers and French defenders suffered commensur-
ately—but the Anglo-Burgundians had the psychological
advantage in as much that they were winning.

Even so, the countryside had been eaten bare by the
succession of armies, regular and irregular, that had lived off it
in recent years and by February, the besiegers as well as the
besieged were in desperate straits. To relieve them, supplies
were collected in England of 'hering and lenten stuffe' and
conveyed through France towards Orléans under a guard
commanded by Sir John Fastolfe. While still some miles north
of Orléans, near the small town of Rouvray, the convoy was
ambushed by French forces under Charles of Bourbon, the
Dauphin's uncle. Sir John's small force fought a sharp,
brilliantly successful action in defence of the wagons, drawing
them up in a laager with the animals in the middle. Important
out of all proportion to the numbers involved, the 'battle of
the herrings', as both sides afterwards called it, seemed to seal
the fate of Orléans.

While the Bastard was defending the city with men and cannon, Georges de la Trémouille was doing his best to save it diplomatically, while simultaneously provoking a split between the Dukes of Bedford and Burgundy. When some despairing Orléannais proposed that the city should be surrendered not to the besiegers but to Philip the Good of Burgundy, de la Trémouille welcomed the suggestion. They argued that there was some doubt as to the legality of the siege under the rules of mediaeval warfare because its lord, the Duke Charles, was a prisoner of the besieging power so that in a sense the city had already been captured in the person of its lord. The proposal to surrender to Burgundy on these grounds was, of course, based on a legal quibble, but if Philip the Good had been harbouring thoughts of deserting his lawful king Henry, he might well have welcomed the opportunity it offered. The Anglo-Burgundian alliance held, however, and, as Charles's chief minister, de la Trémouille could think of nothing further to suggest but retreat, either to the south-east, into Dauphiné, or out of the country, to exile in Spain or Scotland.

No one shows any signs of having been aware of it but there had been one very favourable development during that hard winter. The minds of ordinary Frenchmen, and especially the peasantry, were turning towards Charles the Dauphin. The signs of this change of heart were small and perhaps easily missed if one lived in a castle on a hill far from the scenes of ordinary life. In large part, it can be explained by the fact that over much of France the soldiers-in-residence were the English and Burgundians, requiring to be fed and housed but doing little to relieve the land of the burden of the skinners. There was, however, more to it than simply that. Joan was far from being the only one who heartily wished that 'their' king might have his own again, and the country find peace.

So when Joan went again to Vaucouleurs the whole atmosphere had subtly changed since the previous year. People wanted to believe that there was hope for Charles, even if they saw none. She quickly found well-wishers in the town. One of them, a certain Henri le Royer, gave her a lodging. When evidence was collected for her rehabilitation, Jean de Metz, another of her supporters, tried to recapture the feeling of those days:

When Joan the Maid came to the place and town of Vaucouleurs, in the diocese of Toul, I saw her there, dressed in
poor clothes, a woman's red clothes; she stayed in the house
of a certain Henry le Royer of Vaucouleurs. I spoke to her,
and said, 'Sweetheart, what are you doing here? Isn't the
king bound to be pushed out of his kingdom, and we,
aren't we bound to be English'? And she answered, 'I have
come here, to the king's place, to talk to Robert of Baudricourt, to see if he will take me, or have me taken, to the king.
But he will pay no heed to me or what I say. But I must be
with the king by mid-Lent, if I have to wear my feet to the
knees to do it. For in truth, there is no one in the world—
neither kings, nor dukes, nor the king's daughter of
Scotland—and he will have no help—apart from me . . . I
must go, I must do as I am doing, because my Lord wants
me to do so'. I asked her who her Lord was, and she told me:
God. And then I . . . promised the maid, putting my hand
into hers in a gesture of fealty, that with God's help I would
lead her to the king . . . And I asked her if she wanted to go
in those clothes. And she replied that she would rather have
a man's clothing. So I gave her clothes and boots belonging
to my servingmen.

Naturally, once Joan was a heroine, everyone wanted the
world to know how much he had helped her while she was
still unknown, but Jean de Metz was of those who actually put
himself out to help her. It may have been he, as he claimed, who
gave her the clothes in which she went to Chinon. At her trial,
she herself was very uncertain about their origin. It was not
important to her. What mattered to her was that she was
fittingly clothed: when her change of dress was made to appear
a sin, she said she did not blame anyone for it, that her voices
had told her to do it, and that she had done it 'from necessity'.
On the face of it, she was merely fitting herself out for a
dangerous journey in the company of men. The law of the
church was quite unequivocal on the right of women to wear
male dress in certain circumstances. There was no objection to
it if it was necessary for the preservation of life or chastity, or
indeed if poverty made it impractical for normal distinctions
of dress to be maintained. There is no question that Joan's

dressing as a male servant for the journey from Vaucouleurs to Chinon was perfectly justifiable. Even the sword she wore would be satisfactorily explained as a natural part of a serving-man's equipment in time of war. But her judges were convinced that it was not merely from necessity that Joan changed her clothes, largely because she refused to change back again. They connected the change with her voices and with notions of magic, seeing it as part of her 'sorcery', linked with sexual deviation. By their standards, they were probably not far wrong in their estimation, as the events of later days showed, but at this beginning of her great adventure in the winter of 1429 no one questioned her decision to travel in male dress because it was irreproachable.

Catherine le Royer, Joan's hostess at Vaucouleurs, told the commission for her rehabilitation a story about the day Robert de Baudricourt finally made up his mind to give Joan his full support which, if it is true, demonstrates how riddled with superstition and Christian magic even orthodox religion could be at the time. 'I saw Robert de Baudricourt, then Town Captain at Vaucouleurs, come into my house with Messire Jean Fournier. I heard him telling Joan that the latter, a priest, was wearing a stole, and that he had exorcised it in the Captain's presence, saying that if there was any evil thing in her, she would draw back from them, and if there was something good, she would approach them. And Joan had approached the priest, and gone onto her knees.'

It seems a chancy way of choosing one's heroines, but no worse, perhaps, than tossing a coin. Once having decided in her favour, de Baudricourt and the citizens of Vaucouleurs were generous to her, finding her a horse and a sword, as well as extra clothes, and an escort of six: Jean de Metz (also called de Novellompont), Bertrand de Poulegny and their two servants, a king's messenger named Colet de Vienne and an archer, known simply as Richard.

It was an uneventful journey. Joan's party left Vaucouleurs on or about Sunday, 15 February, and according to Jean de Metz reached Chinon eleven days later,[2] travelling by way of St Urbain near Joinville, Auxerre, Gien (where it crossed the Loire), Sainte-Catherine-de-Fierbois, and so to the little town overshadowed by the great castle where Charles was wintering.

Joan dictated a letter to her king from Sainte Catherine, no doubt announcing her name and mission, but it has not been preserved.

Her own account of her arrival at Chinon, and her approach to Charles was brief to the point of taciturnity: 'I found my king at Chinon, where I arrived about midday and put up at a hostelry. After dinner, I went to the king, who was at the castle.'[3] Not unnaturally, perhaps, Charles refused to grant her an audience, that day or the next. According to the president of his exchequer, Simon Charles, what made him change his mind was the arrival of a letter from Robert de Baudricourt confirming that it was he who had sent this woman to the court.

Neither Joan, nor Charles, nor yet anyone else ever convincingly explained how Joan was able to win Charles over so quickly once she had gained admittance to his presence. The English said that she bewitched him, and if bewitching consists of taking control of a person and persuading that person almost against his will to do yours, then bewitch him she did: 'She . . . was sent to the Dolphyn by Sir Robert Bandrencourt, Capteyne of Vaucolour, to whome she declared that she was sent from God, both to ayde the miserable citie of Orleaunce, and also to restore him to the possession of his realme, out of which he was expulsed and overcommed: rehersyng to him visions, traunces and fables, full of blasphemie, superstition, and hypocrisye, that I mervelye much that wise men did beleeve her, and learned Clerkes would write such phantasyes. What should I reherse, howe they say, she knewe and called him her king, whome she never sawe before? . . . that she declared such privie messeges from God, our Ladie, and other saints to the Dolphyn, that she made teares ronne down from his eyes? So was he deluded, so was he blinded, and so was he deceyved . . .' Grafton's choice of words may be indefensible, but his wonder was genuine, and his bald account of what happened does appear to be more or less true. According to Joan herself, 'When I entered the king's hall, I recognized him among the others there by the advice of my voice which revealed him to me'. Several contemporary writers confirm that she did recognize him instantly, and the picture that seems to emerge from their accounts is of the prince childishly and even maliciously hiding himself among his courtiers 'trying the spirits' in Joan as the priest at Vaucouleurs had tried them: if she really has a message from heaven for me, she will know which is me. The story should probably be discarded, except as an example of the kind of legend to which the speed of Joan's establishment of ascendency over Charles later gave rise.

Throughout her trial, Joan steadfastly refused to divulge what message she gave to her king. She refused to take the normal oath because she felt there were certain matters about which she was bound not to tell the truth: 'If she had leave from our Lord to reveal (things) she would happily speak,' she told Jean Beaupère at the fourth session of the court of enquiry, 'but with regard to her revelations and the King of France, she would say nothing without permission from her voices'—permission that was never forthcoming. The revelations made to her were 'intended for the King of France, and not for those questioning her'. Naturally, all kinds of stories circulated as to the nature of that first interview: Beaupère had heard that she had seen an angel over the king's head the first time she had an audience with him. She vehemently denied it: 'By Saint Mary, if there was any such, I knew nothing about it, and did not see it.' Some believed that she had taken him some physical object as a pledge of her value to him, probably a crown. When growing tired and ill towards the end of her trial, she no longer troubled to deny it: 'asked again about the sign she gave the king, she said, It should be realized that it does exist, and will exist for a thousand years or more, and added that the said sign was in the king's treasury'—but it was not in fact in his treasure chests. Pressed about its nature, she said, 'I shall tell you nothing more', and stood by that declaration. There was, in fact, no more to tell. The treasure she gave the king was self-confidence, through trust in her which she later demonstrated was not misplaced.

Jean Pasquerel, who acted as Joan's confessor, is himself a good example of a man fascinated by her, as Charles was, to the point where he put the direction of the course of his life into her hands. His account of his first meeting with her is worth quoting here, because it shows how her spell (whatever it was) could fall on a man:

The first time I heard talk of Joan and heard tell how she had come into the presence of the king, I was at Puy [the pilgrimage-centre], and there was in the town Joan's mother and some of those who had taken Joan into the king's presence. And as they knew me a little, they told me I must go with them to Joan, and that they would not let me go till they had brought me to her. And I went with them to the town of Chinon, and from there to the town of Tours, to the monastery where I was a Lector.

In that town, Tours, Joan was staying in the house of Jean Dupuy, a citizen of Tours. I found her in his house, and those who had taken me to her said, Joan: we have brought this good father to you: if you knew him well, you would love him greatly. Joan said that pleased her very much, and that she had already heard talk of me, and the next day she would like to make her confession to me. The next day I did hear her confession and sang mass in her presence, and from that time on I followed her always, and remained with her till Compiègne, where she was taken.

To historian-speculators about Joan's first interview with Charles of Valois, Jean Pasquerel is of particular importance because he purports to report the actual words that she spoke when brought into the presence of her king: 'Noble Dauphin (*gentil dauphin*): I am called Joan *la Pucelle*, and the king of heaven sends word to you through me that you will be anointed and crowned at the town of Rheims, and will be the viceroy of the king of heaven, the king in France . . . I tell you from the Lord that you are the true heir to France, and the king's son, and that he has sent me to you to lead you to Rheims, that you may obtain your coronation and consecration there, if you so will.'

Was this really and precisely what Joan said that first evening to Charles of Valois, Yolande of Aragon, and her daughter Marie, Georges de la Trémouille, Charles the Duke of Clermont and the rest? A great deal of historical speculation has been built upon the assumption that it is as accurate as a shorthand note taken in a courtroom, it being apparently overlooked that Pasquerel was not at Chinon that day, but →

first met Joan at Tours nearly a month later, when the general tenor of her promises to Charles was well known.⌉

If in fact this report is literally accurate, a possible interpretation of the message it records is that Charles had no need to be inhibited in his claim to the throne by the fear that he was not Charles VI's son. Despite his rejection by his mother and the Council of Regency as 'the so-called Dauphin of Viennois' in the Treaty of Troyes, he was the late king's eldest surviving male descendant and 'the true heir to France'.

Those who like to believe that this was the main purport of the message that converted the Dauphin to belief in Joan's mission support their view with the testimony of Simon Charles to the effect that immediately after Joan had been announced—or had announced herself—she had a fairly lengthy private talk with Charles and 'after he had listened to her, the king looked radiant', an unusual thing in one whose natural face was lugubrious, even sour.

The theory is that this was the moment for private, even intimate revelations, and speculation as to what could make the king's face glow has grown ever wilder with the years. The earliest story was that like a character in a fairy tale, Joan was able to tell Charles what he had been thinking about one particular morning which he had spent in his oratory all alone. As his thoughts were not particularly unexpected, but in the form of the tale that has come down to us were based entirely on the existing political situation, the whole thing is probably an invention with no more truth in it than in the rumour also once current that Joan had seen an angel sitting on Charles's head: she was, the story runs, able to tell him that 'he had made a humble petition and prayer to our Lord in his heart, without speaking a word aloud, in which he had devotedly besought Him that if he really was the true heir descended from the royal house of France, and if the kingdom should in justice belong to him, it should be granted to him to guard and defend it, or at least that he should be given the grace of escaping without death or imprisonment, and that he would be able to take refuge in Spain or Scotland, the most ancient brothers-in-arms and allies of the kings of France, chosen by him to be his last refuge'.[4]

As for the modern theory that what Joan told the Dauphin

privately consisted of family secrets relating to his legitimacy known to her because she herself was the bastard daughter of Isabella of Bavaria and the long-dead Louis, Duke of Orléans, it is far less credible than the English soldiers' tale that she gave him a golden crown. It is one of the legends of Joan of Arc, and as such will find its place in the last chapter of this book.

Charles may have been attracted, even half-bewitched, by Joan, but he was not a gullible fool, or willing to be represented as one to the waverers in his disputed kingdom. Although he himself might have wished that whatever she promised him might come true, he was not willing to accept her whole-heartedly without some 'trial of the spirits' of a more juridically acceptable kind. It is on record that Georges de la Trémouille committed himself to opposition to this new, transvestite female favourite, and there were others who shared his view. Nevertheless Charles installed her in the Couldray Tower of the castle—which can scarcely have been an inviting retreat, as it had been disused for more than a century, when it had served as the prison of Jacques de Moulay, the Grand Master of the Templars—and agreed to talk with her again. He instituted an enquiry by the Friars Minor into her credibility and stability, and at the end of the week sent her to Poitiers, where doctors of theology and law favourable to his claims had established a rival university to the English-orientated University of Paris.

She was at Poitiers for about three weeks. The examination she underwent there must have been gruelling, for two years later, when being interrogated by the court at Rouen, she referred to it time and again: 'if you do not believe me, send to Poitiers' . . . 'it is all in the book of Poitiers'. It is obvious from the record that Joan did not like having her word questioned once, let alone several times over. She probably admitted the need for some enquiry into her credentials—though she herself believed that the fulfilment of her promises and prophecies ought to provide enough proof of her mission for anyone— but she deeply resented having to tell the whole story twice to lawyers and churchmen, even though they were on different sides. Unfortunately, the report of the commission at Poitiers has not survived. It is the biggest gap of all in Joan's story.

Obviously, the examiners decided that she was telling the truth as far as she knew it. What claims to be the summary of their conclusions is included among the documents of her rehabilitation, but even if it is authentic, it has been greatly edited, and is evidence of very little. If it could be found, the original, unedited 'book of Poitiers' would be a rare treasure indeed.[5]

Joan is said to have expostulated while at Poitiers, 'In God's name, I have not come to Poitiers to make proofs—but take me to Orléans, and I'll show you the sign for which I have been sent'. She is said to have given four promises, or made four predictions, to the court of enquiry: the English would be defeated and the siege of Orléans raised, the king would be anointed at Rheims (with the sacred oil of anointing of the kings of France, allegedly miraculous in origin, and magical in its lasting qualities), the city of Paris would return to its true allegiance, and the Duke of Orléans would return from England.[6]

As a symbol—the rôle she was being fitted to play—Joan's main task was to inspire courage in the Valois and their supporters, and terror in the English. From Poitiers, in a moment of exultation, she dictated the first of several letters of defiance to the English leaders and their men:

+ Jhesu Maria +
King of England—
And you, Duke of Bedford, who call yourself regent in the kingdom of France—
William de la Pole, Earl of Suffolk—
John of Talbot—
And you, Thomas, Lord Scales, who call yourself lieutenant to the Duke of Bedford—
give way to the king of heaven and his royal lineage—render to the Maid sent from God the king of heaven to proclaim royal lineage: she is full ready to make peace, if you will give way to her . . .
And you archers, squires, gentles and others, standing before the good town of Orléans, go away in God's name to your own countries . . . King of England: if you do not do so, I am leader in the battle, and in whatsoever place in France I

shall come upon your people, I shall make them quit it, whether they will or not . . .[7]

However, these were only threats, promises, predictions, propaganda. Their fulfilment could alone prove Joan's credibility—and that fulfilment lay in the future. The commission assembled at Poitiers under the presidency of Archbishop Regnauld of Chartres (himself a refugee from the English) had to decide whether Joan was a fit adviser to their Dauphin. The problem of what proofs she gave them of her fitness remains unsolved. Perhaps they were merely carried away by her rhetoric, or captured by her undoubted ability to charm and conjure men. The only real evidence there was that Joan was telling the truth in any respect was Yolande of Aragon's report that she was a virgin as she claimed. Whatever form of words the lawyers and theologians used in 'the book of Poitiers', they cannot in fact have said more than that they could find nothing unorthodox in Joan's theological views, and that they could see no harm in letting her go to Orléans and prove herself there. Anything she achieved at Orléans could only be profit to the Valois: as matters stood, the city was as good as lost, with only the eastern Gate of Burgundy still sometimes useable by very small convoys, and the citizens close to despair. Sending Joan there would not be dangerous: if the outcome was bad, Charles had safeguarded himself by allowing the commission to interrogate her.

Whatever form Archbishop Regnauld's report took, it was clearly favourable to Joan, and so represented another victory for Joan's personality—or, as she would have said, for her voices. Not the least important advance she made there was to win over the royal observer at the hearings, Jean, the Duke of Alençon, who championed her cause thereafter.

The feeling is inescapable that there was something essentially frivolous about the court at Chinon. Despite the urgency of the military situation, days and weeks were wasted fitting out Joan as a knight of France. She never, in fact, received the accolade of knighthood: 'Asked if she had a shield and bearings, she replied that she never had them, but the king had given arms to her brothers, to whit, a blue field, with two gold fleurs-de-lis and a sword between'.[8] But otherwise she was given the full equipment of a knight, and while she was at Tours, early in April, there gradually formed around her the kind of entourage a knight would be expected to have: Jean Pasquerel, her private chaplain, Jean d'Aulon, her squire 'the steadiest of soldiers of the most proven integrity', two pages— Louis of Contes and a certain Raymond, and two heralds, Ambleville and Guyenne. It is possible also that her two brothers, Jean and Pierre, joined her at this stage: they were later formally knighted as the brothers 'du Lis'.

These were busy days, at Chinon and at Tours. Although Joan had told Jean de Metz at Vaucouleurs that she was in a hurry, and wanted to get to the king 'Rather today than tomorrow, and rather tomorrow than later', and had impatiently told the Poitiers commission 'Take me to Orléans', it is obvious that she thoroughly enjoyed this period of her preparation for war. Her sword and her standard were specially dear to her. When she talked about them to her judges at Rouen, after they were both lost to her, there is a warmth in her words that even the official prose of the court reporter cannot conceal:

'She said that she had a sword, that it was brought to Chinon from Sainte Catherine de Fierbois, and the sword was [buried] in the ground behind the altar of St Catherine, and when it was found it was all rusty.

'Asked how she knew that the sword was there', she did not answer the question but repeated, obviously remembering, pursuing her own thoughts, 'It was in the ground, rusty, with five crosses'. Then she said that her voices had told her that it was there.

It was obviously a crusader-sword, marked with the five crosses of Jerusalem that several of the families in the region were entitled to include among their arms: both the lords of Champagne and their liegemen, the lords of Brienne, had risen to royal rank in the crusader kingdom of Jerusalem.

'She added: she had not known who it was who put the sword there. It was not very deep in the ground. She believed it was behind the altar, though truth to tell she did not know whether it was before it or behind.

'And when the sword was found, the people of the church there rubbed it over, and the rust came off without much trouble, and an armourer at Chinon sharpened the sword. And the people of the church of St Catherine gave her a sheath, and those at Chinon another. So there were two sheaths, one of red leather and the other of beaten gold. And she herself had another made of *corium*, very strong . . .

'And she said that was not the sword she had when she was captured, but she had always carried it, until she had laid it up in St Denis [as a votive offering, after she had been wounded at Paris].

'Asked if anyone had blessed the sword, or had had it blessed, she replied, No, she did not know how to do it herself: added that she was very attached to the said sword, because it had been found at St Catherine's.

'Asked if she had ever laid up her sword upon any altar [as new-made knights were expected to do] replied, No, as far as she knew—but it would have been a good thing to have done. Asked if she had a sword of her own when she was captured: replied, No, but she had one taken from a Burgundian . . . it was a good war-sword, good for hearty slashes.'

Obviously, she was a girl who enjoyed weapons, and everything that went with them—and equally obviously her ecclesiastical judges must have been horrified, fascinated and delighted with her enjoyment.

'Asked if when she was at Orléans, she had a banner or a standard, and what colour it was, she replied: Yes, the field was sown with lilies, and on it was depicted [the orb of] the world, with two angels at the sides; coloured white . . . and on it written the names Ihesu Maria, if she remembered rightly, and they were in silk thread . . .'[9]

Attempts were made to persuade her to admit that she attributed magical powers to this standard, but she would have nothing to do with the idea. The angels, Michael and Gabriel, were there 'solely to do honour to our Lord who was shown on the standard . . . the representations of angels were made solely to honour our Lord, who was shown holding the world . . . The whole standard was ordered by our Lord by the voices of Saints Catherine and Margaret, who had told her: Take this standard from the king of heaven. She had this representation of our Lord and the two angels made there, and the colour, and everything done there, by their command'.[10]

There was nothing special, nothing magical, about any of it —except that God had given her the sword, and the palace armourer had sharpened it, God had given her the standard, and the palace heralds had, necessarily, approved it . . . The excitement, the tension mounted day by day.

4

Orléans

While Joan was being equipped for her part at Tours, Charles of Valois mustered an army at Blois, and Georges de la Trémouille, by no means convinced that the war was yet won, addressed urgent despatches to Alfonso the Wise, king in Aragon, asking for troops to support the fight against the English.

Alfonso replied that all his forces were fully committed in Spanish affairs, and Charles of Valois would have to save himself. During the next few weeks, de la Trémouille made himself some very strange allies among the lesser French nobility, preparing, without much subtlety, his own line of retreat if the whole centre and south collapsed. He could not bring himself to accept Joan, but was too careful of his own position to oppose her openly.

Meanwhile, in Orléans itself supplies were so short that the breaking of the blockade by a packtrain of three animals bearing loads of gunpowder for the seventy-one heavy guns, and several dozen smaller culverin guarding the walls, was a matter of special note.[1] The defenders could do little but watch while day by day the English strengthened the links between the bastilles built in January to complete the offensive stranglehold around the city with a total of something like sixty strong points, some big enough to hold only a handful of men, but all menacing and in the long run deadly.

There is unfortunately no eyewitness account of the arrival at Blois of Joan the Maid, the _Chef de Guerre_, the Director of the War. It is impossible to imagine that it was anything but

61

dramatic—and intentionally so. She was a spectacle calculated to raise hearts and hopes as she rode to the muster with her newly assembled household around her, her white banner embroidered with royal fleur-de-lis floating overhead, and above all, her claimed and admitted right to meet as an equal with such proven leaders as Jean, Duke of Alençon, Charles, Duke of Bourbon, and Etienne de Vignolles, La Hire, a mercenary captain of such repute that he had incredibly held the loyalty of his men through five years of retreat since he had been forced to surrender Vitry to Pierre Cauchon, the Count and Bishop of Beauvais.

Welcome as a symbol though Joan was, however, she was not yet universally trusted. De la Trémouille's suspicion of her was shared by others. At Rouen, her judges naturally asked her about her position at the French court, and she maintained that she had known nothing about state secrets—a statement they seem to have accepted, because they did not press the point.[2] One account of her life, however, maintains that she was present at a secret debate at Loudres a few days before the march on Orléans began, and was so conscious of the reluctance with which she was admitted to the real work of the meeting that she was stung into protesting, 'It seems to you my Lords Captains that because I am a woman I do not know how to guard a secret. I tell you: I know all that you have talked about, but I assure you that I shall never reveal what ought to be concealed'.[3]

On Wednesday, 29 April 1429, Joan, dressed in full armour, rode out from the camp at Blois to the relief of Orléans. It was not, at this stage, a particularly secret operation. Blois is only thirty-five miles from Orléans by the direct route along the Loire, and the English held Beaugency and Meung, which had to be passed before any attempt could be made to force the blockade that way. The whole French force numbered some three or four thousand under the command of Alençon, La Hire, Marshalls Sainte-Sévère and Gilles de Rais, and the Admiral of France Louis de Culen. Joan's voices had told her that the attack should be made from the north, towards the suburb of St Pouair and the bastille guarding it, but Alençon and La Hire, having consulted with emissaries from the city who had slipped through the English lines, ignored their

Director's advice and kept south of the river, to bypass Portereau and the bastille of St Jean le Blanc guarding Les Augustins, and camp along the Jargeau road, opposite the Grand Ile aux Boeufs.

The importance of the advance on Orléans both for Charles the Dauphin and Joan the Maid cannot be overemphasized. Until now, Charles's commitment to his unusual ally had been merely verbal. He was now risking his best troops under his most skilled commanders on his intuition that Joan's inspiration was genuine, or at least genuine enough to inspire others to victory. It is difficult to see how he could have recovered from a decisive defeat at Orléans. Joan's reputation would certainly not have survived one. Perhaps the knowledge that these days were decisive for her added to her tension—an inner tension that burst out in bitterness when she discovered, on the morning of the 28th, that the tactical advice of her voices had been overruled and the Loire lay between her and the main English camp to the north. During the night, the city's commander had crossed the river at no little risk, to meet the Maid and confer with the captains. Joan greeted him with, 'Are you the Bastard of Orléans? . . . Was it you who advised that I should come here, to this side of the river, and not go straight to where Talbot is, and the other English? . . . In God's name! The Lord's advice is surer and wiser than yours!'[4] Throughout the campaign, her belief was, as she told the Bastard, that 'On the petition of St Louis and Charlemagne, God is taking pity on the town of Orléans, being unwilling that the English should have both the person of the Duke of Orléans and his town'.[5]

The day was wasted. Joan wanted an attack on the English bastille of St Jean, followed by a direct assault on Les Augustins and so ultimately Les Tourelles, but it was much more important that the supplies the little army had brought should be taken into the city. The defenders had collected a flotilla of small boats between the islands in the middle of the river, and as darkness came they were loaded with supplies, and soldiers to guard them. Joan went on board also to be smuggled into the city, and a feint attack was organized on the bastille of St Loup, on the north bank of the river. But a strong north-east wind kept the boats pinned to the south bank of the river, and

a disaster threatened. By now, Joan had recovered her confidence: her voices had spoken to her. She announced, 'Wait
a while, for in God's name, all will enter the town . . .' The
story may be apocryphal, but it is a matter of history that the
wind changed, the boats sailed, the supplies were saved, the
worst want of the city relieved, and Joan credited with it all.
She herself would not enter the town that night, but rode on
to Reuilly, leaving the news of her seemingly miraculous
intuition to spread and do its work. By next morning she was
held in such prestige that she was able to insist that the
commands of her voices be literally obeyed, the army being
withdrawn from the south bank of the Loire, so that the attack
could come from the north. On that Friday morning, the 29th,
the English watched the French apparently retreat. As darkness
fell that evening, Joan herself rode into Orléans on a white
horse, with her standard flying above her. It seems that no
effort was made to stop her. She was accompanied by La Hire,
and welcomed by the Bastard and a great crowd of soldiers and
citizens, 'rejoicing as much', the *Journal of the Siege* records,
'as though they saw God himself coming down among them'.[6]
She was lodged with Jacques Boucher, the duke's treasurer,
and everything would have seemed wonderful to her but for
one disappointment: she was told that there could be positively
no battles till further reinforcements arrived. However, on the
Saturday there was a skirmish around St Pouair, on the Paris
road, and while La Hire was busy there, Joan made sure that
the English knew with whom they were dealing by dictating
a letter to Talbot warning him, 'My Lord (God) bids you
go back to your own country, for that is his pleasure for you.'
A few hours later, too tense to remain inactive, she sent
down to the last French outpost on the river bridge and
shouted to Glasdale, the commander of the garrison in Les
Tourelles calling on him to surrender 'in God's name'. By
this time, the English knew who she was: the 'King of
Bourges's Cowgirl'. When they told her what they would do
to her before they burned her, what she may have started as a
genuine attempt at a parley degenerated into a slanging-match
which went on till dark.

Although the Anglo-Burgundians seemed to be in good
heart, the siege was in fact already crumbling—perhaps

because they had become the prisoners of their own siegeworks, and could not manoeuvre quickly enough to meet sallies into or out of the city. On the Sunday, the Bastard went to Blois to confer with Charles. His escort (which included Joan) rode out through the English lines and returned to the town once he was safe in open country without meeting any opposition. On Monday, 2 May, Joan made a tour of the English trenches and strongpoints, finishing it before the besiegers could organize a counter strong enough to challenge her escort of five hundred. The following day, the reinforcements that the town longed for arrived, marching in from Gien and Montargis to the east. On Wednesday the 4th, Joan rode out with her escort to meet the Bastard on the Paris road, returning from Blois by the northern route, and led him back into Orléans unmolested. With such incompetence on the English side, there is no wonder that the Orléannais believed that God was fighting for them.

Joan was a genius if in nothing else then certainly in self-advertisement. Two and a half months earlier, she had been nothing but a thorn in the flesh to her father and a nuisance to Robert of Baudricourt. Now she was the inspiration of a whole city, rapidly becoming famous throughout her country. Arthur of Richemont recognized it, and came hurrying to Orléans to ally himself with her, and so side-step the block to his further advancement represented by her adversary, his former friend de la Trémouille.

If there is a panic that can sweep a people to defeat, there is also an emotional tide of victory. That day, the first visible waves of it were sweeping through Orléans. At midday, while Joan was resting, a party of Orléannais made a sortie from the Gate of Burgundy, along the Autun road to the bastille of St Loup, commanded by Talbot himself. Louis de Contes, Joan's page, later related how suddenly waking she cried out, 'In God's name! My counsel has told me that I'm about to get to know the English!' and shouted at him, '*Sanglant garçon!* You did not tell me that France's blood was being shed!'[7] Armed and armoured, she reached St Loup in time to witness a very sharp encounter between the Orléannais and an English counter-attack from the bastille at St Pouair. In the next hour, the first actual victory of the siege was won, the counter-

attack beaten off, and St Loup overrun. Talbot escaped, but
few of his men. A great deal of the credit for the victory was
ascribed to Joan.

Even so, the next day, when there was no fighting because it
was Ascension Day, yet another attempt was made to keep her
out of the inner councils of the war leaders. When plans to
clear the south bank of the Loire and the southern end of the
bridge had been finalized, she was told only that there was to
be a feint on the bastille of St Laurent, closing the main road
along the north bank of the river towards Meung, Beaugency
and Blois. She saw through the deception, and was justifiably
incensed, refusing to be pacified till she had heard the whole
plan. When she had heard it, she approved, and dictated a third
letter of defiance inviting the English to 'abandon your
bastilles, and return to your own land, for if you do not, I
shall make such a *hahay* for you that it will never be forgotten:
so I write to you—and I shall not write again. Signed: Jhesu-
Maria. Joan the Maid'. Not satisfied with pouring out her
contempt in words, Joan herself, so the story runs, fired this
message, wrapped round a cross-bow bolt, into Les Tourelles,
and burst into tears of outrage and distress when an Englishman
shouted that here was the latest news from the Whore of
Armagnac.

The attack on the southern forts was mounted as planned,
beginning in the east from almost the point where the French
army had camped on 28 April and sweeping towards the
bastille of St Jean le Blanc. The garrison withdrew into the
fortified monastery, Les Augustins, and the attack faltered, till
Joan and La Hire suddenly appeared among the attackers and
spurred them on to renewed efforts. By nightfall, Les Augustins
was firmly in French hands, and the twin towers of Les
Tourelles alone kept the southern end of the bridge closed to
French traffic. A council of war that evening—from which
Joan was again excluded—decided that the little army had
done as much, and more, than could reasonably be expected of
it. There would be no more fighting till more men and more
supplies reached the city. When Joan was told of this decision
she said that she too had been at her council, 'and believe me,
the council of the Lord will stand . . . and yours come to
nothing'. That night, she warned her chaplain that she would

need him early in the morning and all next day, because she had 'more than ever' to do, and that he was to be ready to see blood flow from her body 'above my breast'.[8]

During the night, the English withdrew from their last remaining stronghold on the southern bank of the Loire opposite the city, the western bastille 'du Champ de St Privé', leaving Glasdale with five hundred archers isolated at Les Tourelles. Gilles de Rais suggested that the English should be starved out, but Joan would not hear of it. Early in the morning, she crossed the river and joined the men holding Les Augustins. Glasdale's men were under continual bombardment from a battery on an island in the middle of the river and under cover of this fire, engineers laboured to restore the arches of the bridge destroyed when the siege had begun six months earlier.

Between Les Augustins and Les Tourelles lay a deep ditch with a road beyond. At seven in the morning, Joan had trumpeters sound the assault and herself went to stand on the edge of the ditch, urging on the attack every time it flagged till she was wounded by an arrow that penetrated six inches into her shoulder, close to her neck. It was a wound that had to be dressed. As soon as Joan left the scene of the battle, the courage of the attackers wavered. The Bastard suggested that the assault should be called off till Joan was fit to stand again. But she would have none of it, though she did propose a temporary halt to the operation—and, as the *Journal* says, 'for a wonder, they obeyed her.'[9] By experiment during the lull she found that she could still sit a horse, and after spending a few moments by herself in recuperative prayer she returned to urge a renewal of the attack, encouraging the men with the promise that the English would not have the heart to face another onslaught.

It was true. The ditch was carried, then the road beyond it. The English withdrew into Les Tourelles, but by this time the repairs to the bridge had been completed and under attack from both north and south, with that terrible woman pushing her horse forward step by step, resistance drained away, till panic ended it. In an immortal scene—whether true or not it would be ungallant to ask—Joan is described as screaming after the fleeing Glasdale: 'Clasdas! Clasdas! Surrender to the king of heaven! You called me a whore, but I am sorry for your soul—and your men's.' Seconds later, the drawbridge over which Glasdale was escaping broke under the weight of those struggling over it, and he fell into the river, with many others, and was drowned. Joan wept—for him, her chaplain said, but probably from pain and shock.

It was from that day on, according to Joan, that her voices began to call her 'the Daughter of God'.

That night, while the French naturally rejoiced, and Les Tourelles burned, Talbot ordered a retreat. It was carried out in relatively good order the next morning, though much of the heavy baggage and artillery was abandoned.

It was universally recognized that the victory of Orléans belonged to Joan and whatever inspired her, whether it was the devil, as the English said, or God as the French had come to believe and she maintained. It was the victory of Orléans that proved to the English high command that Joan was a witch: they could find no other way of explaining the effect she had on soldiers who until that week had proved steady and reliable. For that victory, when they caught her, they burned her, as Glasdale's soldiers had threatened they would. At Orléans, she had by 'false enchantments and sorcery', as the Duke of Bedford wrote years later to Henry VI, caused many casualties among the English, and worse 'withdrowe the courage of the remenant in merveillous wyse'[10]—and for this she could not hope to be forgiven. The shock of the defeat at Orléans was so great that the battle receives hardly any mention in the accounts of Joan's trial, though other engagements in which she took part were put under close judicial scrutiny. The fact was that Joan frightened the English, not only the men-at-arms but also the high command. There was something horrifying in the thought of her inexorable advance upon the wall of Les Tourelles, till she could touch it with the end of her standard, and so give it to its attackers, dedicating it like a sacrifice, with a shout of 'It is all yours—go in!'[11] That was the French propaganda picture of Joan circulated after Orléans. There was no English survivor from the final assault sufficiently authoritative to deny it effectively, even if it was untrue—and there is no evidence that it was. Joan the witch dedicated Les Tourelles to destruction: Joan the witch called on Glasdale to surrender to the king of heaven, and within minutes he was dead, drowned. It is not surprising that the oldest known miniature painting of Joan, an illustration in Martin le Franc's *Champion des Dames* dating from 1451, shows Joan in the company of one of the most terrifying women in the Old Testament, that Judith who assassinated Holofernes while he slept. Both of them might be heroines to their own people, but no one in the whole male world could ever really feel comfortable at the thought of either of them.

'By general repute,' a chronicler said,[12] 'this same Pucelle bore off the fame and honour of having been the principle guide (to victory), although the majority of French captains were there'. After the fall of Les Tourelles, and the English withdrawal from Orléans, Charles would have found it difficult to rid himself of Joan even if he had wanted to do so. 'And those captains who were earlier at Orléans entered into great debates with those lords who had come there later, taking counsel as to whether they should pursue the English so as to throw them out of the places they held in the Beauce region, or not; the Pucelle was always called into those consultations, she being in full reign over them, they being willing that everything should be governed by her, and done according to her will'.[13] The great captains, especially Duke Jean of Alençon and La Hire, had made Joan into the most successful of symbols, just as Charles of Valois had intended (whether consciously or not). Not everyone was delighted. Georges de la Trémouille certainly was not, and seems to have had a part in Charles's regrettable decision that he would not officially recognize what had been done for his cause at Orléans by visiting those who had suffered privation there, and those who had rescued them.

No excuse was offered for this royal indifference. Charles always did what he felt like doing and especially avoided those decisions and actions that seemed distasteful to him. When he left Blois it was to double the distance between himself and Orléans, himself and the decisions that still had to be made. He went downriver to Tours. As soon as she fittingly could— there are duties that a successful *chef de guerre* cannot avoid at the scene of victory—Joan hurried after him. Throughout her brief public life she was acutely conscious of having no time to waste. She had forced the fulfilment of the first of her four predictions within six weeks of having made it. Now she wanted to press on to fulfil the second, Charles's coronation at Rheims. With the English in disarray, their Burgundian allies badly shaken, and the French countryside all for the Valois, a determined march across country to Rheims might well have been successfully completed before any coherent attempt to stop it could have been made. But Charles was for caution. De la Trémouille supported him—and so too naturally did all realistic military opinion. Joan's argument, that this was not a natural military situation, but one supernaturally controlled, was unacceptable while the main English forces in the Loire region were still undefeated. On Friday, 13 May, less than a week after Les Tourelles had fallen, Joan and her voices were overruled. The fight for the Loire was to go on.

5

'And now we must go to Rheims'

From his castle of Loches near Tours, Charles announced that he had given command of the army of the Loire to Joan's ally, Jean of Alençon, with the title of Lieutenant General of the Armies of France. Satisfied in this at least, Joan announced that she would fight with him and for the first time in years a Valois commander found himself with as many men as he wanted: 'he had plenty of them,' a chronicle says, 'because everyone was following her'.[1]

It is on record that de la Trémouille and some of the great captains were not happy with the situation even after the decisions of the council had been ratified by the Dauphin. Some of the military men wanted to leave enough men on the Loire to contain Talbot's army there and march north with the rest from Tours into Normandy, the key to English interests in France. De la Trémouille supported them, perhaps from conviction, perhaps in automatic opposition to Alençon, but most probably because he felt his influence over Charles slipping and wanted his master to himself for a while, with all the fighting men busy elsewhere, preferably several days' march away. However, he was overruled. Every man who could be spared from garrison duties was brought into the army of the Loire.

Meanwhile Talbot's envoys were in Paris, trying to explain

away the failure at Orléans, and begging for reinforcements to lead south to the Loire. The remaining English forces there were concentrated in Jargeau to the east of Orléans and Beaugency to the west, with a smaller garrison at Meung, between Beaugency and the city. Their overall commander was William de la Pole, the Earl of Suffolk, a man whose situation at the beginning of June was, to say the least, unenviable.

On 12 June, Joan told Alençon that the time had come to take Jargeau: the army advanced on the town, and Jargeau fell to it—or rather, collapsed into Joan's arms. Suffolk concentrated his forces at Beaugency, while possibly that same day reinforcements led by Sir John Fastolfe made contact at Janville, about twenty-five miles north of Orléans, with a small English force under Lord Talbot. Hardly had they united their commands and decided to march to the relief of Jargeau when they were informed that the town had already fallen. Fastolfe concluded—rightly as events showed—that the whole Loire was as good as lost and argued for a strategic withdrawal to Paris but Lord Talbot overruled him and orders were issued to the army—numbering some five or six thousand men—that would take it south-west to Beaugency and Meung, where Suffolk was waiting.

On 15 June, Meung was surrounded and the bridge with its bastille captured. Then the French army marched on to Beaugency, leaving a force to hold the bridge and threaten Meung from the south, the river side. By the evening, the two forces were within striking distance of one another, the French waiting on a low hill for the English to march out and meet them. Instead of marching out in force, the English sent heralds to call for three champions to fight for France *comme ilz ont coustame de faire* 'if they were brave enough to come down the hill and come to them' . . . to this, the reply was made from among those with La Pucelle, 'go and get some rest. It is late. But tomorrow, by the grace of God and our Lady, we'll see you from closer to'. By the next morning, Beaugency was under close siege and the English had withdrawn into the castle.

Talbot, marching south far too slowly with his relieving force, came within a mile or so of Beaugency then, learning that it was very close to capitulation, turned east to Meung, gathered up the garrison there, and retreated northwards. Beaugency surrendered, and the main body of the French set off in pursuit of Talbot. On the morning of 18 June the two armies met at Patay, a village only twenty-five miles north-west of Orléans.

The battle which developed that morning was probably more damaging to English prestige and English morale in France than the defeat at Orléans had been. At Orléans, a relatively small force had been overcome by a courageous and determined enemy sent berserk by the magic of a woman-devil . . . But there were no excuses for the massacre of Patay. Joan was not even on the field.

Advancing rapidly from Beaugency, the French vanguard faltered when it found itself threatened with a fight so soon, giving Talbot time to make some hasty plans. Under his orders, his own troops took up positions ready to fight a rearguard action, while the main body of the Anglo-Burgundian force continued the retreat to the north, under the general command of Fastolfe. No one, it seems, really wanted a battle that morning—no one, that is, except Joan.

When reports of the impending action reached the French high command, the Duke of Alençon asked Joan what she and her voices thought ought to be done. She told him, 'Use your spurs!' This brief admonition worried those who heard it: was Joan predicting a rout? She explained that they would all need their spurs for the pursuit: 'The English will turn their backs on us. You will need good spurs to catch them'.[2]

Joan was a good prophet, on this as on many other occasions. There is no natural line of defence at Patay, but only open, gently rolling country, with an occasional stand of trees. The French cavalry easily outflanked Talbot's rearguard and were soon among the English stragglers; while the men-at-arms destroyed Talbot's line piecemeal, a massacre developed further forward. The French lost two killed; the English nearer two thousand killed and made prisoner. Among those taken for ransom were Talbot himself and Lord Scales. In a retreat that threatened to become a rout, Fastolfe led the remnant of his army back towards Paris and one by one the garrisons left in Beauce packed what they could and burned the rest, hastening to join him there. Although the victory of Patay was owed largely to La Hire's skill in handling his mounted troops, it was Joan who was honoured for it. The Burgundian soldier-historian Wavrin, an admiring enemy, said that after Patay she was held in such honour everywhere that 'everyone felt powerless against her': 'in all these affairs,' the chronicler wrote, 'Joan the Pucelle won such great honour and renown above all others that it really seemed to everyone that king Charles's enemies lacked the power to resist in any place where she was, and that shortly through her the king must be restored to his kingdom despite all those who would gainsay it'.[3]

The victory was so unexpectedly complete that no one was ready to take advantage of it. Immediate, unrelenting pursuit might have brought the French to the gates of Paris and perhaps even carried them through; but for such a move to succeed it needed the express encouragement and, better still, the active participation of the Dauphin. But he was not at Patay, any more than he had been at Orléans. When he left Tours, it was to go with Georges de la Trémouille to Sully, to celebrate there the recovery of the castle from its occupation by the English under his brother, Jean. Left without orders, the Duke of Alençon felt compelled to order a withdrawal, first to St-Benoît-sur-Loire, then to Chateauneuf. Everywhere, the army and its leaders were fêted, Joan above all the rest, but behind the scenes there was constant bickering and mounting discontent. Some wanted to march on Paris—though the moment when that would have been practical was retreating hour by hour, as the English recovered their nerve. Others still hankered for an attack through Normandy. Charles seemed quite uncertain what to do, and not much interested in doing anything. To whatever proposal was made Joan, who was now a member of the privy council,[4] replied always: 'All that means nothing to me: now, we must go to Rheims'.

There were two practical routes from the Loire to Rheims: through Paris, or through Burgundian-held Auxerre. De la Trémouille was most strongly opposed to any suggestion that Joan should lead the Dauphin to his coronation at Rheims through Auxerre. Years earlier, Charles had named him governor of the region after it had been liberated, and in later times it emerged that the Auxerrois were paying him to make sure that they stayed un-fed and un-sacked. For days Charles hesitated, first swinging to this opinion, then to that. But Joan's influence was now so great that in the end she had her way. The army remustered at Gien on 25 June with orders to march north-east to Rheims. Charles prepared letters summoning all loyal men to his coronation. Joan wrote to the people of Tournai in a style that fell little short of regal: 'I request and require you that you will all be prepared to come to the anointing of the noble king Charles at Rheims, where we shall shortly be.' She also addressed a letter to the Duke of Burgundy. It no doubt contained her usual mixture of threats and pleas, designed to make him give his allegiance to Charles or shake his people's loyalty to him. Unfortunately, the text is lost.

Impatient as always, Joan did not wait till the army was ready to march but set off with her own band of adventurers on a wide sweep through the country in the general direction of Auxerre. There was virtually no resistance. When the army did march, it left Gien on 29 June, and reached the outskirts of Auxerre, nearly fifty miles away, the following evening. Given backbone by de la Trémouille's secret promises, the town at first refused to surrender to Joan or anyone else, then, threatened with immediate sack, its emissaries explained that they were cowards, afraid of the wrath of their overlord Philip the Good: they would surrender the keys without a struggle immediately they heard that Troyes, Châlons-sur-Marne and Rheims were in Charles's hands. This compromise—which sounds typical of de la Trémouille—was accepted. Such was the army's confidence that few voiced doubts about the wisdom of leaving an unreduced stronghold in the rear as the march into enemy country continued. Confidence was not misplaced. The little towns along the route to Troyes surrendered one by one.

Troyes, however, felt it had a reason to fear Charles of Valois, for it was there that the treaty excluding him from the succession in favour of his nephew Henry of England had been signed nine years earlier. Charles wrote to its leading citizens as his army drew near, ordering them to 'Give obedience to those to whom they owed it . . . without fear of things past, for which they need not fear that he wanted to take vengeance on them, for that was not in his mind.'

Joan also wrote them a letter, urging the 'Lords, citizens and inhabitants of the town' to give 'true obedience and recognition to the noble king of France who would shortly be in Rheims and Paris', but the people of Troyes still refused to yield, fearing perhaps that if they opened the gates the garrison of *Français reniés*, renegade Frenchmen in the castle would fight on till the whole town was devastated.

The delay may well have worried Charles's advisers very deeply because although the army seemed in good heart 'the king had no money wherewith to pay its charges'[5] and the success of the whole venture depended on carrying it through to a successful conclusion before lack of pay and shortage of rations dried up the enthusiasm that made everyone happy to 'serve the king in his travels with the Pucelle, saying that they would go wherever she wanted.' At a council of war at the end of the first week in July Joan urged an immediate attack, telling her 'noble dauphin' (as the Bastard afterwards recalled) not to waste too long in council, because within three days she would bring him into Troyes 'either by love or by force'.

While they were still waiting outside Troyes, there occurred one of those odd little scenes that remind us how far away in thought those times were from our own. The story that Joan was a witch, or perhaps even a devil in female form, had obviously reached the city, for at the urging of his parishioners a certain popular preacher named Friar Richard came out to the French camp, 'trying the spirits' in a practical demonstration of exorcism. As Joan herself told the story at her trial: 'As I remember, when the people of the town of Troyes sent him to me, doubting me, and saying that they were not convinced that all this came from God, when he came close to me, he made the sign of the cross, and threw Holy Water. And I said to him: "Approach boldly! I shall not disappear!".'

After interviewing Joan, this same Brother Richard seems to have convinced himself that she was rather a saint than a devil. He carried a good report of her back to Troyes and in later times appropriated to himself the standard that she laid up in Rheims Cathedral 'quite close to the altar'. 'She did not know,' she told her judges, 'that Brother Richard had it'.[6]

The next morning, the army prepared for an assault on the town, but before any bombardment began, the citizens called for a parley, and after protracted negotiations it was agreed that the garrison should be allowed to march out of the castle and the keys of the city handed over peaceably to Charles's officers. The Dauphin actually entered the city on Sunday, 10 July.

The next garrison town on the route was Châlons-sur-Marne. The march to it was begun on the 12th: Charles's herald presented himself there on the 15th and was so warmly welcomed that he reported back that there would be no need for an assault. Nor was there. When Charles himself arrived on the 16th, the keys were ceremonially offered to him to touch, by one who had been among the staunchest of Burgundians, the city's Count-Bishop Jean de Montbéliard-Sarrebrück. But it was not Charles—or not Charles alone—that the people wanted to see. It was Joan the Maid, the Daughter of God, the Saint as they were already calling her. At Châlons, she was within a relatively few miles of her home country, and among those who came to stare at her were people from Domrémy, including her godfather, Jean Morin.

That same evening, Charles entered Rheims. The Burgundian threat was evaporating, although in theory the alliance between Bedford and Philip the Good was as firm as ever. The citizens welcomed him as though they had always been loyal to him.

Charles had actually assumed the title of King of France on 30 October 1422 in the chapel of his uncle the Duke of Berry's castle at Méhun-sur-Yèvre, while Paris was still debating whether it should acquiesce in the proclamation there of Henry VI and II, so that for nearly seven years there had been, as Pierre de Fenin put it, 'two kings in France, that is King Charles and King Henry, the which King Henry called himself king of France and England'.[7] But neither of them had undergone the solemn ceremony of anointing with the holy oils of Rheims which in mediaeval French theory set the seal of God's approval on a French king. For Charles of Valois, that omission was made good in a somewhat hurried coronation the day after he entered Rheims. Archbishop Regnauld of Chartres presided over the ceremony, and Joan stood close to the altar, holding her banner till the end, when she did homage

to King Charles VII among the great lords of his court, saying
to him (according to the anonymous author of the *Journal of
the Siege of Orléans*, to whom, as to every historian since,
Charles's anointing was the real end of that siege): '*Gentil Roi*,
today is fulfilled the good pleasure of God whose will it was
that I should raise the siege of Orléans and bring you to this
city of Rheims to receive your holy anointing in demonstration
that you are the true king, and him to whom the kingdom
should belong'. If in point of truth she said not a word, her
mere presence there on that day was enough. She had said at
Chinon that God's good pleasure was that the siege of Orléans
should be raised and Charles anointed. She had forced fulfilment of those two prophecies. It remained now only to bring
Paris back to its allegiance (which looked as though it might
happen within days) and Charles of Orléans back from his
English prison (which could be expected to be achieved by an
exchange of prisoners after France had risen for Charles VII).
In Rheims Cathedral, Joan's brief career reached its peak. She
acknowledged it by leaving her standard there as a thanks-
offering.

In solid terms, not a great deal had in fact been done:
Orléans had been relieved, the French had won a major battle
at Patay, and Charles had demonstrated his ability to march
from the Loire into Champagne. That was all. But it was
enough to change the whole climate in France. Over the next
weeks Soissons, Senlis, Beauvais and even part of the Ile de
France would swear allegiance to Charles as the true king.
Auxerre would surrender. There would be talk of peace with
Philip of Burgundy. Everything would feel different.

In fact, Joan herself seems to have felt that having achieved
Charles's anointing, she had done all she had been called to do.
On the day itself she wrote to Philip of Burgundy, suggesting
that it was all over now: he would lose nothing by surrendering
to Charles's claims.[8] At about the same time, she told Archbishop Regnauld wistfully, 'May God grant I may retire, to
go and see my father and mother, and look after their flocks
with my sister and brother, who would be so happy to see me
again.'[9] If Charles had been a different character—even the
character he was later to develop into—she should have been
able to retire at this moment, provided always that her voices

and the people who all but worshipped her had allowed it. She had given the French resistance movement the symbol it needed—King Charles VII in place of herself—and she had given it the impetus it had lacked until that year. Others ought to have been able to carry on. Charles, however, was not yet ready to bear the burden of decision himself.

6

'I want to see Paris from closer to'

People have always wondered why Joan did not in fact go back to Domrémy after Charles had been anointed. Her inspiration seems temporarily at least to have left her then and to go home was what she said she wanted to do. The answer must surely be sought in the impossibility, as she saw it, of trusting Charles to live up to the image of him she had created. What was needed was a quick, decisive thrust against Paris. It took three days to persuade Charles to leave Rheims and begin a slow progress in a generally westerly direction.

Perhaps he was tired of action and activity: he was certainly unused to it. Perhaps he was very conscious that the closer he came to Paris, the thicker on the ground his enemies would be. Perhaps he genuinely hoped for a real peace with Burgundy. Georges de la Trémouille, still first-favourite despite all the fighting men had done for their prince in recent weeks, was able to encourage that hope by reporting real progress in the peace talks he was conducting secretly with Philip's ambassadors . . . Charles was expending a lot of energy and a lot of money, and he had no great reserves of either, while to him English resources must have seemed inexhaustible. His intelligence was that Bedford was being strongly reinforced and it was true: King Henry's guardian and god-father, Henry Beaufort, the Cardinal of England, who in his capacity as papal legate had been raising an army to lead to Bohemia against the Hussite rebels and heretics, allowed himself to be persuaded to take that army to France and put himself and it under Bedford's command. That army was moving into positions around Paris while Charles of France was wandering, apparently aimlessly, wondering what to do. All he wanted to do was what Joan herself wanted to do: he wanted to go home, back to the Loire, to Chinon, to his friends. On 2 August, at Provins, still forty miles south-east of Paris, he announced that he intended to withdraw and quite understandably threw all the towns that had recently turned their coats for him into a panic.

Fierce, unrelenting argument held him where he was for three days longer, but on 6 August he forced the army to move south, away from the capital, and Joan had to write reassuringly to the people of Rheims, telling them they had little to fear: a two-weeks truce had been concluded with Philip of Burgundy and at the end of it the surrender of Paris was confidently to be expected. Fifteen miles or so out of Provins Charles met a check that he had not reckoned with. The English had moved forces into position along the Seine to cut off his retreat and were holding the bridge at Bray that the French army was to have used. Disconsolately, the king ordered his army back to Provins. Another week went by. Charles marched north, in an arc around Paris, from Provins to Chateau-Thierry, from Chateau-Thierry to Dammartin, Bedford moving troops continually to prevent a breakthrough to Paris, but constantly just out of sight of the French.

Inevitably, the moment came when the two armies met head-on. It happened at Montépilloy near Senlis, but neither commander would commit himself to a battle, Bedford for fear that Joan would display her standard and his troops panic; Charles for fear that he might lose both that fight and the chance of the negotiated peace with Burgundy that de la Trémouille was promising. There was some skirmishing, and Joan did carry her pennant to the English trenches and issue a challenge of her own in reply to one Bedford had sent to Charles on 7 August, but there was no panic, perhaps because Bedford himself was with the army, having made the ally allegedly betraying him, Philip the Good, governor of Paris.

J.A.—6

Militarily speaking, they were wasted, futile, boring days, but they were not without their political reward. Senlis itself surrendered to Charles, together with Beauvais, and the important town of Compiègne. Charles's personal ambassador to Philip, Archbishop Regnauld, proposed not only a general amnesty but relief from all 'pains and penalties', and the release of all prisoners: Philip's counter-proposals, carried to Charles by John of Luxemburg, a bitter enemy of the Valois, were all but contemptuous in their demands. Philip offered to extend the truce for four months, in exchange for all those towns east of Paris from Compiègne to Provins which had recently submitted to Charles, together with a promise from him that he would enter no town north of the Seine except to pass through it on his way back to his base on the Loire. The brusqueness of these demands was an indication of how quickly the initiative was slipping away from Charles VII. Another, smaller, but in its way equally ominous, item of news was that Pierre Cauchon, the Count-Bishop of Beauvais, who had so recently surrendered the keys of his town to his new king had defected back to the Anglo-Burgundians, deserting his city and making his way to Paris.

Joan and the Duke of Alençon now decided that they would have to take the future into their own hands if the advantages already won were not to be frittered away. On 23 August they took their troops out of the royal army encamped at Compiègne, and occupied St Denis, so offering a direct threat to Paris. Joan made it clear at her trial that this was entirely their own idea, when she was asked if it was by the advice of her voices that she had advanced on Paris and replied with a simple 'No'.[1] Five days later, Philip of Burgundy's proposals for a truce were made public. While Charles was apparently still wondering what attitude to take to them, Joan rejected them out-of-hand. She was hot for war. At Compiègne before they had set out on their adventure she had said to Alençon, '*Par mon martin*! I want to go and see Paris from closer to than I have seen it yet!'[2]

Seemingly it was only now that the garrison of Paris recognized that the threat was real. Everyone realized that Charles would have to march west in support of his victorious lieutenant-general and the fiery Joan or no one would ever trust him again. Accordingly, they began to prepare for a siege. On 1 September 1429 the Duke of Bedford despatched the following order to 'Oure righte trusty and welbeloved squire Thomas Goule, lieutenant of Falaise':

Right trusty and wellbeloved. For as much as my lordes ennemis and oures ben assembled in great puissance at Saint Denis in France and other places aboutez, for to laye the siege unto Paris, and there to abide til thai have the town or elles the bataille, as we ben creditably informed, and fully purpose us, with our Lordes mercy, for to merch for to gif thaim there saide bataille by the viij or ix day of this moneth of Septembre, we pray you hertly and also charge and commande you straitly, upon pain of alle that ye may forfaite anenst my lord and us, that ye comme unto us in al haste possible, so that ye be with us at the last by the saide ix day, with al the feleshipe that ye may raise or gete in any wise, on horsebac and in fote, your place seurly ordeinde fore and kept. And the bailly of (Caen) shall both receve the monstres and telle yow where ye shal have redy paiement of your wages. And failleth not her of, as ye love the con-servacion of this londe, and as ye wol answere to my lordes and us, therefore, in tyme comyng. And weteth wel for certain that hit lay never in oure power sith we had the regency of France so wele as it doth now bothe of lordes, landes and other, to rewarde men. The whiche thing we promette yow for to do largely unto al tho that come to us at this tyme. And owre

Lord have you in His keping.

Yevene under oure signet at Verdun, the first day of Septembre

And failleth not her of, as ye love the conservacion of this londe.

Everything was at stake in those few days. Why then was no public acknowledgement of it made in Paris earlier than this? Partly perhaps because it was hoped that the truce-proposals would be welcomed by the French if they seemed to be proved genuine by lack of warlike activity on the Anglo-Burgundian side, but partly also from fear that stripping the

garrisons too soon from Normandy and the west would lead
to rebellion there. A footnote in a different ink to the orders
issued to the lieutenant of Falaise spells out the English
dilemma: what may well be the last battle is at hand, but a
watch must be maintained for traitors:

> more over we pray you hertilye that ye sende unto us
> Henrye Montone with al the retinue and felaship that ye
> hade last, or moo, yif ye may moo gete. And that ye send us
> of the best marchers and the best horsed men that ye can or
> may gete in the countree. And at Caen we have ordenned
> your saide retinue to have a hoole monneth waages in hand.
> And we wol that your self abide stille upon the sauvegarde
> of Faloize, and that ye take good heed thereunto, boothe
> day and nighte, and that ye bee wel wer of traisons.[3]

Charles, as weak and indecisive as ever, pulled this way and
that by his advisers, as frightened as ever, probably, by the
thought of a confrontation with the duke whose father he had
murdered, gave Bedford and Burgundy far too long in which
to activate plans for the defence of Paris. Bedford, the old
campaigner, foresaw a battle on the 8–9 September: it was not
until the 7th that Charles moved with the utmost reluctance
from Compiègne to Saint Denis, in the cathedral of which
town his father had been buried, with the Duke of Bedford
as his only royal mourner, as long ago as 1422.

Another night was wasted while Joan and Alençon tried to
persuade the king that he must order an immediate attack.
Finally, Joan's patience gave out: 'There was there with king
Charles,' a French chronicler wrote, 'Joan la Pucelle, who had
great fame with everyone, and who daily argued with the king
and his princes to make an assault on the city of Paris, saying
that if he did so, she knew of a certainty that it would be
reduced to obedience to him. At her insistence, an agreement
was reached that they would make an assault on Monday,
the twelfth day of September' (actually 8 September). 'Which
decision having been made, they brought up all kinds of
fighting men, and on the Monday aforementioned King Charles
went into battle between Paris and Montmartre with his
princes, and the Pucelle leading the vanguard.'[4]

Charles had at last committed himself. Let an English chronicler take up the story:

'(Charles) lodged his armie at Montmartir and Abeevilliers nere adjoinyng and lying to the Citie of Paris. And from thence sent Iohn Duke of Alanson, and his sorceresse Ioan (called the Mayde sent from God) in whom his whole affiaunce then consisted, with three thousand light horsemen, to get again the Citie of Paris, eithe by force, or by fayre flatteryng, or reasonable treatie, and after them he, without delay or deferrying of time, and with all hys power, came betwene Montmartir and Paris and sodeinely approached the gate of Saint Honore, settyng up ladders to the walles, and casting faggots into diches as though he would . . . sodeinly have gotten the fayre citie. But the Englishe Capteynes, every one kepyng his warde and place assigned so manfully and fiercely with a noble courage defended themselves, their walles and towers, with the assistance of the Parisiens, that they rebutted and drave away the Frenchmen, and threwe downe Ione, their great goddesse, into the botome of the towne ditche, where she lay behind the backe of an Asse, sore hurt, till the tyme that she all filthie with mire and durt, was drawn out by Guyshard of Thienbrone, servant to the Duke of Alanson . . .'[5]

Allowance having been made for English prejudice, that was approximately what did happen that unhappy day. The French account says: '(Joan attacked St Honoré) beginning precisely at ten o'clock in the morning and continuing for four or five hours without respite . . . During this assault, many of the attackers were thrown down dead and wounded by the cannon, culverins and other guns fired at them by the Parisians; among them, Joan the Maid was gravely wounded and lay in the trench behind an ass until the hour of Vespers when Guichard de Tienbronne and others went and searched for her, but several of them too were wounded by the defenders . . .'

It was a battle that Joan herself did not want to talk about. The only point about it on which she could pride herself was that 'she was wounded in the trenches of Paris, and was healed of the wound in five days'. She did not like to be reminded by her judges that her voices had not authorized her to fight, 'and asked if the skirmish was on a feast-day', had to be asked 'several times' before replying that 'she was very well aware that it was a feast'. Then 'asked if it was a good thing to make an assault on a feast'—something that most commanders would not have worried about, but which had concerned her several times, when her voices had been guiding her—all she would say was '*Passés oultre*: Go on to something else'.[6] The point was raised again during an interrogation in her prison cell: 'she was asked if it were well done on the birthday of our Lady, being a feast-day, to attack Paris: replied, It is a good thing to keep the feast of our Lady . . . asked if she had not said at Paris: Surrender the city to Jesus; replied, No, but, Yield to the king of France'[7].

Charles VII made Joan's wounding the excuse for ending the battle and the campaign. While her wound was healing, he ordered that all French forces should be pulled back from Paris, and the bridge of boats constructed over the Seine demolished. As Perceval de Cagny remarked, 'It seemed that at that time he was content with the grace that God had already shown him, undertaking nothing else.' He signed the truce offered to him by Burgundy, and ordered a retreat into Berry and so back to the Loire. Joan was not alone in feeling very bitter at this turn of events, but like everyone else, she had to acquiesce. Before the army abandoned St Denis, she hung up in the cathedral 'a white suit of armour, complete, for a soldier, with a sword . . . from devotion: for so fighting-men are accustomed to do when they are wounded . . . she offered it to St Denis, whose name was France's battle-cry'.[8]

Less than a fortnight later, the army was disbanded at Gien, and the Duke of Alençon and the other lords dismissed to their holdings, graciously but peremptorily nonetheless. For the moment, the favourites Regnauld de Chartres, Goncourt and above all de la Trémouille were paramount over the policies of Charles VII: there can be no doubt that it was by their influence that 'the desire of the Pucelle and the King's army was betrayed',[9] a triumphant campaign brought to an untimely end and the war prolonged for twenty years.

7

The Living Legend

When the army was disbanded at Gien in the winter of 1429, Joan did not go home, as she had earlier said she would like to do. She stayed with the court, first at Gien, then at Bourges. She was a member of the privy council, supposedly kept informed about everything that was planned. To Charles himself she was a token, a pledge of his legitimacy, a living witness and proof of his success. Just as during the summer 'Joan La Pucelle was always in front of everyone with her standard', the visible symbol of unity, courage and victory, so now in the winter he had to have her either close to him or fighting for him.

To his ministers, however—and Georges de la Trémouille in particular—she was a nuisance that might easily become a threat. Contemptuous though Burgundy's offer of a truce had been, the fact that he had offered it was the first taste of success they had ever enjoyed in the political sphere. Joan's often expressed hatred of Burgundians was an obstacle to the further improvement of relations while she remained so close to the king. While they were talking to emissaries from Burgundy led by John of Luxemburg, she was telling Catherine de la Rochelle—and no doubt anyone else who would listen—that 'it seemed to her they would never make peace, except at the point of a lance'.

To make the position more difficult, Joan's warlike stance was publicly approved by the greatest soldier in Charles's forces, Jean, the Duke of Alençon. The relationship between

88

the duke and the peasant was a most unlikely one but very
genuine, built, apparently, on a foundation of mutual trust and
respect. It was Alençon who had first supported Joan, during
and after her examination at Poitiers. It had been to him she
had turned time and again for help and support during the
summer campaign. He was her 'gentil duc': for her, he was
willing to disobey orders he had received, seize St Denis and
attack Paris. Such a combination of talents was dangerous at
all times and could be very dangerous indeed in certain
circumstances. The favourites decided that the time had come
to break up this strange alliance and it was to that task that
they addressed their efforts throughout the early part of the
winter.

Whatever story they told Charles (and they may, for all
anyone knows, have gone as far as suggesting treason to him,
though it is more likely that they flattered him with a plan
which he could afterwards call his own), they were successful.
The duke wrote to the king, suggesting that the time had now
come to put into effect the plan favoured by de la Trémouille
after the relief of Orléans, for an attack north from the Loire
to Chartres and Caen and ultimately the Normandy coast, so
cutting off the English from England. He said that with Joan
fighting beside him, he was certain of success. De la Trémouille,
Raoul de Goncourt and Regnauld of Chartres were united in
their horror at the very idea. By all means let the duke fight in
Normandy—if he could raise an army and pay it—but for the
king to allow Joan to go with him was unthinkable.

Whether Joan found it thinkable or not, we do not know.
In any case, the plan was probably impractical from the first.
As the stubborn Angloys-Francoys defence of the Porte St
Honoré had shown, the English and their allies were regaining
their nerve and with it the initiative. A Normandy campaign
on a large scale would have been expensive in both men and
money. Given Joan's leadership together with the duke's,
the men could probably have been found, but the money was
another question altogether. There simply was none. The only
man who could possibly have found any, Georges de la
Trémouille, was the leader of the peace party. He was certainly
not going to help finance a new campaign. So for weeks, Joan
hung moody and unemployed about the court, while de la

Trémouille bustled about importantly, glowing with the glory
of the new title granted him after the coronation of Duke of
Sully.

She was just discovering the bitter truth, that no one can
find work for a living legend. Bona Visconti wrote to her,
asking for her help in the recovery of Milan. But she was not a
universal saviour. Her mission was to save France. The Lord
of Armagnac wrote to her, asking her which was the true pope,
the one in Italy or the one in Spain. But she was not the Holy
Ghost, to judge between candidates for the papal throne.
At Bourges, staying at the house of René de Bouligny, the
Councillor-General for Finance, she planned a new adventure
and in October, only a month after the truce with Burgundy
had come into effect, persuaded Charles that she must be
allowed to ride out on it. He gave her the Lord of Albert, yet
another Charles, as the commander of her troops and together
they took a small force to St-Pierre-Les-Moutiers, in the
Burgundian-held upper Loire region, and captured it with
very small losses. Encouraged by this success, they moved on
to lay siege to Charité-sur-Loire, but the attempt to take the
town was ill-conceived. They were short of troops and
supplies of every kind. It was an exceptionally early and cold
winter. Appeals for help were sent to Rheims and Clermont.
The supplies were promised, but did not come. Perhaps
safeguarding the reputation of her voices' infallibility, Joan
later denied that they had told her to attack La Charité.[1]

It must have been at about this time, when there was no
money to pay the soldiers and long rides had to be undertaken
foraging for supplies, that Joan encountered Catherine de la
Rochelle at Montfaucon, and heard from her the story of the
pale lady dressed in cloth-of-gold who was offering the secret
of a golden treasure that would be lost and found again, and
finally used for the payment of Joan's soldiers. Neither the
pale lady nor anyone else actually provided the money the war
required and in December 'because the king had made no
finance available to send her supplies or money for the maintenance of her force, she decided it was better to raise her
siege, and left there in great displeasure'.[2]

Returning, very disgruntled, from La Charité in time to
spend Christmas with the court at Meung-sur-Loire, Joan was

rewarded for all that she had done by the awarding of letters patent of nobility, signed by de la Trémouille, in the names of herself, her parents, and her brothers, who now became formally 'du Lis'. She refused the honour herself: as she was to tell her judges, she 'had asked nothing of her king, save good weapons, good horses, and money to pay the people where she lodged'. It was these essentials that had failed to reach La Charité. There is little wonder that Joan was in an ungracious mood. As she herself said, she never had a shield, though in most representations, beginning with the first known miniature, that in the *Champion des Dames*, she is shown with the arms accepted by her brothers, 'a blue field, with two gold fleurs-de-lis, and a sword between' transfixing a crown, 'given to her brothers by the king without petition or revelation'.

Meanwhile, in the Anglo-Burgundian camp, more immediately meaningful titles were being bestowed. On 13 October, Philip the Good was named at Paris, where he and Bedford both were, lieutenant-general of the King of England and France within the French realm and so officially second-in-command to Bedford the regent. In January, Philip married the princess Isabella of Portugal and in naming the first knights for the Order of the Toison d'Or created to celebrate the marriage, took the opportunity to reward those who had been most prominent for their opposition to Charles VII, among them John of Luxemburg 'Lord of Beaurevoir and Choques', the ambassador who had presented impossible truce-terms to Charles and a former governor of Paris during the time when Charles's exclusion from the succession was being plotted there. Meanwhile, in England, on 6 November, King Henry—not yet quite eight years old—was presented to the Parliament at Westminster by Warwick, and solemnly crowned in the abbey. Parliament immediately ruled that Gloucester's protectorship was over, though the regency continued and Warwick remained 'about the king's person . . . to teach him to love, worship and dread God . . . to chastise him when he dothe amiss; and to remove persons not behovefull nor expedient from his presence'. The remote preparations were already being made for a coronation in France and a victorious campaign against Charles the pretender.

In February 1430, Charles moved his court from Meung to Sully, to spend what was always the hungriest part of the year with his richest vassal, Duke Georges of Sully. At about the same time, Philip of Burgundy, exercising his new commission for the first time, moved Anglo-Burgundian troops into Brie and Champagne, in preparation for a reconquest of all that Joan and Alençon had won for Charles VII the previous summer. The city of Rheims, seeing itself cast as the chief villain in the drama of Charles's coronation as seen through Anglo-Burgundian eyes, anxiously appealed to its heroes for help. Joan dictated reassuring letters to the citizens on the 16th and again on 28 March promising them aid before it was too late in the name of the king. But in fact the king was not prepared to help them even if he had been well enough supplied with men and material to do so effectively. To the growing horror of their inhabitants, it became ever more apparent that the cities from Compiègne to Auxerre which had declared for him more or less willingly the previous summer were now to be left to their fate.

What that fate was to be was left in no doubt as men and supplies were amassed outside Paris, and small towns in the direction of Compiègne such as Choisy-au-Bac were reduced by siege and sacked. Philip the Good set methodically about his work as lieutenant-general, like a man who knew that time was on his side. It seemed that the tide had turned for the Anglo-Burgundian alliance from the moment that Joan had fallen wounded into the fosse at Paris. On 23 April, King Henry VI and II, attended by the Cardinal of England, and a considerable army of noblemen and men-at-arms, landed at Calais, in a demonstration of English confidence the significance of which no observer could miss.

Her king's pusillanimity in the face of the impending triumph of the hated Burgundians was altogether too much for Joan. At some time early in April she left Sully secretly with her brother Pierre, her squire Jean d'Aulon and a small company of men-at-arms and made her way north, believing that nothing but herself stood between Burgundy and the loyal towns: if anything could keep them loyal, it would be she herself showing herself in them and fighting beside their men.

How right she was in her judgement of Charles's impotence

was amply demonstrated by the hand-wringing self-pity of the letter he addressed to those towns on 6 May: Burgundy 'having beguiled and deceived us for some time with truces and in other ways—without a shadow of good faith, because he had said and declared that it was his aim to achieve the blessing of peace the which we ourselves have powerfully desired and do desire for the solace of our wretched people who to the discomfort of our heart have suffered so much and are so suffering every day—has now disposed certain forces to make war against us and our land and loyal people' and there is (after a lot of verbiage) nothing effective that we can do about it.

On 17 April, Joan arrived at Melun and it seemed that she had been right in her estimation of the magic of her name for the townspeople declared for Charles.

A few days later she appeared at Lagny-sur-Marne, and again, people welcomed her. But they were now well within Burgundian lines, life was tense and could be harsh. It was at Lagny that occurred two of the oddest incidents in Joan's life, the one noteworthy because it shows how superstitious people had grown about her (and how far she was now willing to indulge, or share in, their near-worship of her), the other because it shows how ruthless she had become.

At the sixth session of her interrogation she was closely questioned about superstitious practices that might be called magical relating to herself and her belongings, especially her rings,[3] and was then asked how old the baby was that she had visited at Lagny. That seemingly simple question evoked the following peculiar story according to the French account of the examination:

The child was three days old. It had been brought to Lagny, to our Lady's [Church]. She had been told that the girls of the place were standing [in prayer] before our Lady and she herself felt a desire to go there and pray to God and our Lady that He might be pleased to grant him life. And she had gone there and prayed to God with the others. And at last he had shown signs of life and had cried out three times: so then he had been baptised and finally had died and been buried in consecrated ground. And as she had said throughout the three days the child had shown no signs of

life but had been as black as her tunic: but when he had
breathed, the colour had started to come back to him. And
she herself had knelt there with the girls before our Lady
making petition for him.

The other story from Lagny—again told by Joan herself—
is quite different. In her prison cell on the afternoon of
Wednesday, 14 March 1431, she was asked if to take a man for
ransom and let him die as a prisoner was a mortal sin. She
replied that she had never done such a thing 'so then they
mentioned to her one Francquet of Arras, whose death she had
brought about at Lagny'.

She could not deny it, and she can hardly have forgotten it,
for letting a prisoner die once he had been offered quarter and
his ransom had been fixed was a shameful and dishonourable
crime against the rules of war. She tried to justify herself: but
even though all she said was probably true, her crime
remained:

> She knew that she had brought about his death. He had
> deserved it, because he had confessed to being a murderer,
> thief and traitor . . . his trial had lasted fifteen days, and his
> judges were the Bailiff of Senlis and the justices of Lagny.
> [But after his condemnation] she had asked for an exchange:
> this man Francquet for a man from Paris, the innkeeper of the
> Bear. And when she had learned that the latter was already
> dead and the bailiff had told her that she would do a great
> injury to justice if she did release this Francquet, she had said
> to the bailiff: 'As my man is dead, I want you to have this
> one: do with him what justice demands'.
>
> Asked if she had given money or caused money to be
> given to the man who had captured the said Francquet:
> replied that she was not the mintmaster or treasurer of
> France, to be giving money away.

The girls in these two stories are so different that they might
be living in different worlds. It may be, of course, that the
story of Joan's 'standing before our Lady' at Lagny church
was invented only long after she was dead to provide material
for the legend of Joan-the-saint. Certainly, it does appear in

only one version of her trial. But it is more probable that Joan *was* two persons at Lagny as she sought to regain contact with the spirit-world that she feared she had lost forever. By her own evidence, she re-established that contact later, but for the time being she was lost, wandering between the world of her country childhood, where the girls of a place would pray for a miracle to allow a baby to be baptized in order that it might be buried in consecrated ground, and the world of the camps, where the mercenary could be handed back to an (admittedly deserved) death in a moment of pique: a moment of which the woman who had felt it would afterwards be deeply ashamed.

At her trial, Joan fumbled among her memories of this time in a most uncharacteristic way. Denying that she had ever held a man for ransom—and so promised him life—and afterwards let him die, she obviously did not want to talk about Francquet d'Arras. Equally clearly, she was uncomfortable when her judges asked her about the theft of the Bishop of Senlis's horse. It was a petty little story. The bishop was obviously being vindictive when he had reported the facts, and the court when it included this theft among Joan's list of sins. But that is not the point here—which is, rather, Joan's groping for reasons, excuses, explanations of that confused period that were not apologies to anyone, even herself:

> She believed firmly [she said] that there was no mortal sin towards our Lord (in the matter of the horse), because it was valued at 200 gold *salus* and she had given her note of hand for that amount: moreover, she had sent it back to the Lord de la Trémouille to return to my Lord of Senlis. Anyway, the horse was worthless to her as a riding animal. She added: she owed the Bishop nothing. Besides, she would not have been willing to keep it, because she had heard that the bishop was not pleased that she had taken his horse and also because she had found it useless to the military. She did not know whether the bishop had received the amount of her note of hand, nor whether his horse had been restored to him in fact. She thought not.

Later the same day, when she was formally charged with several offences, including the theft of the horse, she said 'It was returned'.[4]

It might be objected that when Joan made these statements, she was tired and ill, after months in prison. She was, however, not more tired and ill when she was making them than when she was making some of her clearest and most decisive points against her judges. It was the subject that worried her: her conscience was not clear on it, and the whole business had happened at a time she preferred not to remember, a confused bitter time, when she was left without the support of her king, the friendship of Alençon, or the guidance of her voices.

The struggle that she conducted in Champagne and the Ile de France to hold the people loyal to Charles VII was not wholly fruitless. But morale was low everywhere, and no one knew quite what to do. Through the first fortnight of May Joan worked her way from town to town northwards, rallying support here and failing to find it there. At most the force at her command seems never to have exceeded five hundred men. Though she denied that it worried her, it must have been on her mind that since Melun her voices had come to her only with dire warnings: 'in the week of Easter last I was in the trenches at Melun,' she told Jehan de la Fontaine in her cell on 10 March 1431. 'My voices told me that I would be taken before St John's Day . . .' He asked her if her voices had repeated their message after Melun, and she replied, 'Yes, many times—almost every day . . . They told me I should take things calmly: these things had to be. But they did not tell me when: if I had known, I might not have gone out. I asked many times that I might know how, but they did not want to tell me. And I asked—*Passez oultre*: go on to something else!'

John of Luxemburg, one of the most able of the Burgundian captains, laid siege to Compiègne. Joan went there on 14 May, and made plans with Charles's ambassador Regnauld of Chartres, and the local commander Louis I of Bourbon, the Count of Vendôme, that achieved their primary object of driving the Burgundians back from the Oise. But the threat was only postponed, and everyone knew it. Four days later, when Joan presented herself with her miniscule force at the gates of Soissons, the citizens refused her admittance. She went on to Crespy-in-Valois, where she was received. While she was there, the news went from bad to worse. Archbishop Regnauld and Louis of Bourbon were reported to have left the area, and crossed the Seine, heading apparently for the safety of the Loire. And on 22 May Philip the Good established his headquarters at the castle of Coudon-sur-Aronde, only four miles from Compiègne, while his troops, a combined Anglo-Burgundian force under captains of such stature as John of Luxemburg and the Earl of Arundel, took up positions along the river opposite the town.

The report of these troop movements reached Joan that evening at Crespy. She realized immediately that the decisive moment had come. With the faithful d'Aulon and her five hundred she rode by secret ways through the woods to Compiègne.

8

Prisoner of the French

Joan entered Compiègne after midnight 'at the secret hour of the night' unseen, she believed, by her enemies. 'And that same day in the evening she made the sally in which she was taken'.[1]

Compiègne lay on the River Oise defended by great walls, a rampart and glacis, a ditch and some rough open fields. The Montdidier road ran out of the town north-westwards and crossed the river by a heavily defended bridge, Pontlevesque, Bishop's Bridge. On the far side of the river the English and Burgundians were encamped. It was over Pontlevesque that Joan led her last sally. Asked at her trial whether her voices had told her to go to Bishop's Bridge, she made two significantly different replies:

> Asked if when she had made this sally she had received a voice to go and make it: replied, she had heard nothing about being captured that day and had been told nothing except to go out.

and

> Although she had a revelation that she would be taken, she had gone all the more willingly to war with the captains.[2] It was a confused and exciting day, perhaps a frightening one, although she would not have admitted to the fear behind her exhilaration. Overt fear came later, when she had been taken by her enemies.

As she told the story of her capture to Jehan de la Fontaine

on 10 March, it was one of over-enthusiasm and miscalculation
of risks:

> I passed over the bridge and the rampart with my people to
> attack the people of the Lord of Luxemburg. And we drove
> them back twice up to the Burgundians' billets and the third
> time up to the midpoint on the road. And Englishmen who
> were there cut me and my people off from the road, coming
> between me and the rampart. So I and my people withdrew,
> and while we were withdrawing I was taken between the
> river and Compiègne, in a field, on the Picardy side, near the
> rampart. All that was between me at the place where I was
> taken and Compiègne was the river, the rampart and the
> ditch to the rampart.[3]

The story is somewhat confused. Perhaps the confusion was
in the mind of the clerk who took it down painstakingly in the
third person (*and they drove them back twice up to the Burgundians'
billets* . . .), but it would not be surprising if it were in Joan's.
The shock of being captured had etched certain scenes on her
mind, but the links between these scenes were lost so that her
memory of that evening was incoherent and incomplete.
Fortunately there is another much clearer account of the
skirmish in the work of a contemporary Burgundian chronicler
who had himself questioned survivors and eyewitnesses:

> While the Duke of Burgundy was at Coudon, as has been
> related, and his people were in the villages round about
> towards Compiègne, it happend on the evening of the
> Ascension, about five hours after midday, that Joan *la
> Pucelle*, Poton [de Santrailles] and other French captains,
> having with them five or six hundred fighting men, made an
> armed sortie on foot and horseback out of the said city of
> Compiègne by the bridge-gate facing Montdidier with the
> intention of charging as far as Messire Baudet de Noyelle's
> quarters which, as I have already said, were at Marigny at
> the end of the road, there being with him at that hour Messire
> Jehan of Luxemburg, the Lord of Crequy and eight or ten
> other gentlemen who had all come on horseback with none
> but light armour, the said Messire Jehan of Luxemburg

having come there to show and advise how the town of Compiègne might be besieged to greater advantage. And the story runs that when the French started advancing on the quarters at Marigny where the for the most part wholly unarmed and unprepared Burgundians were, there quite quickly developed a fairly big skirmish during which the alarm was sounded in several encampments on the Burgundian side and some Englishmen came to the support of the Picards, they setting themselves to fight outside Venette, in the fields where they were camped. There may have been as many as five hundred fighting men all told. Over on the other side, Messire Jehan of Luxemburg's people encamped at Clary, learning that there was an affray, came from that direction to help their master and captain—he being involved in the skirmish—and most of them rallied to him. At this point, the Lord of Crequy was seriously wounded. Finally, after the skirmish had lasted quite a time the French seeing the number of their enemies increasing greatly retreated towards their town, La Pucelle being always with them at the rear, giving great support to her people and bringing them back safely without loss. But those in the Burgundian party, realizing that they would shortly have help on every side, crowded in on them strongly, throwing themselves at them. And in the end, according to my information, the so-called Pucelle was pulled right off her horse by an archer close to the Bastard of Vendôme and she gave her parole to him, and he took her swiftly to Marigny as a prisoner, where she was put under close guard. Poton de Santrailles in Burgundy and certain others were taken with her. And, very grieved, the other Frenchmen went back into the town of Compiègne where they greatly bemoaned the loss they had sustained, and were especially unhappy and vexed by the capture of the Pucelle, while on the other hand those of the Burgundian party, the English, and people generally of all sorts were very delighted at it, reckoning it above having taken five hundred of the other side's fighting men. And fairly soon afterwards the Duke of Burgundy came with all his force from the quarters at Coudon to the camp in the meadows before Compiègne. The English and all sorts of people gathered around the duke, all shouting and crying out together on account of the capture of the so-called *Pucelle*. The Duke of Burgundy went to see her in the quarter where she was, and exchanged a few words with her, and then went back to his quarters, as also did everyone else for the night. And La Pucelle Jehanne was kept under the guard and control of Messire Jehan of Luxemburg who a few days later sent her under strong escort to his castle of Beaurevoir, where she was for a long time a prisoner.[4]

Ironical coincidences are frequent in civil war. It was one of history's small ironies that the man to whom Joan gave her parole on the evening of her capture, the Bastard of Vendôme, was half-brother to the French captain Louis, lord of Vendôme who had deserted Compiègne when the first probing attack by John of Luxemburg's Burgundians had reached the river.

It is another of those ironies that the man into whose custody she was surrendered, the same John of Luxemburg, was the cousin on his mother's side of her old comrade-in-arms Jean the Bastard of Orléans; he was the third son of Marguerite d'Enghien and John I of Luxemburg, and had always been as unswervingly loyal to the dukes of Burgundy as the Bastard had to Orléans. In 1414 he had been governor of Arras for John the Fearless; in 1418 he had governed first Senlis and then Paris, which he had held for Burgundy until he had handed it over to the Duke of Clarence in 1420. Poton de Santrailles had been his prisoner in 1423 and freed for ransom. In 1424 he had captured Guise for Burgundy and shortly after making Joan a prisoner he accepted the surrender of Soissons: already lord of Beaurevoir and Choques by inheritance from his father, with the title Count of Ligny and a share in its revenues, his reward for the capture of Joan was the title of Count of Guise.

Although Joan knew from her voices that she was to be taken prisoner and that it was her duty, as explained by them, to be calm whatever happened, it cannot have been easy for her to accept the fact of having been captured. The English soldiers, who called her 'the cow-girl' and 'the Armagnac Whore', had long ago threatened to burn her when they caught her. It is easy to imagine what their behaviour was like on the night she was taken. Actually within hours of her capture debate had begun on the highest diplomatic levels about her fate but she can have known nothing of it at that time. All she knew was that she was surrounded by jeering and rejoicing enemies and closely guarded as much for her own physical protection as to prevent her escape.

Probably as early as the day after she was captured she was sent beyond the reach of a sudden rescue attempt to John of Luxemburg's castle of Beaulieu in Vermandois where she was, by her own account, imprisoned in the tower, and from where she made a desperate attempt to escape: 'I was a prisoner there, and most anxious to escape. I was kept in confinement with a guard around the tower. There was only the door-keeper to advise and help me. It seemed to me that it would be pleasing to God if I were to escape then: I had to see the English king—my voices told me so.'[5]

What she wanted to tell the English king was never revealed. She attempted to have herself carried out of the castle in a bundle of wood, but was detected, and sent to Beaurevoir under heavy escort where, although she was desperately unhappy, John of Luxemburg's wife, Jeanne of Bethune, and the Lady of Beaurevoir were some comfort to her, although she could not accept their urging that she should give up her male dress and let her hair grow.

Joan was afraid—and her fear was justified—that her attempts to escape from Beaulieu and elsewhere would be held against her. The question was: had she ever surrendered in technically correct form? If she had in fact given her parole, breaking it was a sin in the eyes of the church and a technical offence against the laws of warfare, heinous in some eyes because it threatened the whole practice of giving quarter to prisoners in the hope of holding them for ransom. The Bastard of Vendôme had received her surrender and given her his protection on the field, but Joan afterwards maintained that she had never given her parole to anyone. At her trial (admittedly in very different circumstances) when she was told that she would be fettered as she had tried several times to escape, she said that 'it was true that she had greatly wanted to escape from prison as it was lawful for every prisoner to do. And she said moreover that if she succeeded in escaping, they could not represent it as being false to or breaking faith with anyone, for she had never surrendered to anyone.'[6]

Even if she had not believed this, however, after she became a prisoner she had another defence when accused of breaking faith. Her voices had returned to her, and she was bound to obey them whatever the consequences to herself, to her good name, to legality as men reckoned it, or to anything else. Their demands overrode everything. At Beaulieu, she claimed, she had to try and escape, because 'it would be pleasing to God: I had to see the English king—my voices told me so'.

The interrogation concerning that attempted escape continued:

'Asked if she had leave from God or her voices to leave prisons when it pleased her: replied, I have tried many times, but have not succeeded yet.

'Asked if she would go then, if she saw a way open; replied, If she saw a door open, she would go through it—that in itself would be permission from her Lord. Added: she firmly believed that if she saw a door open, and the guards and the other English in no position to resist, she might understand that as leave and that God was sending her help. But without [his] leave she would not go.

'She would not make an attempt to break out, to see if our Lord would be happy—though she agreed [with the proverb] "Help yourself and God will help you". And she was saying that so that if she were to go they could not say she had gone without permission'.

This is a remarkable statement of peasant morality, with nothing whatsoever in common with the thinking of lawyers. It reveals Joan's motivation as personal expediency and confirms the view expressed earlier in this book, that Joan's 'voices' were fundamentally the projection of her own desires and wishes, presented by her to herself in a form such that they had to be obeyed. She gives two reasons why she tried to escape from Beaulieu and in the last analysis those reasons are in fact one and the same: she did not like it there, and her voices told her to get out and see the English king. She probably did surrender in due form to her captors, but the promises she made meant nothing to her. This is not a moral judgement on Joan—though her judges tried to make a moral issue out of it—but a statement of how her mind appears consistently to have worked. It was a very human mind indeed. There was nothing unusual about wanting to get out of prison. Joan's singularity lay in her tenacity of purpose; not in the mechanisms by which she 'forgot' unpleasant facts (her giving of her parole, for instance, or her responsibility for the death of Francquet d'Arras) and substituted new and more pleasant duties (haranguing the English king in the one case, or serving the ends of true justice in the other) for those distasteful to her.

While Joan was at Beaulieu planning her escape, those interested in making sure that she was never free again were already arguing over how best permanently to dispose of her. The news of her capture reached Paris on 24 May. Within two days the doctors of the university had already written to the Duke of Burgundy demanding that as a person 'suspected most strongly of many crimes touching on heresy' she should be handed over to the university for trial before 'by the malevolence and subtlety of evil persons your enemies and adversaries . . . she be in some fashion taken out of your control'. The university feared a rescue attempt by Charles VII —the kind of attempt that John of Luxemburg had made more difficult by sending Joan to Beaulieu, fifty miles from the nearest town loyal to Charles. The fear was a reasonable one, but apparently unnecessary. Neither immediately after Joan's capture, nor at any other time before her execution, did Charles make any move to save her.

Philip of Burgundy did not immediately hand Joan over on receiving this letter, partly, perhaps, because he expected to be able to bargain with Charles VII over her, but not least because she was not his prisoner but John of Luxemburg's, and there was an etiquette in these affairs. After her attempted escape, John moved her to his castle of Beaurevoir, which lay between Cambrai and St Quentin, further than ever from the battle zone.

More than a month passed, while the siege of Compiègne dragged on, and at Paris the doctors argued. The university had been consistently the enemy of the Valois—had, in fact, nearly always been a centre of revolt against whoever had power in France. During the Great Schism, it had opposed French candidates for the papal throne, and so found itself allied with the English, who had also constantly opposed them. It had welcomed first the Burgundians and then the English in Paris (though it was not a wholly united body: its former chancellor Gerson flattered Charles VII by dedicating work to him, and wrote a study vindicating Joan).[7] Now, as a body, it was as determined as any group in the country that Joan should be condemned. How far was its enmity towards her based on a cool judicial assessment of her actions? It is tempting to say: given the university's political affiliations, not at all, or hardly so. But it indicted Joan for religious offences and there is no proof that some at least of its members did not believe that she had committed crimes for which, under the laws of the time, she deserved to be condemned.

However that may be, there is little doubt that Joan's worst enemy at Paris was politically motivated. He was Pierre Cauchon, the Count-Bishop of Beauvais, who had first apparently welcomed and then unambiguously deserted Charles VII the previous summer. When the university decided to exert pressure on the Burgundians, it was Pierre Cauchon who was chosen to carry out its wishes. On 14 July he dictated the following letter to Joan's captors, delivering it two days later himself:

What follows is what the Bishop of Beauvais requires of my lord the Duke of Burgundy and my lord John of Luxemburg, and the Bastard of Vendôme, on behalf of the king our lord, and on his own behalf as Bishop of Beauvais:

that this woman named Jhenne the Pucelle, a prisoner, be sent to the king to be handed over to the church and tried, in as much as she is suspected and accused of having committed many crimes, such as sorceries, idolatry, invocation [of spirits] and many other matters touching our faith and contrary to it. And although, taking into consideration what is said here, she cannot be a prize of war nevertheless to recompense those who took her and have detained her, the king wishes liberally to reward them, up to the sum of six thousand *livres*: and to the said Bastard who took her . . . rent for her maintenance, up to two or three hundred *livres*.

Item, the said bishop requires from the abovementioned

[persons] and from each of them individually that as this
woman was taken in his diocese and under his spiritual
jurisdiction, she should be handed over to him to be tried,
as is his right.[8]

On the same day, the university's seal was set to a letter
addressed to John of Luxemburg personally:

Your noble prudence is well aware that all good Catholic
knights should use their power and might primarily in the
service of God, and especially [that] the first oath of the
orders of chivalry is to guard and defend the honour of God
the Catholic faith, and his Holy Church. This oath you were
serving well when you used your noble power and personal
presence to apprehend the woman called La Pucelle through
whom God's honour has been immeasurably offended, the
faith excessively injured, and the church overmuch dis-
honoured. For through her idolatries . . . irreparable hurts
have ensued in this kingdom. We are bound to thank you
greatly for having done so great a service to our holy faith
and to all this kingdom . . . but it would be a terrible thing
were this woman to escape punishment for her crimes.
Therefore we beseech you send her . . . to the Inquisitor of the
Faith . . . Please give her up, handing her over to the
reverend father in God and our most honoured Lord, the
Bishop of Beauvais . . .[9]

Two things stand out from these letters: the first, that the
church, the university, and the English authorities in Paris
were all working together to secure Joan's condemnation; the
second, that for reasons undisclosed John of Luxemburg and
Philip of Burgundy were suspected of wanting to keep her
themselves. Appeals are made in them to their political loyalty,
religious faith and cupidity—as though no one was sure which
was the key that would unlock Joan's prison and admit her
executioner. The question as to why John of Luxemburg held
on so long to his prisoner is one that has never been satisfactorily answered. French historians have long speculated that
she was protected by the Demoiselle of Beaurevoir, John of
Luxemburg's cousin Philippe, the Countess of St Pol: it has

often been pointed out that Philippe died on the 13 November and only a few weeks afterwards Joan was surrendered to Bishop Cauchon.

Despite the kindness of the Lady of Beaurevoir, however, Joan grew increasingly depressed in confinement at the castle. All the news she was allowed to hear was bad: the siege was continuing, the English were demanding that she should be given up to them . . . At some time before the siege was lifted (25 October) she attempted suicide—though, naturally, she afterwards did not call it that, but thought of it in terms of 'escape'.

She told the story—though somewhat haltingly—at her interrogation:

Asked why she had leapt from the tower at Beaurevoir: replied, that she had heard tell that those at Compiègne, all down to the age of seven, were to be put to fire and blood, and that she would rather die than live after the destruction of good people in such a way. That was one of the reasons. The other, that she knew that she was to be sold to the English and would rather die than be in the hands of the English, her enemies.

Added: 'Truly: it is something I could have done without seeing: I had rather die than be put into the hands of the English.'

Later in the same session, she was asked if when she had jumped it had been in her mind to kill herself: she denied it, though obviously when she had jumped, dying had been on her mind. Her reply was summarized by the notaries as: 'No. But when she jumped, she commended herself to God, and thought by means of this leap to escape and get clear, so that she might not be handed over to the English.'

Clearly, she did not believe that her voices had promised her that she would escape by jumping from the tower, for she said that 'after she had fallen, she did not want to eat for two or three days; she had in fact been hurt so gravely that she could neither eat nor drink. But nevertheless she was comforted by St Catherine, who told her that she should confess and ask forgiveness of God for having jumped, and that without fail

those at Compiègne would receive help before the feast of
St Martin in the winter. And she had begun to recover, and to
eat, and was soon cured.'[10]

Joan's powers of recuperation were almost as wonderful as
her skill as a prophet: from the wounds she had received at
Paris, she had recovered in five days; the injuries she sustained
at Beaurevoir were obviously much graver, for when she was
first picked out of the castle moat 'some said she was dead',[11]
yet she apparently made a total recovery, both from the fall
and from the depression that had led to it.

Perhaps it was the failure of the siege at Compiègne that
decided the Duke of Burgundy that he owed a gesture to his
allies and led to his re-opening negotiations relating to the
handing-over of Joan, or perhaps it was indeed her loss of the
protection of the Lady of Beaurevoir. Certainly it was little
more than a week after the countess's death when Burgundy
sent a reply to the summonses delivered to him by Pierre
Cauchon on 16 July. That reply was not satisfactory, but at
least it showed that the matter was not unmentionable as far
as he was concerned. Pressure on him and on John of Luxemburg was renewed and at some unknown date between 23
November and 3 January Joan was sold to the English,
ransomed to them, in the jargon of the times, for the sum of
10,000 gold crowns, the money being raised from Normandy.
And the English had sworn to burn her as a witch.

There is a modern school of thought, inaugurated by
Margaret Murray, which would like to imagine Joan as a full-
fledged initiate of a witch-cult allegedly widespread in Europe
in the middle ages and perpetuating the worship of the old
gods at the time when Christianity was outwardly triumphant.[12]
There is however no evidence to suggest that the lawyers and
theologians of Paris University believed that she belonged to
any organized society with coherent religious beliefs. To them
she was simply a witch, one who practised magic in league with
the devil, whom she called 'my Lord'. They noticed—as
modern commentators have—how infrequently she spoke of
Christ or even God. To them, her voices proved her magical
powers, and her victories proclaimed her value to the devil
who so rewarded her.

During the months that she was in Burgundian hands

evidence was collected from Lorraine and elsewhere in support of this belief about her. There was, in fact, remarkably little of it.

People in the western world today have difficulty in sympathizing with those who believed strongly enough in witchcraft to want to stamp it out by judicial means. But to understand the case against Joan and see it as more than mere vindictiveness, it is necessary to stretch the imagination to embrace the idea that witches exist, that they serve evil effectively, and that from the devil they receive powers of second sight and prophecy, the gift of the evil eye and powers of enchantment such as will steal the hearts out of soldiers on the battlefield or bring babies back from death.

Mediaeval churchmen indubitably did believe that witchcraft existed. There are laws against it, and against making black magic, in the canons of almost every synod and council of the church from the early dark ages onwards.[13] There were probably self-proclaimed witches and wizards in Lorraine when Joan was a child. They certainly existed, and were tolerated, in France a generation earlier, for when Charles VI had become insane their help had been called in together with that of more orthodox medical practitioners, certain astrologers, and the saints at pilgrim shrines, in attempts to cure him. Her judges convinced themselves that Joan was a witch. She herself, however, not only steadfastly denied it but also showed an unfamiliarity with familiar aspects of witchcraft which if it was wholly assumed demanded more inventiveness and steadfastness of purpose in denial from her than she showed in any other field.

Was Joan a witch? Once again, the only real evidence comes from the notoriously incomplete court records. Imperfect as they are it is only fair that they should be allowed to speak both for Joan and for her accusers. The questions they asked were based on the information they had received and the laws they felt it necessary to enforce if civilization was to survive. Joan's is one of the earliest of the great witchcraft trials. It is more sober—and therefore more informative—than most later hearings. There is nothing hysterical about Joan's questioning, crazy though the logic on which it was based may now seem.

From their questions, it is clear that the interrogators were seeking to prove that witchcraft was practised in Lorraine, that Joan was familiar with and shared in its practices, and that therefore it was beyond reasonable doubt that her voices were occult in origin, her mission to Charles of Viennois was inspired by the devil, and the victories to which she led the French rebels against King Henry were victories of hell over heaven. In a debate about such insubstantial matters, of course, almost anything can be made to mean almost anything else and in this context even Joan's admission that although she went into the fields and woods she was not a shepherdess by profession (her father had not allowed her to herd the animals after she started to grow up, for fear of soldiers and skinners)[14] could be turned against her, as 'the pagans', the 'heathens', worshipped in the woods and fields and to suspicious minds ordinary decent Christians had no cause to go there unless either they were working or they had been ill and needed to relax.

It was discussion of Joan's voices which, during her third interrogation, gave a natural lead into the subject of witchcraft. Her voices, she said, had told her things for her king and not for Bishop Cauchon's ears, and added that 'that night the voice had told her certain things important to the king which she wished the king might know that day'.

Instant communication over long distances and the ability to be in two places at once are two of the talents with which witches have long been popularly endowed. Cauchon asked why Joan could not speak with her king now, 'as she could when she was in his presence'. She replied that 'she could if it were the will of God' and added that if it were not for the grace of God she would have no powers at all.

Had Joan realized that the great witchcraft debate had opened? Perhaps she had, for she here used the name of God twice in two sentences, linking her psychic powers not with an anonymous 'Lord', but with Cauchon's own deity.

There were more questions about the voices, then suddenly the question was shot at her: in her childhood, had she gone to relax with others in the fields? The word here translated 'relax' was *esbattre*, given in the Latin version as *spaciare*: the *esbat* was what in later times French witches called the meetings of their covens, the English witches' sabbath.

Joan replied that she had on occasions, but she did not recall what age she had been.

Later the same day, she was again asked if she had taken the beasts to the fields and replied that she had already answered that question 'but as to whether in her infancy she had herded cattle or not, she could not recall'. (At her rehabilitation, her former neighbours were willing to swear that in fact she had done so—and also from time to time later in life.)

Then came the key-question. Unfortunately its wording is not preserved in the record but merely the fact of it: 'Asked about the tree: replied, that quite near to Domrémy there was a tree that [a gap] was called the Ladies' Tree, and which others called the Fairies' Tree, and nearby was a spring (*fontaine*) and that she had heard tell that people with fevers drank of it and that they visited this spring in this way seeking a cure. But she did not know whether or not they were cured.'

'*Item*, she said that she had heard tell that sick people when they could get up again went to the tree to *esbattre*, and that it was a big tree, called a beech, from which came *beau may*: and that it belonged to the Lord Peter of Bourlemont.'[15]

'*Item*, that she had gone sometimes with other girls in summer time and made garlands for our Lady of Domrémy there.'

'*Item*, that she had heard from many old people, not of her own generation, that the fairies frequented the place; and that she had heard tell of one named Jhenne, wife of the mayor of the town of Domrémy, her godmother, that she had seen them there. Whether or not it was true she did not know.'

'*Item*, that she had never seen a fairy, as far as she knew, there or anywhere else.'

'*Item*, that she had seen branches of the said tree put on as head-coverings [*chapeaux*: *invenculas*: hats, sunshades, crowns, garlands: the word itself has no magical colouring] by the girls, and she herself had put them on with the other girls. And sometimes they had taken them away and sometimes left them there.'

'*Item,* that since she had known that she had to come into France, she had little time for holidays, less than she might otherwise have done. And she did not know whether she had

danced around the tree since she had reached the age of reason
[*or* years of discretion]. But she may well have danced there
sometimes with the children—but they had sung rather than
danced' (unfortunately, the words of the song were apparently
not asked for).

'*Item*, that there was a wood that was called *Bosc Chesnu* which
could be seen from her father's house, a little way away, not
as much as a league: she did not know, but had heard that the
fairies repaired thither.'

'*Item*, she said that she had heard it said to her brother that
they said in the countryside that she got her revelations from
the tree and the fairies, but she did not and she had told him
clearly to the contrary. And she said moreover that when she
had come before her king, certain persons had asked her if in
her district there were not woods called Chesnu Woods,
because there were people who said that from Chesnu Woods
would come a Maiden (*pucelle*) who would come to do wonders,
but she had not put any faith in that'—though manifestly
others had when she had appeared calling herself *La
Pucelle*.[16]

To anyone committed to demonstrating that Joan was a
witch, there were some damaging admissions here: not only
was magic believed in around Domrémy but Joan's name was
connected with it at the level of village gossip and she herself
admitted to knowing what was believed although she 'put
no faith in it'. At a seventeenth-century witch-trial that
knowledge itself might well have been enough to condemn her,
but the fifteenth century was less credulous and wanted more
evidence than that as a very small child Joan had sung and
danced around a fairy-tree, made garlands for 'our Lady' of
Domrémy and worn beechleaves in her hair. Her judges
returned to the witchcraft question again and again, trying to
prove that her rings, her sword, her lance and her standard
were treated as magical objects, which she consistently denied.
But of course whatever she said, her voices, and her refusal to
repudiate them, were enough to condemn her.

There is one exchange between Joan and her judges which
shows woeful ignorance (or brilliant powers of deception and
obfuscation) in one who was allegedly an adept of the black
arts since childhood: it also illustrates how deeply her judges

had probed the beliefs of the Burgundian countryside and casts further light on how their minds worked when they were framing the charges against her.

Towards the close of the fifth session of her interrogation, she was asked what she made her *mandagora* from.

The question itself was a trap to determine the extent of her knowledge. The mandrake-plant was well known to all witches. It was obviously in the news at the time among inquisitors and bishops (and so presumably among witches and wizards) for *The History of Charles VI and VII* records that 'at that time were burned several *mandagoires* which foolish people keep in the bedroom, having such great faith in this filth that they genuinely do firmly believe that as long as they have it—though it must be properly wrapped in fine cloths of silk or linen—they will never in their lives be poor'. From its supposed likeness to the *phallus* the mandrake-root was a very potent fertility-charm, bringing increase in men and cattle (*cf.* Genesis 31) as well as in all-round prosperity.

What Joan had to say about mandrake testified only to her ignorance, whether real or assumed. She said, 'she had heard of one of them in her village but had never seen it. And that she had heard that it was a dangerous and evil thing to keep but she did not know what it was used for.'

She was then asked where the Domrémy mandrake was and replied not that it was in a bedroom but that 'she had heard in the ground near a tree, but did not know the spot—but she had heard tell that over the spot was a tree called a *corilus*'.

So far she had revealed only the kind of garbled information about the magical plant that any village child might pick up in a superstitious society, so the next question was much more direct: did she know what purpose a mandrake served? She replied that 'it made silver come—but she did not believe it' and added that 'her voices had told her nothing about it whatsoever'.

Weeks later, she was suddenly asked if the godmother who had seen the fairies was said to be a witch and replied 'that she was said to be a good, valiant woman, not a soothsayer or a witch',[17] but asked if she believed that fairies were evil spirits, replied 'I know nothing about them'. Later the same day an attempt was made to tie her saints in directly with her alleged witchcraft, when she was asked if she had ever given them garlands: she replied that 'in honour of them she had (perfectly orthodoxly) given them to their representations or images in churches, but she had not given them any when they had appeared to her, as she could recall' and went on to deny that she had ever put garlands 'in the tree'. Asked about what she knew concerning those who 'erred with fairies' she said, 'she had never done it or heard anything about it (directly), but had certainly heard tell of it, and (heard) that they went on Thursdays—but she did not believe it, though it would be sorcery'.[18]

Joan was certainly a difficult, prickly character. She was certainly not 'normal' (whatever that may be) but was driven on by forces with which most human beings never have more than the faintest contacts in dreams, whether we think of those forces as coming from God, or the devil, or deep within herself. But she knew no more about witchcraft—or the Christian art of 'discerning the spirits' as it was practised in her own times—than anyone else brought up in her ignorant, superstitious peasant community. When Gerson reviewed the material collected against her by the university (with which he had quarrelled) he concluded that she was not devil-possessed and was therefore not a witch: 'what she did proceeded not from an evil mind'. Her judges, of course, did not accept her good will and intentions: they found that she was possessed by evil spirits and practised magic—though they failed to establish that she ever took part in an *esbat* and was a member of a coven.

How beautifully John Beaupère's thinking about Joan's voices—reviewed in chapter two—would have tied in with proof that Joan was a fully fledged witch. The argument would then have run that fascinated since childhood by *the* power— the power of the tree, the fountain, the mandrake, and the earth with which they were all linked—at adolescence (an adolescence which did not take a normal course) Joan began to hallucinate, especially perhaps when her metabolism was low, during her fasts, and convinced herself that her witch-religion was true, that she herself was filled with 'the power': that she was 'the Virgin from Chesnu Woods coming to do miracles'. Her victories would then be explained not merely by the strength of her own conviction about herself but also by the fact that every other member of her cult in France was fighting with her.

But unfortunately for the theory—which opens up thrilling vistas of a vast 'underground' movement dedicated to the overthrow of Christian civilization in Europe, awaiting only its leader, the Fairy Queen or the Virgin from Chesnu Woods, to sweep aside the nonsense of Christianity and restore pre-Christian normality—unfortunately for all this, dig deeply though Cauchon's investigators did, they failed to establish any connexion between Joan and other witches. They brought charges against her relating to such things as the mandrake. But it was her voices—personal to her alone—which let them condemn her.

9

Prisoner of the English

For most of his life and in most of his public acts, there was nothing exceptionable about Pierre Cauchon.[1] He was the loyal servant of the man who had made him, Philip the Good, to whom he owed his bishopric and the opportunity to play the prominent rôle in French political life for which his qualities fitted him. His surrender of Beauvais to Charles VII was an aberration which he soon regretted: it was his defection to Paris, his return to his true loyalty, that was typical of him. The one thing in his life which truly marred his reputation in his own times, and has left it besmirched through all the years since was the depth of his personal hatred and fear of Joan *la Pucelle*. It was deep, bitter, warping. It has made thousands, perhaps millions, hearing Joan's story for the first time, despise him.

What gave birth to his hatred is not known. Perhaps he hated all women, and the victorious Joan forcing him to surrender the city that was doubly his, by birth and the pope's gift, symbolized for him everything that he hated. He may or may not have had a hand in the production of the pamphlet against her that is known to have circulated in the University of Paris during the winter of 1429–30: he certainly approved of it, employing both the various charges it brought against her and the men who found them justified in his campaign to have her indicted, brought to trial, and executed. His personal malice is obvious in the letter he wrote from Paris and sealed on 14 July 1430 demanding that she should be handed over, either to the king's officers or to himself. There was nothing illegal in his demands. Joan was captured within the limits of the diocese of Beauvais, and under canon law it was his duty to examine and question her, and present her for further interrogation to the inquisitors of the Holy Office if he believed the case merited it. But there is prejudice in the style of the letter, and collusion rather than coincidence decided that the university's summons to John of Luxemburg to surrender his prisoner should be dated the same day. It was Bishop Cauchon himself who carried these letters to 'the fortress of the most illustrious prince my lord the Duke of Burgundy, installed in siege before Compiègne' and personally delivered them to the duke in the presence of a Notary Apostolic named Triquelot, requiring him to make an affidavit that they had been delivered.[2] It was Bishop Cauchon who, not trusting his own officers or the king's, finally took delivery of Joan at Arras, the chief northern stronghold in Burgundy's domains, brought her to Rouen, the most English of Norman cities, and gleefully reported the facts to the little king and his mentor the Earl of Warwick in person—as Nicholas de Houppeville later testified: 'I saw the Bishop of Beauvais come back after he had been to fetch her, and when giving account of his embassy to the king and the lord of Warwick he spoke with joy and exultation.'

No doubt the documents in the case against Joan La Pucelle were already forming thick piles in the rooms of the bishop's clerks, and many hours had been spent in sifting the statements of those who had known her and might be induced to say something that could be used against her. The delay in opening the enquiry, however, suggests that in January, when she came into Cauchon's hands, plans for her trial had not yet been drawn up, but the way the bishop's mind was working emerges from the single document from this period which has been preserved, a French translation of the royal letter authorizing Cauchon to hold Joan prisoner and conduct her examination in the king's name:[3]

Henry by the grace of God king of France and England, to all who may read these presents: Greeting!
It is wholly notorious and common [knowledge] how, for some time past contrary to the divine law, a woman causing

herself to be called Joan La Pucelle leaving aside the dress and
vesture of the female sex has vested herself, dressed and armed
in the estate and dress of a man, a thing abominable to God,
repugnant and forbidden by all law, [and] has made and
exercised cruel homicides, and, as is said of her, has given
simple people to understand, in order to seduce and abuse
them, that she has been sent by God and has knowledge of
his divine secrets, together with many other dogmatic
statements most dangerous, prejudicial and scandalous to
our Catholic faith . . . and that while pursuing the said
abuses, and exercising hostility towards us and our people,
she was taken in arms before Compiègne by one of our loyal
subjects and then brought a prisoner to us. And because of
the superstitious, false dogmatic teachings, and other crimes
injurious to the divine majesty . . . suspected against her . . .
we have been requested most urgently by the reverend
father in God, our beloved and loyal Counsellor, the Bishop
of Beauvais, the ecclesiastical and natural judge of the said
Joan (in as much as she was taken and apprehended within
the boundaries and limits of his diocese) and equally
exhorted by our most dear and beloved daughter the
University of Paris that we should require the said Joan to
be handed over, given and delivered to the said reverend
father in God to be interrogated and examined as to the
said charges . . .

. . . [wherefore we hereby] ordain and agree that . . . the
said Joan should be given and handed over in act and fact to
him by our people and officers, so that he may have her in
keeping to interrogate and examine her and procure her trial
in accordance with God, reason and the divine laws and holy
canons by the said reverend father in God . . .

Given at Rouen on the third day of January in the year of
grace one thousand four hundred and thirty, and of our
reign the ninth.

Cauchon had fought to wrest Joan from John of Luxemburg: he had fetched her personally from Arras acting as the
king's officer: he now received her as 'her ecclesiastical and
natural judge' and imprisoned her—but not in her 'ecclesiastical and natural prison', for that would have been the convent

at Beauvais where women were kept awaiting examination by him, their bishop; Beauvais was still in Valois hands. The prison Cauchon chose for Joan was the royal prison of the castle at Rouen. He had no rights in Rouen, except those given him by the king. His ecclesiastical jurisdiction extended only to the limits of the diocese of Beauvais. Yet he was ordered to keep her, interrogate her, and procure her trial *by himself*.

Joan could have been tried as a traitor, sharing the fate of the unlamented Francquet d'Arras. She could have been ransomed —and what a price could have been demanded for her, when the king had to pay ten thousand crowns to buy her from his allies! But an ecclesiastical court, even if it were regularly constituted, could not condemn her to death. The 'inter-rogation and examination' that Cauchon was ordered to procure was primarily a propaganda exercise, intended to show Joan up for what she was in English and Burgundian eyes: a combination of whore and sorceress, not at all the kind of person the king's French subjects ought to honour and venerate. A political show-trial in a secular court would have been bound (if it was to appear honest at all) to examine the quality of her leadership and detail the victories her king's armies had won over the Anglo-Burgundians. An ecclesiastical court could avoid discussion of tactics and concentrate on her moral behaviour and motives. It was therefore much the better propaganda weapon—especially if it were presided over with real vehemence by a man who genuinely deplored her conduct in all its aspects, including her success, as Cauchon indubitably did.

In a normal situation, an ecclesiastical inquisition into Joan's beliefs and conduct which left her examiners convinced that she was totally unfit to live among Christians and was beyond redemption in this world should have led to her being surrendered 'to the secular arm' not for immediate execution (as in fact Joan was surrendered) but for a second trial, however cursory, which might well, but would not inevitably, lead to her condemnation and execution by the authorities of the state. It is notorious that Joan had no secular trial, and from the wording of the royal letter of 3 January it would appear that already by that date it had been decided that she should have none: it directs that Beauvais should conduct both the interrogation and the trial. It is, of course, always possible that the meaning of the letter has been distorted in translation and transmission, but if it has not it combines in Cauchon the functions of both ecclesiastical and secular judge—this being perhaps neither its formal intention nor strict legal effect if it were examined by a panel of jurists, but rather a betrayal through its wording of the mind of those collaborating in its composition.

From the propaganda point of view it was, of course, infinitely preferable that Joan should be interrogated and condemned by a church, not a secular court. A church court, however constituted, could be represented as impartial, and even as in some way possessing the universality believed to reside in papal institutions: Cauchon was a bishop of the Catholic Church and whatever we may think of him, in his day the aura of his consecration clung to him, giving him an authority and status with the average man in France that no English secular judge could have had. The charges, too, were universal charges. Witchcraft, magic and heresy were forbidden throughout the Christian world: so was treason in theory, but to prove as Joan's main crime a charge of treachery against Henry VI and II could not have been expected to awaken abhorrence of her in those dedicated to the English king's overthrow in France. Joan had to be tried on charges which everyone abhorred, not only to destroy her, but to make Charles VII appear guilty in the eyes of as many as possible through his association with her. Any kind of trial could have been used to condemn Joan and end her life. She could have been strangled in her cell without the doubtful dignity of any trial at all. But only the kind of trial that Cauchon planned for her with the active co-operation of the regent and the university could hope to achieve that wider and deeper destruction of her which her opponents desired.

All this does not mean that Joan would not have been found guilty by a more normally constituted church court, in which the chief investigator's only prejudice was against sin and error. The chances are that in that world at that time any church court would have condemned her for most of the sins with which she was ultimately charged—just as any English secular court would have surely been bound to find her guilty of

armed rebellion. There were certain relatively fixed standards
of judgement in these cases: Joan did not so much fail to
measure up to them as trample upon them, ride rough-shod
over them in her armour on the horse that may or may not
have been stolen from the Bishop of Senlis. Eminent legal
historians have disagreed over whether an impartial court
must have found her guilty as charged. They all agree that the
procedure of the interrogation was fairly regular[4]—and that
the court was as prejudiced as a court could be. The outcome
of a drumhead court martial conducted against Joan by the
survivors of her capture of Les Tourelles would not have been
a more foregone conclusion.

There were two problems to be solved before Joan could
actually be brought before her judges. The first was that of
Cauchon's status in Rouen. The natural ecclesiastical judge in
the Rouen diocese was the Archbishop of Rouen, but the
holder of that office had died a short while before and the see
was vacant. In fact, this suited Cauchon admirably. An
archbishop actually in residence might well have insisted upon
his rights. As it was, armed with the king's letters of appoint-
ment, he was able to ask 'all the great persons, and the most
clerkly and literate, the advocates and notaries' then in Rouen
if he might try Joan with little fear that anyone would say no.
'Because the archbishop's see was vacant and jurisdiction was
in the hands of the chapter of the church at Rouen . . . he went
to the said chapter, to the dean and canons . . . for leave and
permission to do what was needful in the territory of the
archbishop. And it was granted to him'.[5]

The second problem was to constitute a court which would
do what was required of it with as little delay as possible, but
would not be so obviously subservient to Cauchon and the
Regent that its decisions would be instantly and universally
rejected. By 9 January Cauchon felt sure enough of his men to
call them together for a first formal session, at which he
reported in some detail all that had happened so far, telling
them that the king, the university, the cathedral canons and
'Brother Martin (Billarin), Inquisitor General to the Faith in
France', were all agreed as to the right and necessity of trying
Joan. The list of judges and assessors—a short but respectable
one—included the Abbot of Fécamps, a doctor in theology,

and the Abbot of Jumièges, a doctor of laws, as well as the
Archdeacon of Eu and the treasurer of the Cathedral at Rouen.[6]

Procedure in ecclesiastical courts varied a little from place
to place, and in accordance with the charges being tried.
Ultimately based on the procedure in civil courts under Roman
law, as modified by the Christian concept of charity towards
the accused, its aim—like that in modern communist show-
trials—was to secure a confession of guilt, so that the accused
would (in theory at least) welcome any punishment inflicted on
him as a penance refitting him for life in the church, whether
in this world or the next. Nothing, those who organized such
trials believed, could be worse than being cut off from the life
of the church, therefore no suffering imposed by the church
would be intolerable provided that at the end the sinner was
rehabilitated. Hence, torture was permissible in gaining a
confession; but there were well-known arguments against
using torture early in a case. Normally it was used only to
extract information from unwilling witnesses and confirmation
from the accused himself of what he had already said.

A church trial normally fell into four parts. It opened with
the taking of a formal statement from the accused and the
collection of corroborative evidence by the statements of
witnesses. Next, these preliminary statements were used for
the detailed interrogation of the accused, every point being
gone into as often as the court thought necessary to dig down
to the truth. The process might take anything from minutes to
months, and torture might be used at the end of it, though it
was usually reserved till the end of the third stage. In this, the
court reviewed the results of the interrogations and drew up a
libellus of formal charges against the accused: if the prisoner
had already admitted his guilt, the judges could pass straight
on to the fourth stage, formally recording its verdict, hearing
pleas in mitigation, and passing sentence. If the prisoner still
denied the charges, however, he was given the right to answer
them all. Sometimes, his answers were satisfactory, and he was
acquitted—but this was rare, because the judges had convinced
themselves of his guilt by their study of the interrogations.
Usually, the prisoner was 'charitably admonished' (in major
cases, on three separate occasions) to tell the truth. If he still
refused, either he might be tortured to bring him to heel or—

as happened in Joan's case—he would be found guilty on the charges and further condemned as 'obdurate' and excommunicated. Only if the charge was a major one would that excommunication lead to his 'remission to secular justice' and execution.

The first stage in the case against Joan, the recording of her formal statement, is reported to have been completed at Bovreuil Castle on 13 January, while Joan was in the hands not of the church, but of the Earl of Warwick. That statement is lost. During the following month, she may well have been questioned frequently, as new witnesses against her were found, but no record of the period was kept, and nothing is known of her reactions beyond the fact that she tried several times to escape: comment enough perhaps in itself on her feelings. She was closely guarded and was not allowed to make her confession. (If she had been allowed and willing to do so, the heresy and sorcery charges against her would presumably have lost a good deal of their force).

By Monday 19 February all was ready for stage two, the interrogation. Six assessors appointed by the university had arrived at Rouen and on the morning of that day they assembled with Cauchon and some members of the local court at the bishop's house in the city to hear the bishop relate the facts once more. At this stage a hitch occurred. The Inquisitor General, who had given his consent to Cauchon's conducting the examination, had quitted Rouen leaving his 'vicar' to represent him there. But the vice-inquisitor had chosen not to attend the court. 'So it was ordained and appointed by the bishop that the vicar should be summoned' in order that he could not claim afterwards that he had not been kept informed of what was happening. The court adjourned until the afternoon, when 'after dinner, about four o'clock in the afternoon, Jean Magistri or Le Maitre), the vicar to the inquisitor', presented himself at the bishop's house, listened to the facts and ruled that 'if his commission and vicariate were sufficient he would agree to do what he should and could to make the said inquisition.'[7]

The delay must have been deliberate. Six weeks had passed since Joan had been brought to Rouen, time enough for everyone in the city to have learned what was to happen to her.

Yet here was the vice-inquisitor claiming that he had not informed himself as to his competence to attend her trial . . . All those weeks it had been known that the presence of a trained inquisitor would be needed to give an air of added respectability to the proceedings as well as actually to oversee them on behalf of the Holy Office. The Dominican convent which was headquarters of the inquisition in the archdiocese was actually in Rouen. Who was creating the delay and why is not clear from the court record, compiled by a notary appointed by Cauchon named Guillaume Manchon. Perhaps Cauchon himself inspired it for reasons undisclosed. He certainly made no objection to it.

On the morning of Tuesday the 20th, the court met again to hear Cauchon's formal announcement that 'by taking advice he had found that he could associate [Magistri] with himself in holding the trial'. He was, however, not fully satisfied. Consultations overnight had convinced him that he ought to summon the inquisitor himself back to Rouen 'to be present at the trial . . . or appoint a vicar with full power'. Magistri then withdrew until such time as a full commission for him should arrive.[8] Every care was being taken to ensure that there should be no mis-trial.

Joan's first appearance before her judges and assessors was made on Wednesday, 21 February, in the Chapel Royal of the castle at Rouen. Before she was brought in, Cauchon read into the record the letter ordering that Joan should be handed over to him, and the documents recording the agreement of the dean and chapter to his holding the trial at Rouen. He then named one Jean Estivet as official promoter, with responsibility for procedure and records, and in what was the first formal move in the case Estivet requested that Joan should be sworn, warned and questioned in accordance with the law.

However, before she was introduced and sworn, the Bishop made a significant statement, to the effect that 'as Joan had begged and requested that she should be permitted to hear mass . . . he had taken council with other wise and prominent persons, from whom he had learned that taking into account the crimes of which she was accused and defamed, and also the fact that she was wearing male clothing, they must refuse the request, and so he now ruled'.

It was to be made crucial to the case that Joan had consistently refused to wear any but male clothing ever since her arrest. As was pointed out earlier, it was not in itself a crime or a sin that she wore such clothes: she could hardly have gone into battle without body armour and a helmet, or slept in a tent with soldiers in the skirts typical of the peasant women of her region. She herself claimed that in a prison staffed and guarded by men, her modesty required her to wear a man's clothes.[9] If this had been the whole truth (and there had been no prejudice in the court against her) her pleas could only have been accepted, and the charges against her relating to her dress dropped. But she herself made much more of her habits in dress than just this. She claimed that her voices had bidden her to wear men's clothes and she could in conscience do nothing else. Therefore Cauchon used her habits of dress—and used them very skilfully—as the weapon with which to break her. His argument was that if she insisted on wearing male clothing despite being begged and ordered not to do so she was being disobedient to the church: while she continued to show outward and visible disobedience to the church in this way, any confession she might make, or any act of faith she might perform, could only be further proof of her general wickedness because it would obviously be insincere. Her reasons for wearing male clothing therefore did not matter: what mattered was that while she wore it, she had not submitted to the church—she had not, in other words, been broken by interrogation. Her voices, her own will, her 'heresy', were still dominant. The other charges were important. Some of them were capital. But to Cauchon, this one mattered above all, because he sensed that to Joan it mattered above all. No one but Joan could see her visions or hear her voices; but everyone could see what clothes she wore. They symbolized what she was. So he ruled that while she still wore male clothing, she was a heretic and thus deserving of practical if not formal excommunication, deprivation of the right to share in the common life of the church.

Joan herself realized the significance of this provisional excommunication. She countered in various ways for as long as her mental and physical health allowed. Then her resistance collapsed dramatically—as the resistance of victims of brainwashing techniques seems so often to do. But of that, more in its place.

After the bishop had made his statement, Joan was finally brought into the chapel. At this crucial moment in her life, she was about nineteen years of age; she had been in prisons of various kinds for eight months and had not long recovered from an attempt at suicide; she was dressed in rough, men's clothing, and wore her hair cut and shaped *en ronde* in a short pageboy style rolled above her ears.[10] Nothing else is certain about her appearance: it has been estimated that she was tall for her times, perhaps five feet five inches, and she was later described as strongly-built (as indeed she would have had to have been to wear full armour through long days in the field) and having a very full throat.

The stir her entrance must have created can easily be imagined. To most there, she was the arch-enemy, the closest they would ever come to the devil in human form. Was Henry Beaufort, the Cardinal of England, present that day to witness her first appearance in court? He may have been. It is on record that he attended several sessions of the court anonymously, and even took the boy-king with him sometimes to see the evil woman who had so damaged the English cause.[11]

While the members of the court examined the prisoner at their leisure, Cauchon explained to Joan what had happened thus far: how he came to be her judge and the authority he had for trying her. He then ordered her to swear on the gospels that she would tell the truth in answer to his questions and the duel between them began with her refusal to do so: 'I do not know what you want to ask me. It may well be that you will ask me about things which I shall certainly not tell you.' This of course was wholly unsatisfactory; Estivet the promoter had correctly ordered that she should be sworn. In the end, she did promise to tell the truth 'in matters touching the faith'—but, as later developments proved, she held herself to be the only judge of what did touch the faith, so in fact her oath meant very little.

Next, her identity had to be established by a review of the material she had provided in her earlier statement, but before proceeding to this, Cauchon had another statement to make— one designed to frighten Joan, and impress on all those present what a desperate character she was. Because, he said, she had tried several times to escape, he had given orders that she should be fettered. Joan replied that it was lawful for every prisoner to try to escape. So Cauchon ordered the three men specially detailed to guard her—John Rys, John Bernard, and William Talbot—to watch her carefully, allowing no one to speak with her except with his permission.

He then began the examination: what was her name, where was she born, who were her father and mother?

The opening interrogation soon ran into trouble as Joan struck back against his virtual excommunication of her. Among his questions were those already discussed asking who had taught her religion and how profoundly, and her reply that her mother had taught her the *Pater*, the *Ave* and the *Credo*. The bishop then asked her to recite the *Lord's Prayer* and the *Ave Maria*. Joan's reply was a brilliant stroke. She would, she said, say them 'gladly—provided that my Lord the Bishop of Beauvais was willing to hear her confession'. And she held stubbornly to that till the bishop declared the court adjourned. On the surface, it looked as though Joan had won the argument and proved that she was being deliberately and probably maliciously prevented from fulfilling her duties as a Catholic Christian by going to confession. But in reality, she had probably damaged herself by her obstinacy, for a large part of the bishop's case was that she would not obey the legitimate orders of the church—that church which he represented as both bishop and judge. In the space of an hour, the court had heard her both refuse to tell the truth and refuse to say the basic Christian prayers: her refusals can only have strengthened the convictions of those who believed that she was a heretic and a witch, for heretics would not obey nor witches pray.

The second day's hearing—Thursday, 22 February—began with a sensation. There were no less than thirty judges and assessors present in a room in Rouen Castle to hear Jean Magistri, the vice-inquisitor, say that he had now agreed to be present at the hearings 'so that the trial should not be null and void, and for the discharge of his conscience—though he did not claim authority above that of the Inquisitor General'.[12] This peculiar statement could only mean that the Inquisitor General had still not given Magistri a mandate to represent

Letter from Joan of Arc to the citizens of Rouen, 9 November 1429

King Henry VI

John, Duke of Bedford, Regent of France

Philippe the Good, Duke of Burgundy

The castle and town of Chinon

Ji luy vint dire vng de ses gens.
Monseigneur vous pouez a plain.

The siege of Orléans (from *Les Vigiles de Charles VII*)

Joan of Arc on her charger (from Martin le Franc's *Champion des Dames*)

The taking of Jargeau (from *Les Vigiles*)

Pour la conclusion ellit.

Comment la puelle fit faire luruice a troijes no obstant que le cosal fauft Sopprunon q le roy son Seuout retournet.

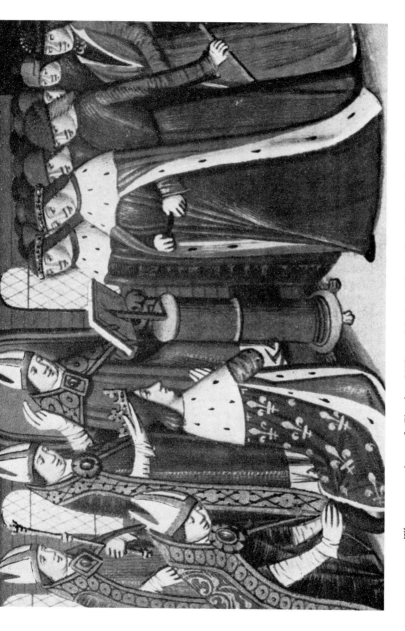

The coronation of Charles VII at Rheims (from *Les Vigiles de Charles VII*)

Rheims cathedral

The church of Saint Denis, Paris

Joan sketched in the margin of the account of the raising of the
siege of Orléans (from the register of the Parlement of Paris for
10 May 1429)

Joan 'La Pucelle' compared with Judith, holding the head of Holofernes

VUE DE LA TOUR DE VEZ.

The tower of Vez where Joan spent her last night

Joan at the stake (from *Les Vigiles de Charles VII*)

Joan of Ark by Gauguin

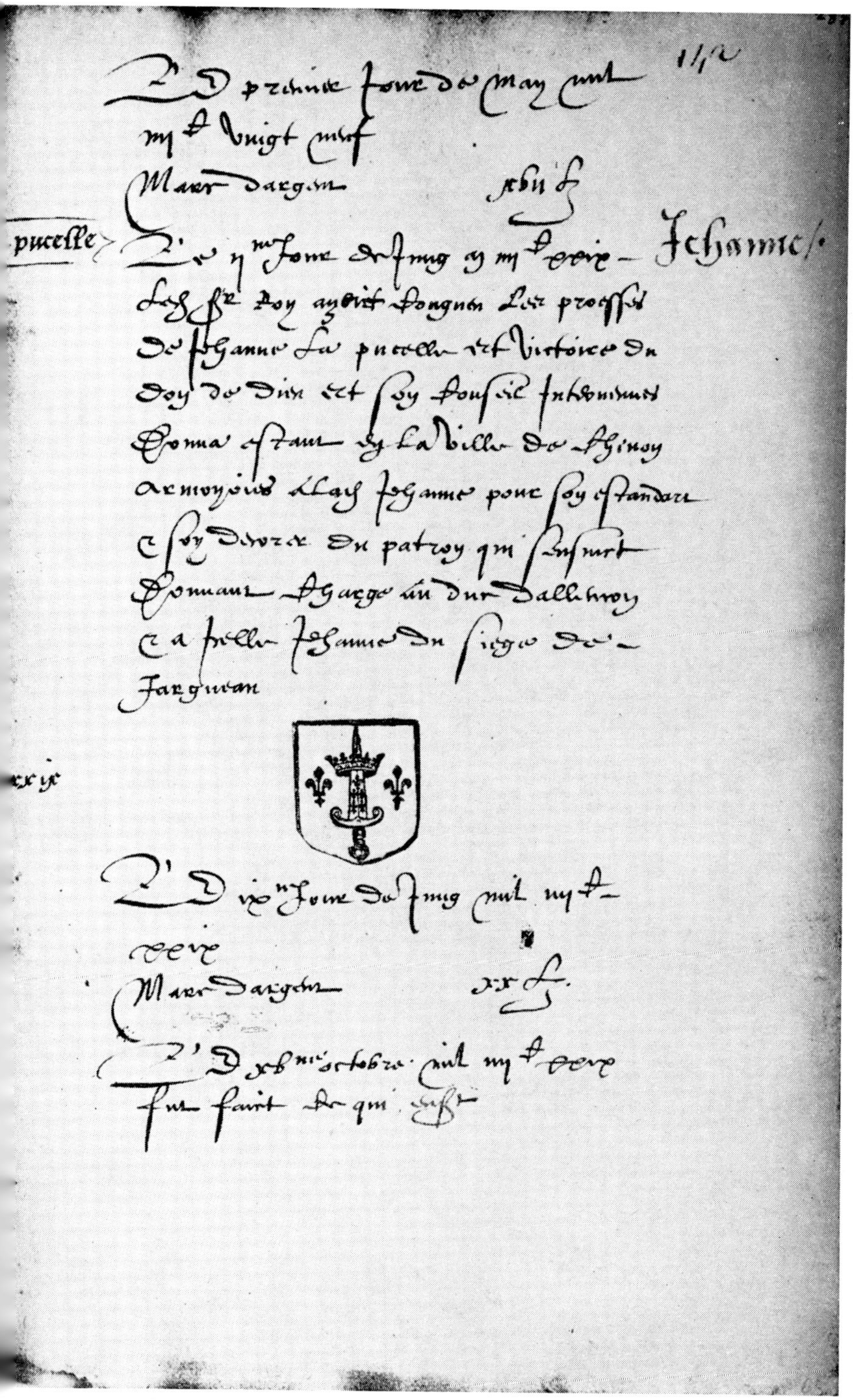

Extract from the trial proceedings. The arms are those granted to the brothers 'du Lis' in December 1429

him at the hearings and that Magistri recognized his superior's right to overrule his decision to attend. It also suggests that extreme moral pressure had been brought on him in the two days since his original refusal to attend the court: probably it had been pointed out to him repeatedly and from many sides that it was his plain duty as the senior representative of the Holy Office then in Rouen to observe the proceedings: he owed it both to the church, whose dignity and integrity he was sworn to uphold, and to Joan, whose soul it was his task and privilege to help to save.

Once he had taken his place among the assessors, every authority in Rouen, secular and sacred, oppressed Joan.

But she refused, that second day, to be oppressed. Brought into the hearing, she refused to renew her oath, saying she had already done so once: 'I did so yesterday. You put on me too much.' The argument continued for some time before she finally promised just as much truth as she had offered the day before, with her own reservations.

The questioning that day was left to Jean Beaupère, a member of the University of Paris, a lawyer and churchman who was prominent in the movement to restrict the power of the popes by the summoning of regular general councils, and who was a few years later to play a very active part in the rebel council of Basle.[13] At Joan's trial, however, he represented strict orthodoxy; sticking closely to the brief that he had been given he continued the process that had been begun the previous day by his master Cauchon, taking her line by line through her original statement, asking what skills she had learned at home, how often she had been away as a child, when her revelations had first come to her, and by what stages they had led her to Robert de Baudricourt at Vaucouleurs and Charles VII at Chinon.

The whole of the rest of the day's hearing was directed, like several of those after it, towards establishing what authority Joan gave to her voices and trying to find out if they had ever misled her. It was obviously a difficult and unrewarding time for the interrogator, for the record here becomes confused and untrustworthy. Some of the evidence has been suppressed. A note in the French version reads: 'Asked who had advised her to take male clothing: to which question I found in one book that her voices told her to take male dress and in another I found that whenever she was asked her only reply was always "I charge no man" . . . And she said that she had changed her dress for necessity'.[14] (This clearly raises the question of the authenticity of the whole record: long after the trial, Guillaume Manchon, the notary apostolic whose duty it was to sit in at every hearing and prepare the official transcript in Latin, maintained that the judges compelled him to change certain words and phrases, to blacken the case against Joan. He swore that two men hidden behind a curtain in a window 'wrote down and reported everything that incriminated Joan and nothing that excused her'; after every session, their version was compared with his own, and there were always serious discrepancies, and 'my lord of Beauvais was greatly annoyed with me about this'. The whole question is confused and difficult. The English observers present, who would have to prepare the case against Joan for treason if Cauchon's should fail, must have been interested in her remark that 'God loved the Duke of Orléans well' and 'she had had more revelations about him than anyone in France, except the king', but there was more meat for the ecclesiastics in her admission that the voices could be overruled: after she had been wounded at Paris, they had said that she should stay at Saint Denis, and she had wanted to do so but 'the lords' had not wanted to leave her there, because she was wounded, and they had taken her away. This answer led Beaupère to the question whether or not it was a good thing to have attacked Paris on a feast-day. Joan, who always maintained that she did nothing against her voices' advice, did not want to answer it, for could an angelic revelation order something that common morality thought evil? After the question had been pressed in several different forms, she flatly refused to discuss the matter any further. At her blunt '*Passez oultre!*' the court was adjourned until Saturday.

Once again at this new session on 24 February, the third in the series, it was Beaupère who put the questions and the day once again began with a tussle over how much of the truth Joan was willing to tell: 'Everything', she said, 'except on the question of the revelations.' It was on this day that Joan's guards had reported what they obviously feared was the beginning of a hunger-strike. She had not eaten or drunk since Friday. Beaupère tried—unsuccessfully as has been shown—to link her fasting with her voices, and then, hardly more successfully, to find a sexual element in Joan's relationship with them, asking how they woke her. It was a very significant few minutes, for during it Joan revealed how objective and substantial her apparitions were to her: Beaupère asked her, for instance, if the Voice (we must write it with a capital here, to mark its personality) was still in her room and she replied: No, as far as she knew. But it was still in the castle. To her, it lived apart from her, in a definite place at a definite time. Did she realize that to a theologian she made it sound not divine or angelic, but diabolical—a 'familiar' attendant upon a witch? Probably not. But she must have sensed a change in the atmosphere, a coldness towards her, perhaps, spreading among those listening, for she ended the exchange suddenly and violently, crying out, 'You say that you are my judge. Take care what you are about. For I am indeed sent by God and you are putting yourselves in great danger.'

'An angel direct from God?' Beaupère asked. 'Or through some saint?'

'I come from God—'

'Then do you think God will be angry with you if you speak the truth?' The questioner this time was Cauchon, angry, frustrated—but still probing, still dangerous. He won the reply that the voices had told Joan certain things 'for the king and not for him' and that during 'that night the Voice had told her certain things important to the king, that she wished the king might know that day.'

Immediately, the sarcastic question came: why could she not speak with her king now, as well as in his presence? If she was, as she said, from God, surely that would be no problem to her.

By now, Joan had recovered herself. No theologian could have taken exception to her answer: 'I could if it were the will of God. But for the grace of god, I should do nothing.'

The argument continued briefly, but Joan was defending herself with as much skill as she was being questioned. Soon Jean Beaupère went back to Joan's original statement for a new line of questioning, beginning again where he had left off

at the previous session, with her childhood, trying to establish
that her political and religious background was altogether
undesirable: she had been brought up to hate Burgundians,
and to take part in provincial magical rites, dancing round the
Fairies' Tree, looking for fairies, making garlands for them,
till the day came when she announced herself as the Virgin from
Chesnu Woods 'coming to do wonders'.

There can be no doubt that this third session of the hearing
was the one that established in most minds the conviction that
all the occult stories about La Pucelle, 'the Virgin from God',
were true, and justified her condemnation as a witch. Yet, as
we saw in chapter eight, they established very little, except that
she had heard certain more-or-less garbled versions of common
European folk stories and joined in universal children's games.
If she had not been so insistent upon the personality and
actuality of her Voice(s) and revelations that she made them
real to others who themselves heard and saw nothing, there
would have been no evidence in support of the charge of
witchcraft whatsoever.

It was Tuesday, 27 February, before the court sat again.
Once more the business of the day began with a wrangle over
the oath. Joan was still fasting—and it apparently annoyed her
that Beaupère knew of it. He asked how she had been since
Saturday.

'You can see—I have been as well as can be.'

'Have you been fasting all Lent?'

'Is that pertinent to your case?'

'Yes. Truly: it is pertinent to the case.'

'Then: yes: truly: I have always fasted.'

'Have you heard your voices since Saturday?'

'Yes: truly: many times.'

'Did you hear them in this room on Saturday?'

'That is not pertinent to your case.'

Assured that it was, she said, 'Yes.'

'What did they say to you on Saturday?'

'I did not hear them clearly, and did not hear anything that
I can repeat to you, before I returned to my room.'

'What did they say when you had returned to your room.'

'May you answer boldly!'

If Beaupère had not been sure that with every word Joan

spoke she was making her condemnation more certain, he would surely have told her to mind her manners. Her answers were clever in the wrong sense, and were making an unfavourable impression: rebellion against the church was one of the charges, and it could not hurt his case if Joan showed herself rebellious and uncooperative. But he let the argument go on so long that he had difficulty in regaining the initiative. When he had succeeded to some extent, he returned to his brief and questioned her closely about the personalities assumed by her revelations as St Catherine, St Margaret and St Michael, then led her on to tell the story of the finding of her sword at St Catherine de Fierboys, and describe the standard she had carried at Orléans.

The story of the finding of the sword at St Catherine was surely one of the strangest that anyone in the court had ever heard, and could have been checked relatively easily—Jean d'Aulon who had been at Chinon at the relevant time was also a prisoner. Yet no one suggested that Joan was lying: the sword with five crosses had been buried behind the altar in the church, where she predicted that it would be found. If this is so, it is surprising how little Beaupère made of it; he merely let Joan tell the story in her own words, and elicited from her that the sword had not been consecrated, as a knight's sword would have been, by being laid on an altar. Nor was the sword given prominence at later stages in the trial: it was merely one of Joan's 'sorceries'. It is as though the story were so remarkable, and so circumstantially told, that no one cared— or dared—to make any comment on it.

In later times, the story of the sword became one of the centrepieces of the Joan legends. Quite early on, the five crosses of which Joan spoke so unambiguously became five fleurs-de-lis, so that the sword could be thought of as having been specially prepared by divine agency for use by Joan the Saviour of France.[15] Later English chroniclers laughed at the story (though a shade uncomfortably), but at the time nothing special was made of it.

At the end of that day's hearing Joan was asked a question that elicited from her another doubtful statement which her accusers chose to ignore. Beaupère asked her which she preferred, her sword or her standard, and she replied that she

preferred the standard to the sword 'forty times over'. Then,
without apparently any prompting, she declared she had never
killed a man.

This statement offered a wonderful opening for a hostile
interrogator, but for the time being the court preferred not to
pursue the question. Murder was one of the main charges, the
murder of the king's subjects in the course of armed rebellion.
She had been in the van of so many assaults carrying—or at
least wearing—the 'good war-sword, good for hearty slashes'
and had been involved in the deaths of so many men, that to
argue over whether she herself had personally killed anyone
seemed wholly immaterial, except to Joan herself.

The fifth session of interrogation, held on Thursday, 1
March, began—according to the only surviving account of it—
with questions relating to Joan's original statement covering
the period of her service with Charles VII. The questions were
primarily political, designed to show that Joan had been high
in the councils of the rebels. She denied that she had ever
been privy to what would now be called state secrets. Quite
quickly, the questions turned back to points that were of
nagging concern to the clergy, and to the real hub of the case
against her in Cauchon's court: to whom did Joan owe
allegiance—God or the devil? Charles or Henry?

As might have been expected, asked directly if she ever had
any doubts about whom she ought to obey, she gave an un-
exceptionable answer: she said that she prayed to know the
will of our Lord and wanted to obey him; and she held and
believed that our Lord the Roman pope ought to be obeyed . . .
she herself did believe in the Roman pope.

Clearly, the court's task was to undermine the credibility of
this statement. The way that seemed most likely to be achieved
was obvious: by attacking her through her voices and her
alleged witchcraft. Had she heard her voices that day? Did the
saints always come in the same dress? What were their faces
like? Their hair? Their voices? Did she practice magic . . .
would she tell the court about her ring—the one the Burgundians now had? (Rings always had played and would play
an important part in magic.) Joan enjoyed remembering her
ring: her father and mother had given it to her, and she
believed it was inscribed 'Jhesu-Maria'—she did not know

who had done the writing. There was no stone in it, as she recalled. It had been given to her at Domrémy. Her brother had also given her a ring—and neither of her rings had ever cured anyone.

For the moment, the matter was allowed to rest there. The interrogator turned his attention back to the Fairies' Tree, and the spring nearby: had Joan heard her voices there? Yes . . . But what they had said she did not recall.

A moment later, pressed about the promises that the saints had made to her, she was driven to make one of the most damaging statements which she ever made to the court: 'the said saints' the Latin report says, 'had promised to lead her to paradise—which was something she had asked of them.'

The rumour was obviously being spread at that time that the saints had promised Joan she would be freed from prison, and had even been specific about the date: 'within three months'. She was asked about it, and tartly replied, 'That is not your business', adding that she did not know yet when she would be freed. On suspicion that there might be a plot to free her—though how she could have been informed of it, with three English soldiers permanently inside her small cell was never explained—she was then asked if she had any other grounds for believing she might be freed, and replied 'Ask me that in three months' time—then I will tell you.'

Still worrying the witchcraft question, the interrogation next turned to the question of Joan's mandrake, and what she made it from, and after that to her visualization of St Michael and whether she was given to sexual fantasies about him. What must have been a generally unsatisfactory session for the interrogators—except for that one priceless revelation, that the saints had promised to lead Joan to paradise—ended with yet another fruitless attempt to break her resolution not to tell the whole truth about everything she was asked and persuade her to reveal what message she had given her king at Chinon.

Some at least among the English found it very difficult to understand why no attempt had been made to rescue Joan, and the fear was a very real one that her talk of the saints having promised her that she would be rescued might be a cover for a plot. At the opening of the sixth session, on 3 March, the interrogator began with the question, did Joan think or know by revelation that she would escape?

Her reply was a spirited, 'That is nothing to do with you. Do you expect me to talk to my own hurt?'

To those already suspecting a plot, this answer can only have seemed to prove their point. Either Cauchon shared their fears or more probably he used them to win a point of his own, for this was to be the last session in open court. All later interrogations would take place in the security of Joan's cell.

Overlooking Joan's impertinence, the interrogator next asked if he was not right in thinking that her voices had told her she would be freed. 'Yes indeed,' she said. 'They have told me I shall be freed. But I do not know the day or the time.'

The question was allowed to rest there, and the interrogator turned once more to the problem of why Joan insisted on wearing men's clothing. She was obviously bored with the topic, and firmly referred her questioner to the transcript—presumably unattainable to him—of her first interrogation, by her own king's experts at Poitiers.[16] However, this time she was not to be allowed to refuse to answer, and when the question was pressed she agreed that 'the Lady of Luxemburg and the Lady of Beaurevoir had offered her a woman's dress, or the cloth to make herself one' and after insisting that male dress could not be wrong for her because God wanted her to wear it added that if dressing as a woman had been right for her she would rather have done so 'at the request of those two ladies than for anyone in France, except the queen'. Beyond that she would not go. To the next question, her reply was, 'You shall have no more from me now.'

At this point, there were only two things the court could do: either allow the question to lapse, or cause Joan to be tortured, to wring an answer out of her. This ultimate pressure, no one was willing to order until Joan had told the whole of her story at least once. It was not squeamishness that restrained them, but the knowledge that a witness broken by torture often became too cooperative and therefore untrustworthy. It was far better if evidence given under the Question could be used to supplement and confirm that obtained by simple questioning. So the subject of Joan's dress was dropped, and most of the session was devoted to taking Joan line by line through her own account of her battle experiences. This was the day that heard the stories of Brother Richard of Troyes, and the baby at Lagny, of Catherine de la Rochelle and then quite suddenly, with the deliberate omission of the stories of the siege of Paris and Compiègne, of Joan's leap—or fall—from the tower at Beaurevoir, ending with the pregnant questions: had she really said that she would rather die than be in English hands? and had she not been angry (when she had found that she was still alive and a prisoner at Beaurevoir) and cursed the name of God? She said that she would indeed rather have died than be in the hands of the English—which the court believed, because it made her a suicide, though a failed one. And she also said that 'she had never cursed a saint, male or female, and that it was not her habit to swear'—which the court chose not to believe, because the idea was firmly fixed in its communal mind that she was a blasphemer.

10

The Breaking-point

In a church court, where a prisoner's ideas were much more important than his actions—for his actions were seen as only the expression of his ideas—the aim was by skilful and persistent questioning to persuade the prisoner to condemn himself out of his own mouth. The theory was that once this end had been achieved, he could be made to look at his faults, recognize them, confess them, be forgiven them—and then be punished for them in this world, so that he might not have to suffer for them in the next.

Many brought before church courts on minor charges were only too willing to acknowledge their sins, be readmitted to the community, pay their fines or make their fasts, and have the whole business forgotten. To be excommunicate was not comfortable in this world for it carried civil as well as religious disabilities—and heaven would not help the man who died in that state, and so passed downwards into the next, bound for hell. Those who were obstinate, those who were convinced that they were right, and the whole Catholic world wrong, were in the minority, offering a challenge to the church's inquisitors that being dedicated men they were only too ready to accept. (What earned the Holy Office its evil name was the zeal of its inquisitors: like good policemen everywhere, they were suspicious of those who too readily admitted to minor crimes and they often used their powers of torture after such admissions, in order to get at the 'real facts'.) They knew that every human being has a breaking-point: the interrogator's problem is to find that breaking-point, and use it.

Cauchon and Beaupère's public battle with Joan had, by the end of the sixth session, taught them a great deal about her, her inner strengths and weaknesses. Her greatest inner strength was manifestly her belief in her revelations—and that they could not subvert directly. Her voices had spoken equivocally, but they had never let her down, or so it seemed. They had sometimes failed to come to her when she thought she needed them, but that was a different matter. They could not be proved ever to have been wrong. If only she could have been persuaded to say they had promised her freedom by a certain date, and then that promise proved empty by keeping her in prison past the date . . . But such a line of attack was not possible while Joan would not make claims that could be disproved.

Her greatest weaknesses were the male dress she insisted on wearing—the court could have forced her to wear female clothes or none, but that would have only strengthened her conviction that she was right and they wrong on the question—and her need for an audience. At Beaulieu she had tried a desperate escape. At Beaurevoir she had been driven to the point of suicide. Both as the result of isolation. She thrived on an audience: the harder she was questioned in the presence of all the great lords, the better she seemed to like it. There is nowhere any record of a conference between Cauchon and his closest advisers at which a decision was made to press on Joan's two weaknesses till she broke, but the change of tactics indicated by continuing her interrogation only after a full week's delay, and then in the confined space of the dim prison in the presence of a relatively small group of persons, is enough to indicate that such a decision must have been taken. The flimsy excuse of a plot to free her may have been used to account for this development to the other judges, but its real purpose was to break Joan, and this it finally achieved, though only after several more weeks of uncertainty.

In her cell, on Saturday, 10 March, Joan was made painstakingly, painfully to relive the story of the day on which she had been captured, and the background to it of the siege of Compiègne and her voices' black warnings that she would be

taken before St John's Day. When that subject had been
sucked dry, Dr Jehan de la Fontaine, interrogator for that
session, and the following one two days later, made a passing
attack on Joan's standard which tried—and failed—to show
that she attributed to it the magical powers the English at
Orléans and elsewhere had claimed that it had, then opened up
a new topic: what had Joan herself earned from her year's
work for her king? Had he ennobled her, given her a shield
and bearings? No, but he had given her brothers arms, 'to
please them, without petition or revelation'. Did she have a
horse when she was taken? Was it a courser or a hack? A
half-charger, she said: a light cavalry horse.

Who had given it to her?

'Her king or his agents had given her the money . . . And
she had five chargers, not counting hacks, of which she had
seven or more.'

And had her king given her rewards in addition to the
horses?

'She asked nothing from her king save good weapons, good
horses and money to pay the people where she lodged.'

Did she then have no treasure?

'Ten or twelve thousand—some of which she kept in coin.
It was not a great treasure to go to war with . . . She thought
her brothers had about the same. And what she had was from
the king's own money [the privy purse].'

It was not a very rewarding line of attack. Joan had
obviously not been in the army for the money to be made from
campaigning. Jehan de la Fontaine did not pursue it, but
brought the day's session to an end with the perennial question,
what was the sign that she had given her king? Joan said that
it did exist, and would exist for a thousand years, and was in
the king's treasury—but she would tell him nothing more. 'In
any case, the sign to you is that God has given me into your
hands. It is the clearest that he could send you.' After that
ambiguous but terrible answer, the questioning went on for a
few more minutes, but nothing further of any significance was
said.

Apart from those points she refused to discuss, Joan had
now been taken through all the stages of her public career,
with her motives and rewards. If time had been short, she

might well have been tortured at this stage, to make her disclose what it was believed she was concealing. But with Charles VII quiescent, and apparently acquiescing supinely in the trial of the girl he had briefly made his first favourite, there was no immediate pressure for a speedy result. When Jehan de la Fontaine reopened the questioning in the prison on Monday, 12 March, he began with some fairly routine questions about the sign (taking up precisely where he had left off, hoping to add, no doubt, to Joan's sense of the inevitability of everything that was happening), and then went right back to the beginning, to the time when the voices had first come to her, when she had vowed her virginity to God, and the man from Toul had wanted to marry her: her voices, Robert de Baudricourt, her loyalty to her father and mother, all these questions were raised in forms designed to make her think about herself, question her motives, and ask herself whether her revelations were really to be trusted. Joan's interrogators have often been represented as mindlessly cruel men, bent only on burning her. To read the transcripts of her trial again with modern parallels in mind is a most revealing experience: cruel perhaps they were, if merciless dedication to the interrogator's task is cruelty, but mindless they certainly were not.

Joan admitted that she had rejected the man from Toul, though her father had obviously welcomed him; she admitted that she had concealed the revelation that she was to go to Vaucouleurs because she knew that her father would have prevented her from going. Was that, de la Fontaine asked, *honouring* her father and mother?—as the Ten Commandments bound her to do. Joan could not answer that question directly: it answered itself. She said, 'In everything else she had obeyed them fully . . . And since, she had written to them, and they had forgiven her.'

So why was it no sin for her to have left her father and mother? De la Fontaine must have known what she would reply: 'Because God asked it, it was right to do it.' As she said the words, she must have felt the hostility around her, sensed as so often before the unspoken question: who made you the judge of what God wants? She added, 'Because God asked it, if I had had a hundred fathers and a hundred mothers—and if I had been the king's daughter—I would have gone.' But the

unspoken question remained, and always would remain. If—
as we, God's clergy, believe—your voices are not from God
how do you know what God wants?

Had her voices called her the Daughter of God, Daughter of
the Church, Daughter of the Great Heart? 'After Orléans, they
often called me Jhenne la Pucelle, Daughter of God'.

Then why, if you call yourself Daughter of God have you
been unwilling to say the *Pater*?

The answer—'She would have been happy to say it. When
she had refused to say it, it was to make my lord of Beauvais
hear her confession'—though perfectly true was irrelevant. It
was the question that counted, and all the other questions
before it—and the hours of loneliness afterwards, with only
John Rys, and John Bernard, and William Talbot for company,
till the next session, whenever it might be.

It came that same day, late in the afternoon. It was brief, and
turned on the two points of her obedience to her parents, and
obedience to the church in the matter of her clothing. This was
the occasion when she was asked about her father's dreams,
and admitted that he had said he would rather have drowned
her than see her run after soldiers, but claimed that 'everything
good' that she had ever done had been at the command of her
voices, adding 'but as for her dress, she would reply another
time.'

There was not much more time. They were almost ready to
list for her the sins that they expected her to confess. But she
was still not broken, though some of her admissions had been
most damaging. Before that session ended, she asserted again
most strongly her faith in the goodness of the military work
she had undertaken. Asked just how she thought she had
served the Duke of Orléans (who was still a prisoner in
London, although she had promised that he would be ransomed) she replied with great spirit that 'she had taken
enough English to redeem him' in an exchange of prisoners.
She was ready to do anything for him—she firmly believed that
God had a special love for him—she was even prepared 'to go
over seas—to go and demand him in England by force'. She
was not proud of the way in which she had treated her father,
but she had no shame about the commission her voices had
given her and the way she had set herself to fulfil it.

In the prison at the castle on Tuesday, 13 March, Magistri, the vicar to the inquisitor who had been so hesitant about his own position when the trial opened, himself directed the questioning for the first time. The one thing that interested him above everything else was the nature of the sign that Joan had given to her king, the sign which had convinced the Dauphin that the war against the Anglo-Burgundians was not lost and that Joan had indeed come, as she said, from God. He had question after question about it ready to put to her. She answered none of them in any way which could be useful to her king's enemies. By this time speculation, based presumably on an unverifiable rumour fed perhaps by some of her earlier evasions, had convinced everyone that the sign was a physical object, and had almost certainly taken the form of a crown.

Joan had told the court time and again that there were matters on which she would tell the truth and others on which she would lie. She had also made it very plain on several occasions that the nature of the sign she had given to her king was a matter for him alone and that she would not discuss it. Pressed hard by Magistri about it at this session, she seems to have lied hard, scarcely troubling to conceal the fact that she was doing so. For her own sake it was a very dangerous thing to do. Among the list of charges finally brought against her was one of having lied to the church about the sign to her king. But on that Tuesday she succeeded in creating such confusion that it is very difficult to pick out any sort of story at all. If the members of the court wanted to believe that the sign had been a crown, she would let them: if they wanted to believe that an angel-messenger had brought it to the king, or to anyone else, she would let them believe that also. By the end of what must have been an exhausting hour she had claimed both that she had taken the sign to the king, and that the Archbishop of Rheims had done so—though she had been at hand to identify it to the king as the sign he had been waiting for:

An angel gave the guarantee to the king, bringing him a crown, and telling him that he would have the whole realm of France entirely.
Asked if the angel had brought the crown to the king, and if

he had put it on the king's head . . . It was sent to the
archbishop—that is, he of Rheims. And the archbishop
received it and gave it to the king, in the king's room at
Chinon . . . I do not know what day. As for the time it was
later rather than otherwise. I do not remember as to the
month. It was April, I think: in the month of April next, or
this month, it will be two years ago: it was after Easter; . . .
When he came into the presence of the king, he made
reverence before the king, bowing before him and saying
that [the crown was a sign] and praising him for the great
patience that he had had, regarding the great tribulations
which had come upon him. And from the door onwards he
walked, stepping on the ground, coming to the king.

The 'he' here is, of course, the angel, not the archbishop.
Joan claimed that she herself went into the room with the
angel and said 'Sire, here is your sign: take it.' Those who saw
the angel that day included the archbishop, the lords Alençon,
de la Trémouille and Charles of Bourbon. Others saw the
crown—presumably floating in the air—who did not see the
angel.

It may be that this whole section is unauthentic—that it was
one of those passages forged by Cauchon to make sure of a
conviction. Whether it was the bishop's invention or not,
Joan was convicted partly on the strength of it, because it was
the kind of story—like Catherine de la Rochelle's of the lady
and the treasure—which was expected to be told about angels.
But my own feeling is that Joan invented it on the basis of the
rumour she had heard and the earlier questions put to her
about the sign ('Had she seen an angel hovering over the
king's head?' when she had first identified him at Chinon). It
was precisely the kind of story needed to lead the court away
from probing too deeply into the truth—the truth which she
never revealed.

Apart from this fantastic story, Joan told the vice-inquisitor
only what he already knew: that her voices had told her to go
to Charles and what to say when she reached him. She had
gone to Chinon and said it because she obeyed her voices in
everything. Only when things went wrong at Paris and La
Charité had she not been obeying her voices but trying to do

things on her own. At Pontlevesque, where she was captured, 'although she had a revelation that she would be taken, she had gone out all the more willingly to war with the captains, and in any case she had not told them that it had been revealed that she would be taken'. Whatever had gone wrong, her voices were not to blame.

Magistri, Inquisitor Bilarin's deputy, was not perhaps an experienced interrogator, but it is doubtful whether anyone could have shaken Joan yet. Ending the session, he picked on the subject of one of the occasions when she had acted on her own initative in order, one feels, to make her realize just how wicked she had been in his eyes. 'Was it well done,' he asked, 'to attack Paris on the birthday of our Lady—a feastday?'

Over the centuries the question looks trivial but perhaps because this attack was one of the few actions for which Joan admitted personal responsibility and concerning which she could not appeal to the superior wisdom of her voices, the sin of having attacked Paris on a feastday was included, twenty-four hours later, in the short list of 'sins' presented to her for her contemplation—the 'voluntary confession' she was expected to make at the end of her period of 'self-criticism'.

The contents of that expected confession were revealed to her only after two more trying sessions in the prison on the morning and afternoon of Wednesday the 14th, during which examination was made of matters that could be tried and tested against generally accepted norms of behaviour. The chief of them, on which she was closely questioned during the morning session, was her attempted suicide at Beaurevoir. On this point, she had already defended herself strongly but un-convincingly; during this examination of it, she admitted that St Catherine, the voice of her conscience, told her afterwards that she should 'confess and ask forgiveness of God' for having jumped, although she still maintained that she had been thinking of escape, not suicide. The other questions raised—whether she had cursed God, why she had warned the Bishop of Beauvais against trying her, and whether indeed her voices had promised her paradise—were passed over more quickly: her evidence on them was well known, and the questions were asked merely to make sure that she had not changed her views. On none of them had she moved in the slightest.

At the afternoon session, two matters were suddenly sprung on her which had not been raised before: the story of Francquet d'Arras—through which, as we have seen, she stumbled somewhat unsuccessfully for justification—and the farcical, if uncomfortable affair of the Bishop of Senlis's useless horse. But these were only the prelude to the real work of the afternoon, acquainting Joan with those faults of which the vice-inquisitor and the bishop felt certain that she ought now to be accusing herself. Joan claimed that she was not conscious of any of them as sins, and briefly refuted each of them as they were read out to her: attacking Paris on a feast-day, stealing my Lord of Senlis's horse ('it was returned'), letting herself fall from the tower ('I did it, but not from despair, but in the hope of saving my body and going to the help of good people in need. And after jumping, I did confess within myself, and asked pardon of our Lord—and had forgiveness for it from our Lord. But I think that to make the jump was not well done, but ill done.') and wearing men's clothes.

Four 'sins', and only one of them that she was the least uneasy about. But that was enough for these men who knew their job so well. They left her for the night, to think about her sinfulness, and first thing next day told her what she already knew: that if she had done anything against the faith, she ought to leave it to the church to judge it . . . Her answer about her fall from Beaurevoir, as well as her general readiness to defend herself rather than submit to their assessment of her moral behaviour, had underlined once more the fundamental element in the case against her. When the formal list of charges against her was published, spiritual pride would be one of the things of which she was accused, and when she was finally condemned the primary accusation against her would be that she had threatened the unity of the church by refusing to submit to its judgements.

On Thursday, 15 March, in her prison, her reply to the reminder that it was for the church to judge was an admission that she was aware of that: 'her answers would be seen by the clergy, and if they told her there was anything in them contrary to the Christian faith, she would confess it, following their advice . . .' But told then that she would have to submit all that she had done to the judgement of the church, she said, 'I shall say no more about it to you for the present.' This was a key moment. Joan knew it, and the assessors knew it. The previous afternoon, she had talked of judging herself, confessing within herself: now she was talking of confessing to the church (though still with reservations). It was because she knew that she had given ground that she refused to say any more. She needed time to think, time to consult her voices—or so she believed, but in fact things had now gone too far for time to save her.

Time was the enemy, a relentless enemy, gnawing at her mental energy and her physical wellbeing, weakening the foundations of her confidence, till in the end it crumbled away. When she fell ill, and with what disease, is not known. The conditions under which she was living, in fetters, sometimes fastened to a block of wood, with guards constantly in her cell, day and night, were such that it is surprising that she kept her health—mental and physical—as long as she did. When she finally collapsed, it was body and mind together . . . But on 15 March, when the first signs of her surrender to interrogation were discernible, that complete collapse seems to have been still some days away.

She had admitted, on that morning, that it was conceivable that there might be something 'against the Christian faith' in what she had said and done: if there was, it was for the clergy to find it. 'If there was anything wrong, against the Christian faith in what our Lord had commanded, she would not defend it, but would be very anxious to repudiate it.' The statement was illogical—as she probably realized and even intended—because nothing Christ had actually commanded could be wrong for the Christian. But the whole question was who *had* directed her actions, and now for the first time she was showing willingness (however grudging) to be told what was wrong with her thinking.

A few minutes later, she was defending herself as ably as ever over the question of whether she had a right to escape: 'If she saw a door open . . . that in itself would be permission from our Lord . . . Help yourself, and God will help you.' But the cracks that had opened in her defences could not be so easily plugged, as became clear when the interrogator next raised the question of her going to mass, as she had constantly requested to be allowed to do. If she were to hear mass would it not be more fitting, he asked, if she did so in a woman's dress?—and which would she rather: wear a woman's dress, and hear mass, or a man's and not hear it? She would not answer a hypothetical question: 'Promise me that if I were in a woman's dress I could hear mass, and I will answer.'

The promise was given, and it threw her into a terrible conflict, discernible even through the bare record of the court reporter: 'What will you say if I have sworn and promised our Lord not to take off this dress? But . . . let me have a long dress, to the ground . . . and let me go to mass. And when I come back, I will put back on the clothes I have now. . . . Give me a long *houpellande*, and I will take it, and even a woman's cap, to go to hear mass.' So the moment had come—and it must have felt like falling into a pit backwards, with the edge crumbling under her feet, for seconds later, she was fighting and scrambling to regain her stance: 'As pressingly as she was able,' the French account says, 'she asked to be left the clothing she was wearing, and to be allowed to hear mass without changing it.'[1]

Immediately, of course, her interrogators asked her if she were not now willing to submit to the judgement of the church 'in word and deed'. She replied, 'All my words and deeds are in the hands of God. With regard to them I bow to him. And I swear to you that I do not want to do anything contrary to the Christian faith, and if I have done or said anything, or if the clergy know anything against me contrary to the Christian faith that our Lord established, I do not want to defend it, but will repudiate it.'

Needless to say, no woman's dress was presented to Joan at this stage. She had surrendered, but she had also drawn back from that surrender. However, twice in one day she had also admitted the church's right—which in her case meant her interrogators' right—to weigh and judge her actions. It was enough. The rest of the day's proceedings were irrelevant beside it, developing into a long wrangle on the nature of angels and saints. Joan had not yet been defeated in this arena, nor would she be until the end.

Friday was a rest day—though to Joan it meant merely a rest from questioning. By the Saturday, 17 March, she had summoned from somewhere reserves of strength, and was ready to defend herself with some of the strongest statements she ever made: 'she believed as firmly in the words and deeds of the St Michael who had appeared to her as she did that our Lord Jesus Christ had undergone death and suffering for us' and 'she had gone to the king of France from God, from the virgin Mary and all the blessed saints of paradise, and the triumphant church on high, and by their command. And to that church she would submit all her good deeds, and everything she had done or would do.'

Appeals from earth to heaven were, of course, totally unacceptable to ecclesiastics who believed that what St Peter and his successors and their delegates bound on earth was bound in heaven. Granting that Joan would be judged by God, they asked the obvious question: would she submit—as they believed every Christian must—to the church militant? This question, she refused to answer. Among themselves they must have talked of her as a very obdurate heretic. She went on further to demonstrate her obstinacy and tenacity by firmly refusing the dress she had hesitated over on Thursday: 'and if that should bring her to condemnation . . . she would rather die than repudiate what our Lord had made her do': and if they offered to free her if she wore women's clothes, she would wear them till she was outside, and then change again 'immediately, and do what our Lord had commanded.'

The subject was dropped at last, and the questioner tentatively raised that of fairies: were they evil spirits? Joan crushed the topic: 'I know nothing about them.'

Then—did St Catherine and St Margaret hate the English? 'They love what our Lord loves and hate what he hates.' But did he hate the English? 'She knew nothing of the love or hatred God might have for the English, or what he was doing for their souls. But she knew very well they would be put out of France—except those who died there . . .'

Joan was still quite unshakable on the subject of her mission: the whole of heaven was fighting for the victory of the 'French' king and would stand behind him till the end. The matter was discussed for some time, but in the end Joan was unmoved.

For the rest of that morning, and the whole of the afternoon, the main emphasis was on magic and superstitious practices. Joan's standard in particular fascinated her interrogators, who had it fixed in their minds that the two angels shown on it were intended to be magical figures and that Joan herself believed, as some English soldiers certainly did, that she owed her victories to it. They failed to win any admissions from her. She carried that particular standard because St Catherine and St Margaret had ordered her to do so. She made no claims for it—any more than she did for the fact of her virginity: it had not been revealed to her, she said, that if she ever lost her virginity she would lose her strength, her 'armament', and the voices would come to her no more. Once again she also refused to attribute any particular powers to the ring inscribed Jhesus-Maria, and denied that she had ever worshipped her saints, or knew anything more about fairies than the stories commonly told about them. From her answers, she felt no guilt or even doubt about these aspects of the charges against her. Questions about them did not give her the uneasy moments that she experienced when made to think about her fall from Beaurevoir tower, or the death of Francquet d'Arras, and certainly did not cause her the distress that the question of her clothes created in her now that it had been firmly linked with that of her submission to the church and her right to go to mass. The question of her obedience to the church came up only briefly that afternoon. She was asked if she would tell the whole truth to the pope 'the vicar of God' and replied that she would like to be brought before him, and would tell him 'all that it was proper' for her to reveal . . . as she had told Cauchon so often, there were secrets that were between her, Charles VII, and God alone, whether Cauchon liked to believe it or not.

When charges as abstruse as consorting with fairies, talking with angels, and knowing hidden and secret things are taken seriously, a confession is the only proof there can be of guilt—if indeed it would be proof of anything but madness. In the absence of a confession, there can only be a consensus of opinion among those insane enough seriously to sit in judgement on such charges. It is a brave man who hearing a girl talk about her friendship with beings he can neither see nor hear will take it upon himself to judge whether those beings are 'good' or 'evil' spirits. But that was precisely the task which confronted the Bishop of Beauvais and his fellow assessors as they left Joan's prison late in the evening of that Saturday in March. The preliminary investigation was over. The time had now come to formulate specific charges.

Some of those charges were self-evident. All those relating to disobedience to the church in the person of Bishop Cauchon could be substantiated—and the more vehemently Joan denied them, while still refusing to do what the bishop told her, the more guilty she would make herself look. But the others needed very careful formulation. It was the practice then to introduce as many charges as might have any foundation, and after preliminary discussion of them all in the presence of the accused, drop those that looked unlikely to be substantiated. When Pope John XXIII had been brought to trial at the Council of Constance in 1415 on charges ranging from heresy to piracy, and including the murder of his predecessor by poison—all in an attempt to persuade him to resign as pope, and allow the Great Schism to be brought to an end by the election of a universally accepted successor to himself—there were seventy-two charges against him, but by the time he was deposed, they had been reduced to one, a new crime, specially invented to fit his peculiar case, the 'heresy' of schism, of having divided the church. A very similar pattern was to emerge in Joan's case—nor was this the only similarity between them, as will be seen later.

The task of drawing up the list of formal charges against Joan was entrusted to Estivet, the promoter of the trial. He was probably assisted in the work by a young lawyer from Paris named Thomas of Courcelles,[2] a man famed for his oratory and his knowledge of Latin as well as for his forensic skill. In the course of the following week, with the transcripts of the hearings readily available to him, and his own memory of Joan's manner and appearance fresh in his mind, he put the finishing touches to a *libellus* of sixty-seven accusations against her.

The court sat again on Tuesday, 27 March, but before the accused could be confronted with the *libellus* there was a lengthy and acrimonious debate about procedure. Joan had consistently refused to swear the oath in due form, or to answer some essential questions with either truth or lies. In the eyes of some of the assessors she was therefore guilty not necessarily of any of the charges about to be formally made against her, but of sinful and criminal obduracy and there was nothing to prevent them proceeding to immediate sentence (as though for contempt of court) on that charge alone. Others thought that by refusing to answer she had in effect pleaded guilty to all the charges. Still others believed that normal procedure should be followed, and she ought to be solemnly warned about her behaviour on three separate occasions before being formally excommunicated.

Joan was then brought in and warned that they were all worried about her spiritual well-being. They were, they told her—and no doubt at that moment they all believed it, such is our capacity for deceiving ourselves—all 'benevolent and pitying, wishing and determined to proceed in this matter with gentleness and grace'. Their only aim was to 'bring her back to the way of faith and salvation'. If she liked, she could have two or three of the clergy there present to help her—or anyone else she liked to name—but in the end she would have to take the oath.

Threatened with instant formal excommunication—which would have meant her immediate surrender to the English, if they could force it—Joan took the oath on the gospels though with her own reservation, that she was careful to explain: 'In as much as you are admonishing me for my own good, and our faith's, I thank you . . . And in as much as you offer me counsel, I have no intention of departing from the counsel of our Lord. And as for the oath that you want to confront me with I am ready to swear to tell the truth in everything pertinent to your case'.

It was another partial but perilous surrender. As soon as she had sworn, Thomas of Courcelles began to read out to her the sixty-seven articles contained in the *libellus* against her. The very first of them accused her of disobedience to the church. Her answer to it—her formal plea of 'not guilty', though to her accusers it proved her guilt—showed that she had not moved at all from her former convictions: 'I know very well that our holy father, the pope of Rome and the bishops and other churchmen are there to preserve and defend the Christian faith and punish those who fall from it. But as for me and what

I do, I will not submit to them, except to the church in heaven —that is to God and the virgin Mary and the saints in paradise. And I firmly believe that I have not erred in faith . . .'

The rest of the charges were a hotch-potch of everything the court had been listening to over the past weeks, ranging from having possessed and used mandrake-root (7) and consorting with fairies (4) to 'having boys about her' but going back on her marriage plans (11 and 9), having a man's clothing and weapons (12, 15, 16), and blaspheming against God (13, 15).

The list was so long, and Joan answered it in such detail— though not always wisely—that only twenty-nine of the charges could be heard that day. None of her pleas was accepted. Some of them—such as her reply to the charge of having done unwomanly things (16), that 'there were enough other women to do them'—she can hardly have expected would be. But in the last resort, none of this mattered beside her damning reply to the first, purely religious charge—and the fact that this was not really a religious inquisition at all, but a political show-trial, at which the accused claimed that she was right to commit treason by working for the 'king of France' (17) and admitted that if she could not have peace, she believed in having war: 'If they will not make peace, I am quite ready to fight' (25).

The whole of the next day's session was given up to the rest of Thomas de Courcelles' reading of the *libellus*. During it, she was as obdurate as ever, refusing to deny her voices (31, 37, 48), or see sin in war (32—'The gentlemen of France wanted to attack Paris. It seemed to me that they did well to go against their enemies'), claiming that her standard was a gift from God (33) and that 'she knew very well that God loved her king and the Duke of Orléans more than anyone else' (35); but worst of all, in her judges' view, was her refusal to make any reply when called on yet again to submit to the judgement of the church except 'send me a priest next Saturday and I will answer you . . . Saturday, after dinner, I will answer', which the Latin version of the record interpreted as refusal to answer at all except under the seal of the confessional.

They gave her the time she had asked for, but did not send her a priest to hear her confession. It was to themselves that they wanted her to confess, submitting herself to the judgement of the church on earth as represented by themselves. On the Saturday, 31 March, they visited her again in the prison and told her she must submit, and she replied that she was only too willing to submit 'in everything they asked of her' provided that they did not demand 'something impossible' of her. Asked what would be impossible, she gave them precisely the same answer as she had continually throughout the trial: 'the visions and revelations she had described, she could not repudiate for anything'. She did not deny that prelates had authority, but 'our Lord is to be served first'.

The adjournment that followed lasted seventeen days. During it, Joan was so ill that she thought she was going to die and was haunted by the fear that she would do so and be buried in the town ditch. A small court of seven commissioners, headed by Pierre Cauchon, had her brought before them in the prison on Wednesday, 18 April. The contrast between her weakness and their assurance must have been extreme, but the legal process ground inexorably on. During the recess, the judges had met together informally to discuss the case. Some of them are known to have protested at the unfairness of parts of the *libellus*, but begging Joan to take his advice and admit the court's competency to judge her, the bishop let no hint of their disagreement reach her, telling her rather that 'the many and notable churchmen' who had heard her interrogation had 'found many faults committed' by her.

At the end of what amounted to a sermon preached at her, Joan replied, 'It seems to me—seeing the sickness I have— that I am in great danger of death: and if this is how God will work his pleasure with me, I beg you to let me have confession, and my service also [the mass that every Catholic had to hear during the Easter season] and holy ground [for her burial].'

Cauchon promised her nothing, but told her that the more she feared for her life, the more anxious she should be to amend it. As a Catholic, if she would not submit to the church, she did not deserve what the church could give her. Joan was too ill to argue or defend herself. All she said was, 'If my body dies in prison, I look to you to have me put in holy ground. If you will not, I must look to the Lord.'

One by one all those present then called on her to surrender to the church. The last of them, Nicolas Midi, a theologian from Paris, talked at length on the text from St Matthew's gospel that was quoted as scriptural justification for religious trials leading to excommunication: 'If thy brother shall trespass against thee, go and tell him his fault . . . but if he will not hear thee, then take with thee one or two more . . . and if he shall neglect to hear them, tell it unto the church: but if he neglect to hear the church, let him be unto thee as an heathen man', and warned Joan solemnly that if she would not obey the church she would be abandoned like a Saracen.

The thought distressed Joan, and she protested, 'I am a good Christian, and have certainly been baptised. And I shall die as a good Christian.'

For two weeks more Joan was left in suspense over the pit of excommunication and an unmarked grave, while around her prison the argument as to what should be done with her went on. Then on Wednesday, 2 May, Jean de Châtillon, a theologian, undertook her public admonition before all the judges and assessors. Once again, the charges were read out, for this was 'telling it to the church' as the scripture advised. Once again, Joan denied everything, and refused to submit to the judgement of the church: 'I know the church militant cannot err or fail,' she admitted, 'but as far as my words and deeds are concerned, I refer them all to God who made me do what I have done.'

By now, this belief of hers that she was above the church had become universally recognized as the most important factor in the case against her: it ranged her with the enemies of Catholic unity: John Wyclif of England, John Hus of Bohemia, and John XXII the pope of Rome.[3] Together with all her other offences, she was a heretic, sinning against the clause in the creed that spoke of the 'one, holy, Catholic church'—the clause that at the Council of Constance had been used to break John XXII and force him to resign. Jean de Châtillon, the preacher on whom the task of admonishing Joan had fallen, actually quoted the clause at her, and asked if she did not realize that she was making herself a heretic by not believing in, and making herself one with, the holy Catholic church—and if she did not also realize that heresy was a fault for which she would be punished by burning? Joan replied: 'I cannot tell you any different. And if I go to the fire for telling you all I have, I cannot do any different.'

'I cannot tell you any different' . . . 'I cannot do any different': it is only a step from Joan to Martin Luther, *Ich kann nicht anders*. Luther was not yet born, but the judges at Rouen and the theologians at Paris saw the danger of the subversion of the whole authority of the church through men and women 'pretending to revelations from God and his angels, sowing lies and errors'. Evil or misguided they may have been in their treatment of Joan, but it genuinely seemed to them that the unity of the church and therefore the authority of the church had to be preserved if civilization was to survive. If Joan had still been a private person, they would nonetheless have felt bound to take steps to end her rebellion against church authority. But she was no longer a private person. She was a living symbol, universally recognized in France and beyond its borders—and what she was symbolizing now was the shattering of Christendom . . . To many, the prospect was genuinely terrifying. As the symbol of so great a threat, Joan had to be destroyed, in the hope—the vain hope—that the threat would disappear with her.

After being publicly admonished in this way, Joan was returned to her cell, where she remained for another full week, until Wednesday, 9 May, while her judges debated whether the moment had not yet come to accelerate her mental and physical collapse into collaboration with them by the use of torture. On that day, she was brought before the court in a room in the great tower of the castle of Rouen, and warned that she would be tortured if she did not submit. She did not really believe that it could happen to her, though others had recently been tortured and executed in Rouen on charges of witchcraft and heresy: 'Truly, if you do stretch my limbs,' she told Cauchon, 'and make my soul part from my body . . . I would say you were making me speak by force.' This is, of course, the strongest argument against the use of crude physical torture—but it was not the reason why Joan thought she would not be tortured. The fact was that St Gabriel had come to her and comforted her (she had known that it was the archangel, she told Cauchon, because he had told her so) and 'she had asked St Michael and her other voices if she would be burned, and they had told her to wait upon God and he would help her'.

Weeks earlier, she had told the court that her voices had assured her that she would escape, though she did not know 'the day or the hour'. Their promises meant more to her than Cauchon's threats, because they themselves meant more to her than he did: they were more real and personal than the flesh-and-blood man before her. After her illness and the deprivations of so long in prison, it would not be surprising if the physical world had become unreal to her, so that the real world was that inside her own mind. But if that was so, she had only gone one step further along the road from exterior to interior living. From the outset, her voices had meant more to her than anything else in the world. How could she doubt them now? All the world had betrayed her, but St Gabriel had come to her, and St Michael and the others, comforting her. They had not told her that she would not be tortured or promised that she would not be burned, but they had promised her God's help. Centuries earlier, pagans with experience of the ambiguity of oracles might have been worried by a vague promise such as this. But Joan was comforted, for her voices were her only real friends. How could she admit to herself the reality of the danger of being tortured when that might lead her to submission, and submission would mean repudiating them?

Whether Joan was willing to face up to the danger of torture or not, however, the threat was real. The expediency of torturing her was the only topic discussed by all the assessors at Bishop Cauchon's house in Rouen on the following Saturday afternoon. The majority were against it—though none of them for the humane reason of sparing Joan. Several agreed with the English priest Erard, that 'the matter was clear enough without torture'. Raoul Roussell, the Cathedral treasurer, was already looking forward to the future. He thought it would not look well to be remembered as one of the men who had tortured Joan, so he voted against it 'for fear of calumny' afterwards. The only two wholeheartedly in favour of it were the lawyer Thomas de Courcelles, who thought she should be tortured 'to make her submit', and a canon of Rouen named Nicol Loyselleur who recommended it 'for her own good'.

Meanwhile Nicolas Midi, who had preached at Joan during her 'charitable admonition' in prison on 18 April, had been working through the text of Estivet's *libellus* of sixty-eight articles against Joan and with the aid of the transcript of the evidence had reduced them to twelve charges. Over the protests of the court reporter, Manchon, that in the document that emerged Joan was made to say things that she had never said, these twelve articles were sent to Paris for debate by the faculties of both theology and law. On Midi's version of the evidence and with Paris garrisoned by Joan's enemies, it did not take the university long to conclude that she was a schismatic and heretic of the worst stamp imaginable. As the decision at Rouen against using torture showed, the majority there shared that opinion. On Saturday, 19 May, Joan was brought into the courtroom in the castle for the last time, to hear the verdict pronounced against her—a verdict which, although a triumph for those who would have been perfectly happy if she had been burned out-of-hand months earlier, was an admission of failure from the legal point of view because Joan had not been broken and brought to submission and confession.

Yet again the proceedings opened with a review of the whole case by the bishop. He ended his summary by introducing into the record the notification from Paris that Joan had been found guilty there of being 'a schismatic, an apostate, a liar and soothsayer, suspect of heresy, erring from the faith, a blasphemer.'

Even now, though the end was obvious, not everyone present would agree that she ought to be condemned. There were those who felt that her submission was necessary— although politically undesirable, for if she could be made to confess, she could not afterwards be 'handed over to the secular arm'. They argued that she should be admonished yet again and that it should be made quite plain to her that if she did not yield she would certainly lose her life.

In the end, they had their way, and Pierre Maurice accepted the task of explaining to Joan what she had been found guilty of, and what it could mean to her. (If there is any point at which the procedure of the trial could be faulted, it would be here: Joan was given no opportunity of answering these accusations):

You, Joan, have said that from the age of thirteen years you have had revelations and apparitions of angels and of St Catherine and St Margaret, and that you have often seen them with your physical eyes and that they have spoken to you—

On this first point, the clergy of the University of Paris have considered the nature of the said revelations and apparitions, the things revealed and the quality of the person [to whom they were revealed]. All things having been considered that should be, they say and declare that all the said things are lies, phantasies, seductive and pernicious things, and that all the revelations are superstitious, proceeding from evil and diabolical spirits.

You have said that your king had a sign by which he knew that you were sent from God, because St Michael, accompanied by several angels, some of which had wings and others crowns, and with them Saint Catherine and St Margaret, all accompanied you to the castle of Chinon, and went up the steps of the castle to the room of your king, before whom an angel bearing a crown did reverence. And on one occasion you said that when your king received the sign he was all alone, and on another you said that the crown, which you called the sign, was sent to the Archbishop of Rheims, who brought it to the king in the presence of many princes and lords . . . As for this, the clergy say that it is not reasonable, but is a presumptuous, seductive, pernicious lie . . .

. . . You have believed too lightly and affirmed too temerariously faith in saints and angels . . . and as for the comparison you made about believing in them as firmly as in Jesus Christ, it is an error against the faith.

. . . You said you knew certain things in the future, and hidden things, and people you had never seen . . .

. . . You have continually used male dress . . . wearing your hair short . . . leaving nothing to show that you are a woman . . .

. . . You have said in your letters that you have used the names Jesus and Mary, and the sign of the cross, to show those to whom you write that they need not fear the contents of the letters, but in other letters you have prided yourself that you would [kill] those who did not obey you . . . The clergy say that you are a murderess and cruel person, desiring the effusion of human blood, seditious, provoking tyranny, blaspheming God . . .

You have said that through revelations . . . you left your father and mother contrary to their will and that they were so distressed that they all but became demented. And that you went to Robert de Baudricourt who, at your request, gave you a man's clothing and a sword and people to take you to your king, to whom you said you had come to drive out his enemies . . . The clergy say you have been wicked and impious towards your father and mother . . . and you made a presumptuous . . . promise to your king.

. . . You said that it was by your own decision that you leaped from the tower of Beaurevoir . . . The clergy say that there was pusillanimity, tending to despair and suicide. And that you made a . . . presumptuous assertion, that God had pardoned the sin . . .

. . . You said that St Catherine and St Margaret promised to lead you to paradise provided you preserved your virginity . . . and if you were in mortal sin, St Catherine and St Margaret would not visit you as they do . . . a presumptuous assertion, and a pernicious lie . . .

. . . You have said that you are well aware that God loves some living people more than others, and that you know by the revelations of the said saints that they speak the French language and not English because they are not on their side. And that since you learned that these voices were for your king you have not liked Burgundians . . . a presumptuous assertion, blasphemous against the saints, and a transgression of the divine commandment to love one's neighbour . . .

. . . You have said that to those you called St Michael, St Catherine and St Margaret you made reverences and knelt down . . . The clergy say that supposing you had had the revelations . . . you pride yourself on, you would be an idolator, an invoker of devils, straying from the faith . . .

. . . [On what concerns your revelations] you are unwilling to refer to the judgement of the church on earth . . . but only to God alone . . . The clergy say that you are a schismatic, wrongly comprehending the truth and authority of the church, and that up until now you have not ceased to err perniciously in your faith towards God.

Twelve points, all deadly. No matter that everyone knew that the story of the sign had been garbled, Joan's assertions about the political allegiances of angels and saints grossly oversimplified, and her views about the relationship between her vow of virginity and the revelations made to her totally misrepresented: all the capital charges that had ever been made against her were found proved.

Having shown Joan the wide range of her sins in this way, Maurice had next to try to make her admit the error of her ways: it would be easy to sneer at the way he chose to do it as mere hypocrisy, but there is no evidence at all that he was not earnestly seeking to persuade her to save her life when after a final warning about the gravity of the charges, especially the last charge of schism, he added, 'Joan, my most dearly beloved, it is now time for you to think well about the end of your case, and what you have said and done . . .

'Think w ↑ll, Joan: if there had come some knight into the court of your king while you were there, a man of your seigniory, saying: I will not obey the king and none of his officers shall make me submit to him, would you not have said that he stood condemned?'

It was a good argument to use with one who had been so proud of her soldierly qualities: Joan was of Christ's seigniory: she had been baptized a Catholic, Christ was her king . . . but it missed the mark in as much as she claimed that she had always obeyed the king and that his officers' commissions did not extend over her. Nevertheless, if she was still capable of following an argument, this one must have had an effect upon her.

By submitting, Maurice told her, 'You will save your soul, and snatch your body back from death, as I hope. But if you do the opposite, know that your soul will be damned—and I fear for the destruction of your body. From which, may God preserve you.'

The prospects were terrible, but Maurice presented them as a moving appeal. Joan answered in words of terrible dignity which suggest that she had at last realized the full danger of her situation. She had spoken of being burned before. Now she believed that it could happen. She was fighting herself as well as repudiating the escape Maurice offered her as she said: 'If I am condemned—and I see the fire lit—and the wood made ready—and the scaffold, where they will put me into the fire, ready for me to be thrown into it—and after, when I am in the fire—I shall not say differently from what I have said, but I shall want to maintain what I have said until death.'

She would want to—but could she?

She had reached the breaking-point.

11

Death at Rouen

For five days they left her alone with her guards and her thoughts—the wood—the scaffold—the fire in this world and, if they were right, the fire in the next also.

By chance, the one human being who could possibly have helped her—though not at this late stage—her king, Charles VII, was involved in a little drama of his own that May.

In 1430 Georges de la Trémouille, concerned at the signs of a return to favour of his old friend Arthur, the Duke of Richmond, had sent men to assassinate him. They had failed in their attempt but Richmond felt that their failure did not excuse his rival's perfidy. Early in 1431, while Joan was on trial for her life and the regent and Cauchon were worrying lest some attempt should be made to rescue her, Richmond was coaching the Vicomte Thouars, the Lord of Lazay and the Lord of Vivonne in the parts they were to play in bringing de la Trémouille down. On 7 May they swore an accusation against him, listing his crimes as including murder, rapine and violent theft, but when they were called upon to justify their charges it was found that they had failed to arm themselves with knowledge of sufficient details to carry conviction. On the following day, 8 May, Charles found them all three guilty of high treason for conspiracy against the king's friend. The Lords of Lazay and Vivonne were both beheaded, though Thouars was spared on de la Trémouille's plea that they were related. So the outcome was that Georges, Duke of Sully, was more firmly established in royal favour than ever—which, in

view of his known animosity towards Joan, may explain why
Charles did nothing, not even protest, while Joan waited to die.

At what moment did Joan realize that she could not hold
out 'until death'? Perhaps not even she herself ever knew. She
did not speak out till her trial reached its formal climax in the
great public ceremony of her excommunication at the cemetery
of St-Ouen on Thursday, 24 May.

Three platforms had been erected in the cemetery for the
occasion, to let all those chiefly concerned see and be seen.
One was occupied by the Bishop of Beauvais and the members
of his tribunal; the second by the bishops and clergy from the
city of Rouen and the towns around; the third by the Cardinal
of England, representing both the regent and the remote
central authority of the church.

A fine patriotic sermon was preached by the Englishman,
William Erard, on the text 'A tree beareth not fruit of itself...'
and containing some bitter attacks on Charles VII which
stirred Joan to shout defiantly, 'Do not talk about the king—
he is a good Christian. Talk about me.'

After the sermon, the formal excommunication was read
into the record, and before the sentence could be pronounced,
Joan surrendered to the pressures upon her.

At first, her surrender was only partial. She asked that the
papers in the case might be sent, 'To our holy Father the
Pope, by whose decision—and God's first—I will abide.' It is
probable that in strict legality this appeal to the pope should
have been allowed, but in practice it was ignored. So at last
she yielded everything: 'she wanted,' she said, 'to hold all
that the judges of the church wanted her to say and to maintain, and to obey their every command and desire.'[1]

What confusion and delay this total collapse evoked is left
to the imagination by all the sources. The state of disorder to
which it reduced the whole solemn morning is obvious from
the fact that no two accounts agree as to what happened next—
a fact which has led some historians to speculate that Joan did
not intend to recant at all. When the essential point that she
had done so had been established, Beauvais pronounced a final
sentence that fell far short of English expectations from the
morning's proceedings, terrible though Joan herself found it:
'That your sentence may be salutary, we have condemned and

do condemn you by a definitive sentence to perpetual imprisonment with the bread of suffering and water of sorrow, so that you may there weep for your sins and henceforth may commit none . . .'

Erard, the preacher, shouted 'Ha! France! France! Till now you have been free from monsters, but now you have been seduced by this woman, who has made a heretic of you!'

Joan shouted back, 'It is not true!'

Before there could be any further disturbance, she was hurried out of the cemetery and back to the prison.

At the process for Joan's rehabilitation in 1456, it was said that she was made to sign a statement in which she formally renounced her errors, that this 'schedule of abjuration' was five or six lines long, and that she signed it with a cross. Two versions of this document exist, one of them incredibly prolix and detailed, the kind of document that Estivet and de Courcelles might have put together neatly to round off the case, the other a short but quite sufficient formula, such as might have been hurriedly put together in the cemetery or during the dinner-hour that followed:

I, Joan, called the Maid, a miserable sinner, having now realized the sink of error into which I had come and having by the grace of God returned to holy church our mother, in order that it may be seen I have returned to her not half-heartedly but with a good heart and will, do confess that I have grievously sinned, by claiming lyingly that I had revelations from God and his angels St Catherine and St Margaret (*here the longer form inserts all her faults*), and all those my words and acts which are against the church I do repudiate, wishing to remain in union with the church, never leaving it.

By the testimony of my sign manual: X

That same day 'after dinner', the vicar to the inquisitor, accompanied by several of the other judges, visited Joan in the prison and pointed out to her 'how gracious the church had been to her, and that she ought to acquiesce quietly in the sentence and obey the church, leaving aside her revelations and madnesses', warning her that 'if she were ever to go back

to her follies the church would never receive her again, and
urging her to accept female dress'.

The totality of Joan's surrender was revealed in her reply:
'she would happily assume female dress and obey the church'.
Immediately women's penitential clothes were brought, and
she put them on, and her hair—uncut during her imprisonment, but worn rolled up *en rons* above her ears—was let
down.

If Cauchon's hatred of Joan had not been so personal, and the
fears of such men as Estivet and Magistri of her heresy so real,
that might have been the end of her story. At least, she thought
so, for later she told Cauchon, 'I am dying because of you. If
you had had me put into a church prison, and I had been
guarded by church people, and not by the English my enemies
this would not have happened to me.'[3] In fact she was legally
the church's prisoner, and if the bishop and the inquisitor had
combined forces to demand that she should be held perpetually
in an ecclesiastical prison even a churchman with such divided
allegiances as Henry Beaufort, the Cardinal of England, would
have found it very difficult to support Bedford in a demand
that she should be handed over to the king's men. But after
her sentencing, she was sent back to the cell she had left that
morning—and that cell defeated her.

Her treatment there after her adjuration was a harsh compromise between the regular and the irregular. In it one can
sense traces of the battle over her final disposal which must
have raged during the next few days. As a prisoner of the
English, she was still guarded by men: as a penitent of the
church, undergoing lifelong rehabilitation she was helped by
two Dominicans from the convent in Rouen, Martin Ladvenu
and Isembart de la Pierre who were appointed to care for her
spiritual needs. But according to Ladvenu himself when he
went to Cauchon and told him that he thought it would be
more fitting if she were to be confined to a church prison the
bishop replied, 'That would not do. It would displease the
English.'

So the scene was set for the tragedy of Joan's recovery of
the state of mind normal to her—for that is in fact what her
ultimate 'relapse into heresy' really was. Psychologically, the

savagery of the sentence and the 'mixed' treatment she received afterwards were wrong if the aim was to maintain in her the penitent state of mind interrogation and the threat of torture had produced in her. On the Sunday after her sentencing— Trinity Sunday, 27 May—or possibly on the Monday morning, she announced her return to her normality in the most dramatic way open to her by once more putting on the male dress which throughout her trial had symbolized to Cauchon her rebellion and to herself her loyalty to her voices.

How she obtained the tunic, hose and cap with which she defied Cauchon and condemned herself has been a matter for speculation ever since. The judges either did not go into the question or, if they did, the story they heard was immediately suppressed. Martin Ladvenu later said that she was violently attacked in prison by 'a great English lord' who tried to rape her, and that she had told him that this was why she had felt driven to put on a man's clothes again, but the story was surely a rationalization after the event and anyway does not explain where the clothes had come from. Jean Massieu, a court officer and mace-bearer to the bishop, giving evidence to an inquiry set up by Charles VII in 1450, suggested that Joan's own clothes had never been removed from the cell but had simply been put into a sack and left lying there, a constant temptation to her, one—he implies—deliberately offered by those who hated her.

That may have been how the clothes came to be there. But Massieu's story of how Joan came to put them on again reads more like a salacious barrack-room tale than the truth. One wonders how many drinks Massieu had earned with it before he told it to the king's commissioner: 'On the following Sunday morning, when it was time for her to get up, she said to her English guards, as she herself told me: Take off my chains. I am going to get up. Then one of the Englishmen pulled off the woman's clothes she was wearing and they tipped out the sack in which the men's clothes were. These they flung to her, saying, Get up. And they stuffed the woman's clothes into the bag. Then—as she herself told me— she put on the man's clothing that they had given her. But first she said: Sirs, you know very well that this is forbidden to me. I will not wear them. Nevertheless, they refused to give her any other clothes and the argument went on till noon. Finally, she just had to get up to fulfil a physical need, so she put those clothes on.'

The whole feel of this tale is wrong, yet it has gained wide credence at various times because it is the best available, more circumstantial than Ladvenu's tale of the great English lord.

However, no matter where the clothes came from or what was the lever which made Joan yield to the temptation to dress in them, once she had done so she would not take them off again—and so condemned herself to the fire as a relapsed heretic. 'The following Monday, 28 May, the judges (acting obviously on information received) went to the prison and found Joan dressed in male clothing. They asked her when she had put it on and she replied that she had just done so.' They asked her why, and repeated the question several times, receiving a different answer each time. First she said that she had done it from her own choice, because 'she liked men's clothing better than women's'. Then she said that 'she had put it back on again because it seemed more proper' in a prison staffed by men. Later she claimed she had done so 'because they had not kept their promise, that she might hear mass and receive the body of the Lord and be taken out of chains, but if they would promise that she could go to mass and be taken out of chains, she would do all the church required'.[4]

Perhaps she was simply too shocked by her own temerity after what had happened to be able to put into words all that she felt. Probably her motives were as mixed as her feelings: she did prefer men's clothes, she did think they were more fitting, she was resentful because promises she believed to have been made to her had not been kept . . . but the chief reason (in her own scale of motives) she kept to herself, till someone asked her the key-question had she heard her voices since last Thursday? Then the whole story tumbled out: 'Yes. They had said God was warning her through them that she stood in great danger of perdition because she had made that abjuration and renunciation in order to save her life: she was damned for having done so. Till last Thursday,' she added, 'her voices had told her what to do and she had done it. And on the scaffold itself, the voices had told her she had answered the preacher most boldly: he was a false preacher, and said

that she had done several things which she had never done . . .'
She had to mention their praise of her, to salve her pride and
self-respect—and perhaps to give herself a moment to steel
herself for what she had to say next which would inexorably
entail her execution. Manchon, the clerk to the court, stolidly
took it down: '*Item*: she said that were she to say that—' It is
easy to restore from his record precisely what Joan said:

'If I were to say that God sent me, I shall be condemned.
But God really did send me. Since Thursday, my voices have
been telling me that I have done and am doing a great injury
to God by making myself say that what I did was not well
done . . . All I said and abjured, I did for fear of the fire.'

A little later, she claimed that she had never intended to
renounce St Catherine and St Margaret, and repeated that
what she had said, she had said for fear of the fire, adding that
if she had repudiated them, it had been 'contrary to the faith'.
Finally, in a phrase in which defiance and despair seem blended
in equal measures, she said that she would rather do penance
(by dying) than remain in prison any longer.

If she could not have the world back as it had been, with
her voices, her friends, encouraging her, praising her, applaud-
ing her, she would rather be dead. In a church prison her
voices might not have returned to her, or if they had there
might have been some compassionate and understanding
human being to talk her out of whatever extravagances her
friends proposed before those follies killed her. But at Rouen
Castle there were only enemies and, by persuading her that she
should defy Cauchon, putting on a man's clothes once more,
her voices betrayed her into their hands.

Cauchon wasted no time. The following evening he himself
read this account of the action he took into the trial record:

On Tuesday 29 May we, the Bishop of Beauvais, caused the
doctors and other clergy in great number to come together
in the chapel of the archbishop's palace. And we revealed to
them that the said Joan . . . [had abjured the previous
Thursday but] now, persuaded by the devil, said that in the
night [following] and for several nights thereafter . . . her
familiar had returned to her and said many things to her;
and similarly that she was not satisfied with female clothing

and had resumed male clothing, finding that acceptable. And the previous day the Lords Judges, having heard a rumour, had returned to her and seen her in male clothing again and reminded her what was in . . . her abjuration. The judges then deliberated on these new crimes and their votes were recorded . . .

In all forty judges voted. Although one or two said afterwards that their votes had been changed by Cauchon it is obvious that the overwhelming majority were in favour of outright condemnation. Such men as William Erard and the Bishop of Fécamps, always opposed to Joan, declared her 'relapsed' and 'to be remitted to secular justice'. Some, including de Courcelles, ruled her 'presumptuous, contumacious, disobedient, and without hope of life in this world'. One canon, unsure of himself in such exalted company, said he thought she was relapsed but would defer to the doctors of theology. A few—including some of those who might have been most inimical towards her, the Englishmen—expressed regret at having to find her relapsed and said that she ought to be remitted to secular justice with recommendations of mercy.

According to Martin Ladvenu who was waiting in the crowd outside the chapel Cauchon was delighted with the result. Coming out of the meeting he called to a group of Englishmen standing there, 'Farewell—farewell! *Il en est fait!*'—which might mean 'That's done it!' or 'That's done for her!' and in either case is a clear expression of his feelings. Or of Ladvenu's animosity towards him twenty years afterwards. Ladvenu was another of the victims of Joan's bewitching personality— almost the last to fall to her during her lifetime. An essential element in her myth is illustrated by the opposite reactions to her of this man and his superior. Magnets attract and repel. During the course of the trial Magistri, the vice-inquisitor, felt his repulsion growing day by day till he feared her as much as Cauchon hated her, but by the time of her execution Ladvenu and his fellow Dominican Isembart de la Pierre were ready to follow her anywhere. By his own account, de la Pierre actually did follow her to the very edge of the fire.

When Joan had agreed to dress once more as a woman Magistri had warned her that 'were she ever to go back to her follies the church would never receive her again'. By putting on male clothing and claiming to have heard her voices again, she had gone back to them. In deciding that she was a relapsed heretic this latest court was admitting that the church had failed with her and the devil had won: there was nothing for it but to admit the defeat and rid the world of the danger of contamination by her. The church itself could not execute her. She was to be 'remitted to secular justice'. Secular justice showed how it intended to deal with her by spending the night building a suitable pyre for so notorious a witch, setting up a stake and building a low stone barricade around it, so that the wood could not fall in on her and quicken her death.

There is no record of who told Joan that her end had come. According to Ladvenu she was allowed to make her confession to him and receive holy communion, just as though she had been a Christian in good standing and not about to be declared an excommunicate heretic and burned to death. She had been begging to be allowed to do so ever since her trial had begun. She 'received the body of Christ humbly and devoutly, and with so many tears . . .' Why was she allowed this mercy? The reasons were never disclosed, though it was against all the precedents in such cases.

There are several accounts of Joan's last hour. They are not all compatible in detail, but the general course of events is clear.

Early in the morning, Joan was brought out from Rouen Castle, walking in the middle of a company of soldiers, wearing a penitential gown and the mitre of the condemned. She was accompanied by a deacon from the Dominican convent. She was led to the Old Market, where soldiers were keeping a great crowd back from the scaffold and the platform erected for official witnesses, assessors and judges. Many of those who had taken part in her interrogation were there, together with Robert Gilbert 'Chapel Deacon to our Lord the King (Henry VI)' and the king's secretary, John Tressart.

At about nine o'clock Nicolas Midi began to preach on the theme of the corporate nature of the church and the danger that infection would spread unless cauterized, taking his text from *Corinthians*, 'If one member suffers, all suffer with him'. The sermon was followed by explanations and justifications of what was about to happen and then Cauchon read the final sentence—the second 'definitive sentence' Joan had heard against her in a week:

> We, Peter, by divine mercy the humble bishop of Beauvais—
> And we, Brother John Magistri, vicar to the inquisitor into the faith—
> being competent judges in this case—
> in as much as you, Joan, called La Pucelle, have been found to have fallen back into various errors and crimes of schism, idolatry, invocation of devils, and other misdeeds, and in as much as if we are to be just judges we are bound to find against you on these charges—
> though the church never folds its arms against those who are willing to return to it, we judge that whereas once in full possession of your mind and with faith unfeigned you withdrew yourself from those errors . . . as is recorded in a paper by your own hand, you did thereafter fall immediately back into them as a dog will return to its own vomit—a fact we record with great sorrow—
> for this reason we declare you to have incurred the sentence of excommunication in which you were formerly embroiled, you having fallen back into those errors aforesaid for which we declared you heretical—
> and by this sentence . . . we rule that like a rotten limb you be cut off and rejected from the unity of the church and we remit you to secular justice, the which we beg to deal with you gently and honorably whether it be by loss of life or of some limb.

There the preliminaries ended, and the church having abandoned any further responsibility for Joan's body or soul, Cauchon, Magistri and the other judges left the platform with Joan standing there, apparently silent and still incredulous: this was the moment from which her voices had sworn that she would be spared.

'And the Bailiff of Rouen, an Englishman, being there, commanded with no further trial, and without giving any sentence against her, that she be led to the place where she was to be burned—the which command being heard by the said

Joan, she began to cry out and groan so pitifully that she moved the people and all who were there to the point of tears.' So William Manchon.[5]

Martin Ladvenu, the Dominican, in his account of the scene, put into Joan's mouth at this moment a wonderfully heroic dying speech: 'She uttered pious and devout lamentations and invocations of the blessed Trinity and the blessed and glorious Virgin Mary and all the blessed saints of paradise . . . asking people of every sort, of her own party as much as other, most humbly to forgive her, and asking also that they would pray for her, forgiving them the evil that they had done her.' Perhaps she did—but brokenly, incoherently, pitiably.

'And immediately,' Manchon adds, 'the bailiff ordered that the fire should be set. And this was done.'

It has always been held against the bailiff that he hurried Joan to her execution immediately the church had relinquished her into the custody of the state. So the second of the Dominicans attending Joan that morning, Isembart de la Pierre, told the commission for her rehabilitation 'The lay judge pronounced no condemnation to death or the stake . . . She was handed over to her executioner, and devoted to the fire [the judge] saying "Do your duty" without any other sentence.' In law, he was no doubt wrong. But he had a near-riot on his hands—and perhaps he too was moved by pity. Joan's fate was sealed. Cauchon's relinquishing of her to secular justice—'which we beg to deal with you gently and honorably whether it be by loss of life or of some limb'—was at best a form, and at worst hypocrisy. The bailiff had no doubt received his orders for an immediate execution: he could have dragged the proceedings out; nothing would have been served by it but empty dignity.

As it was, thanks to the stone parapet around the stake, Joan took long enough to die.

'She asked for a cross and hearing this an Englishman who was there made a little one from wood at the end of a pole which he gave her' Ladvenu said, while by Isembart de la Pierre's account, 'she bore witness to so great and astonishing contrition, and made utterance in words so devout and catholic that she made the vast crowd present weep, and even the Cardinal of England and many English'. Moreover, he

said that he 'being beside her there till the end she asked him
humbly to go to the nearby church and bring the cross, and
that he held it standing before her till her death, before her
eyes so that she could see it always and unceasingly . . .'

But the executioner said that the fire was so hot he could not
stand near enough to hasten the end. She choked on the
smoke; because of the wall, the heart and other parts did not
burn.[6]

Secretary Tressart cried out, 'We are lost: we have burned a
saint.' There is no record that he had classed her as such before
the mass catharsis of her execution.

'And it was,' Secretary Manchon wrote, 'a wonderous cruel
thing.' So cruel, in fact, to all the eye-witnesses that they were
overcome by it, and reduced to near hysteria. None of the
accounts tally because none of them were seeing what happened,
though they were all watching. Afterwards, they remembered
what they imagined they had seen, or wished (as in the case of
Isembart's cross) that they had done to help her.

When the fires had died down, the ashes and unburned
remains were collected meticulously and thrown into the Seine,
so that there should be no relics for use either in religious or
magical practices.

'And many people of property as well as common people,
Manchon noted, 'muttered much against the English.'

The first formal complaint came from a Dominican belonging to the same convent as de la Pierre and Ladvenu. Cauchon
imprisoned him for saying publicly that Joan had been
wrongly condemned. The official inquest—the 'Posthumous
Enquiry'—had still to be held. Cauchon himself conducted it
at the archbishop's house at Rouen a week after the execution
after news of it had already been welcomed by the University
of Paris. Predictably, the enquiry found that Joan had been
rightly condemned. The court was, however, so dominated by
the bishop that Manchon declined to include a record of it in
his account of the affair.

The official announcement of the execution addressed to the
Duke of Burgundy by the court at Rouen has been preserved
in a French version. It gives a very full account of the events
leading up to Joan's trial, and describes her abjuration and
ultimate relapse into heresy before going on to suggest that

t the very last she realized how her voices had misled her, and hat her prayers at the end were a recognition of the fact: . . . she was again publicly preached to and . . . left to secular ustice, which immediately condemned her to be burned. And here she, seeing her end approaching, realized that the spirits . . were wicked and lying, and that the promises which the aid spirits had previously made to her of saving her were false, nd so she confessed to having been made a mockery of and eceived, and she was taken by secular justice . . and publicly urned.'[7]

This is, of course, precisely the view of events taken here— ut it is one totally opposed to the view which later gained round, that Joan's voices were genuine, she went to the stake elieving in them *and* in the church, and that she was a saint. he regent was most anxious that the view 'We are lost: we ave burned a saint' should not spread among the allies. lready the previous year, the Duke of Burgundy had been trangely unwilling to see Joan handed over to the English. lthough the official announcement of the execution is recisely that, a public announcement, a public-relations andout, it is also more than that. It is a propaganda document, nxious to reassure doubts that were already making them- lves felt. My own judgement is that it is a true account of ne facts—but also that it would have taken the form it does, mphasizing again and again Joan's guilt in the eyes of a ompetent church court, even if the facts it relates, and the xplanation it gives of them were not true. The English knew ney were right to have executed Joan—but they did not xpect anyone else to believe it. They would have preferred oan not to have relapsed into heresy—although that made her ecution certain—because once she had so relapsed, once she as ready to die defending her voices, the whole question of hether she was 'from God' or not was re-opened for those illing to think that a church court, directed by the English, uld make a mistake. Their only hope of scotching the rumour nat Joan's voices were genuine (and therefore her king also enuine) was if she could be shown to have repudiated them the end. They used Joan's manifest anguish in her last hour r that purpose. The irony is that though they were justified, ney failed. In the very long term, the verdict of orthodox

Catholics was both that Joan's voices were genuine revelations
and that it was Cauchon and his associates, not she, who were
disloyal to the church.

In the short term, very little was achieved either by Joan's
mission, or her execution. Charles VII was too busy with his
own little affairs south of the Loire to take any account of what
was happening north of it. After the executions there on 8 May
de la Trémouille returned to court in triumph, with still
greater glory lying in store for him before an alliance between
Yolande of Sicily and the Duke of Richmond finally ousted
him in mid-1433. It was only after he had retired into obscurity
that the French cause began to prosper again through en-
deavours made on the French side, with Alençon, Richmond,
the Bastard of Orléans (soon to become the Count of Dunois
and many other of Joan's good captains rediscovering their
loyalty to the king they had seen anointed at Rheims, and that
king himself finding the energy to inspire them.

The English cause north of the Loire had, however, begar
to lose ground long before this French renascence in 1434, and
though the memory of Joan and her hard death played a part
in it, it would be simplistic to see this as its only cause. The
economic situation was worsening in both France and England
Unpaid and dispirited English soldiers were deserting the
armies in France to return home, and it was proving very
difficult to raise new recruits. A deep-laid family quarrel
between the king's uncles and great-uncles had led to an
agitation—fostered by the Duke of Gloucester—for the
Cardinal of England's trial for treason as soon as he should
return to England from attending to the king's business in
France. Nevertheless, the year 1431 closed in apparent triumph
with the king making a royal progress from Rouen to Paris
at the beginning of December for his coronation. His entry
into the city on the second, followed by a visit to his grand-
mother, dowager Queen Isabella of Bavaria, at St-Pol, was
triumph, and nothing marred his coronation by Cardinal
Beaufort on the sixteenth. Scarcely had he returned to London
in February, however, to open Parliament in person and
preside—at least nominally—over the hearings which cleared
the cardinal's name, when three hundred Normans seized the
castle at Rouen and the citizens of Paris sent a despatch to

England, warning of uprisings everywhere, pleading for re-inforcements 'else we cannot see you remaining sovereign in your kingdom as you ought to be.' Rouen was retaken, and the survivors of the three hundred beheaded in the square where Joan died, but their failure did not deter others. Worse still, the collapse of the siege of Compiègne in October 1430 seemed to mark the end of Philip the Good's real efforts on behalf of the alliance. Relations between him and Bedford were already strained before his sister Anne, the Duchess of Bedford, died on 14 November. She had been a bond between them and once she was dead, they began to drift apart. The breach was considerably widened when, without consulting Burgundy, Bedford married Jacquetta of Luxemburg—a betrayal, in Burgundy's view, for he was lord of Luxemburg,[8] as he had been lord of Hainault, whose princess had been illicitly married to Gloucester a decade earlier. In mid-1435 Philip forced the regent to send representatives to Arras for talks on the future of the alliance and of the whole of central France. The head of the English delegation was Bishop Cauchon, who had been rewarded for his services to the English crown not with the archbishopric of Rouen that he had longed for, but with the minor Norman see of Lisieux. Bedford died at Rouen Castle on 14 September and a week later, on the 21st, the Treaty of Arras was signed between Philip and Charles VII neutralizing Burgundy. On 13 April 1446, Paris opened its gates to Arthur of Richemont, Constable to the King of France.

The English were now unquestionably the foreigner and the enemy everywhere in France, apart from Normandy, parts of Maine, and Gienne, but though there were patriots for Charles VII everywhere, there was little room for them to act.[9] Both the French and the English faced a deadly enemy, anarchy. The skinners, reinforced by English and Burgundian deserters and discharged mercenaries, harried the population month after month, year after year, and in their wake followed disease and famine. The English peasantry could not and the English nobility would not spend to save France, where villages were abandoned by their inhabitants for fear of brigands, and the towns thus overcrowded were depopulated by plague. For more than ten years after the signature of the treaty the situation was allowed to worsen day by day. By 1444, both the French and the English in France were exhausted, and on 16 April that year a five years' truce between them was signed at Tours.

It was during these years of truce that Charles VII at last grew up to face his responsibilities. He was never a great king, but he learned to judge men and use well those who genuinely wished to serve him. They repaid him with loyalty and hard work, so that he was remembered by French historians as 'Charles the Well-Served'. Georges de la Trémouille, the evil genius of his late twenties, was finally charged with murder and expropriation on an information laid by his step-son Louis de Giac, whose father he had had assassinated just twenty years earlier in 1426: Charles did nothing to save him, but he managed to fend off condemnation till he died a natural death in May 1446. Just two months before his death he was an official witness at a scene which must have recalled for him the strange years of Joan the Maid, when he was negotiating peace with Burgundy while she was urging the French captains to attack Paris. On 4 March, Francis, the new Duke of Burgundy, came in state to Chinon and did homage there for the holdings in France he had just inherited from his father, Philip.

Meanwhile, Constable Richemont, ably supported by Joan's old friends Jean, now Count of Dunois, and the Duke of Alençon (who was making himself a great expert in the use of artillery to reduce fortifications) reorganized the French fighting forces to provide a standing army garrisoning selected towns, policing the area around Rouen, and permanently prepared to repel invaders. Charles VII wanted peace with England, though his ministers believed that a war, if it could be sufficiently intense and sustained, could throw them off the continent for ever. In 1445, Charles's niece Margaret of Anjou was married to Henry VI of England who now, at the age of twenty-three, was directing his own policies, and favoured peace with France. There was a secret clause in the marriage treaty, providing for the gift of the County of Maine to France as a gesture of goodwill when a suitable opportunity arose.

French troops moved into Maine in 1448. When the news broke in England that they were being allowed to do so peaceably and the king's enemies revealed why they were not being opposed, anger and shame brought the country to the point of revolution. A few months later, an English captain in Normandy expressed the feeling of his countrymen by breaking the truce and attacking a party of French soldiers. On 17 July, Charles VII declared the truce at an end. Three months later, on 29 October, Rouen surrendered to Richemont and Alençon. In April 1450 all Normandy with the exception of Calais fell into French hands; in summer 1453 Gienne, the dowry which Eleanor of Acquitaine had brought to Henry II disappeared in the same terrifying dust created by the cannon at the siege of Chatillon, though Bordeaux held out till 19 October.

Two months after Rouen was captured, Charles VII briefly took up residence there. He was immediately presented with petitions for an official enquiry into the death of Joan La Pucelle, the angel sent from God to foretell and bring about his restoration to his kingdom. The facts around her trial and execution had remained largely unknown in 'Free' France where the only written description of what had occurred was contained in a letter from the king of England 'to the emperor, kings, dukes and other princes of Christendom' dated 8 June 1431, very similar in content to that addressed individually to the Duke of Burgundy on the 28th of the same month. There were even doubts as to whether Joan had died on the morning of 30 May 1431.

The king granted the petitions made to him, appointing 'his beloved and faithful counsellor' Guillaume Bouillé to investigate the 'faults and abuses' in the trial.[10] Bouillé was a famous theologian, formerly rector of Paris University, who had recently been acting as the king's ambassador at Rome. The week-long enquiry he made in March 1450 ought at least to have settled the question of whether or not Joan had been burned to death once and for all time, for among the handful who gave evidence were Martin Ladvenu and Isembart de la Pierre, who had watched her die. But Joan was a legend now —had been for nearly twenty years—and a legend cannot be allowed to rest.

12

Afterwards

Even while Joan was still alive, there were those ready to call
her a saint, if only because in those times the popular heroes
were the saints, and it was difficult for people to separate the
two ideas. (Those in authority in the church had, of course, very
clear notions about the distinction.) It was with this in mind
that she was asked at the sixth session of her interrogation if
  'She had ever seen or had made any image or picture of
  herself in her own likeness . . .'
The charge, of course, was to be blasphemy and idolatry,
a breach of the second commandment 'Thou shalt not make
unto thyself any graven image, the likeness of any thing . . .'
The interesting point is that the question reveals that such
pictures were known to be circulating, and Joan's reply
showed that she knew of at least one of them, though there was
nothing blasphemous about it. She said 'that she had seen at
Rheims a picture in the hands of one of the Scots: it bore the
likeness of herself in full armour, kneeling on one knee,
presenting a letter to her king. Otherwise she had not seen or
had made any image or picture in her likeness.'[1]
  So, in the earliest known picture of Joan she was a heroine—
but her ecclesiastical accusers were afraid that the heroine was
being regarded as a saint. Over the four and a half centuries
since her death, she has been both—as well as a token and
symbol of success to those who believe themselves witches,
or wish they could—and it is interesting to watch the process
by which the legends grew.

Although it may be supposed that La Pucelle was never forgotten by those who had fought beside her, had heard her prognostications and watched them come true, and had seen her outface Georges de la Trémouille and argue her case with her king, there is no record of her having been mentioned at all in French royal circles between her capture at Compiègne and the enquiry into her death that Charles VII set in motion at Rouen in 1450. During that time, however, the groundwork was laid for the growth of both aspects of her legend, not publicly and deliberately, but in the minds of those who had cause to remember her as a prodigy, either for good or evil. Brother Richard of Troyes, who threw holy water at her when he first met her, and later stole her standard, so great was his esteem for her . . . Bishop Cauchon's man-about-the-place, Massieu, who had enjoyed such notoriety in Rouen from his story of how Joan came to relapse into heresy that he had to relate it to the king's commissioner as the truth . . . All those children to whom she had stood godmother—'to the boys among whom she had happily given the name Charles', as she admitted, 'and to the girls Joan—or other names at other times, as the mother wished'[2]—and who had since grown up to ask why they had been named as they had . . . Her squire, Jean d'Aulon, and the faithful five hundred who rode with him to Compiègne . . . All those who had called her the angel from God—or the whore from Armagnac . . . The villagers of Domrémy, who had watched her rise—and her fall. None of these forgot, or could do so. Some of them did not want to believe that she was dead. Others hoped she really was.

Naturally, false Joans appeared—the first of them apparently as early as 1436, when the chronicler of the church of St Thibaud in Metz noted, 'This same year, on the twentieth day of May, there came Jehanne la Pucelle to speak with the lords of Metz: and she was calling herself Claude . . . the same day there came to see her there her two brothers, the one being a knight, and called Sir Peter, and the other a squire Little John (Petit Jehan), and as soon as they saw her they recognized her, as she did them . . . She was recognized by many tokens for the Maid Joan who had led the king to his anointing at Rheims'.[3] Nicolas Groga, the governor of the town, gave her a sword, and she made off with her brothers to 'Bacquillon'—a place unknown, which might as well be the back of the moon, where things impossible are to be found, according to the ancient legend.

As long as it were indeed the brothers 'du Lis' who identified her at Metz (deep in Burgundy, where the living Joan had never been) and it was certain that they were not rogues, profiting by their sister's memory, all this might look decisive for Joan's survival—until we remember the nineteenth-century case of the Tichbourne Claimant and the twentieth-century survivor of the massacre of Ekaterinberg, both of whom were so convincing that some people have never accepted the decision of the courts disallowing their claims, the one to valuable estates in England, the other to the treasures of imperial Russia.

A little later, Jean du Lis visited Loches and announced there that his sister was not dead. The town spent twelve pounds on entertaining him, noting the facts in its records: *Jehan Dulils, frère de Jehanne la Pucelle par feu donc pas mort*: (not then dead by burning). A couple of years after this, Claude, now calling herself Claude des Armoires, escorted by her 'brother' Pierre du Lis, is said to have visited at Orléans Joan's mother Isabelle Roumée, the widow of Jacques Tart, who was certainly then living in the town as the pensioner of the commune. Claude des Armoires has been identified as the wife of Robert of Armoires, a cousin of Robert de Baudricourt of Vaucouleurs. Orléans was inclined to accept Claude as the true Joan on the evidence of Pierre du Lis's identification of her. At the house of Jacques Bourcher, the duke's treasurer, where the real Joan had lodged during the siege, she was brought face-to-face with Charles VII. That ended her imposture (though some modern writers would prefer not to believe it) and no more was heard of her.

Two other girls who also claimed to be the original Pucelle were quickly unmasked and for most of those who did not trust the English announcement of 1431 the results of Charles's enquiry at Rouen in 1450 were decisive: the seven witnesses heard never questioned that it was Joan who had been burned and neither it seems did the king's notary Guillaume Bouillé who conducted the investigation. The aim was to establish that Joan's trial had been improper and her execution illegal. It

turned up a good deal of evidence blackening the dead
Cauchon's name but nothing to suggest that Joan had survived
beyond 30 May 1431.

Nevertheless, there were still those who wanted to believe
that she had, and later chronicles describe—often in vivid
detail—how she fought beside Gilles de Rais and other
captains, first against the skinners, and then in the last battles
against the English. Not unexpectedly perhaps, the stories
grow more circumstantial the further their authors were from
the events they purport to describe, till they reach the fantasies
of 'historians' like Don Alvero de Luna in his *Coronica de la
Pucella*, who tells such tales as this:

> The Pucelle of France being (in siege at) La Rochelle,
> something of great significance happened. She wrote to the
> king (of Castile) sending to him her ambassador with those
> whom the king himself had sent abroad, urgently beseeching
> him to send her some ships of his fleet, as his court was
> bound to do in fulfilment of the confederation existing
> between his court and the king of France. And these
> ambassadors having come to Valladolid, where they were in
> the year 1436, he gave them a great reception and put on
> several feasts in their honour. And when the Constable was
> shown the letter la Pucelle had sent to the king, he showed
> it to all the important men of the court, as though it were a
> most venerable relic

—as indeed it would have been, had it not been a sixteenth-
century invention.[4]

The enquiry at Rouen in 1450 was no more than that: it
had no juridical significance. Joan had been tried by a church
court, properly constituted under canon law, and only a
higher church court could overturn the verdict that she was a
relapsed heretic. The necessary proceedings to effect the
reversal of the decisions of Cauchon's court were instituted at
Rouen in 1452 by Cardinal Guillaume d'Estouteville, the
legate from Pope Nicolas V to Charles VII, and the Dominican
Jean Bréhal recently named as inquisitor in France, at the
instigation of Guillaume Bouillé, who had conducted the
earlier enquiry.[5] In May of that year, d'Estouteville heard the

evidence of twenty witnesses establishing not so much Joan's innocence of the charges as the invalidity of the trial procedure. On the basis of what they had to say, he ruled that a petition could be made for the case proper to be re-opened.

There the matter rested for another three years till a petition to a new pope, Calixtus III, brought an order that proceedings were to be opened to revoke and annul the sentence. They were begun on 7 November that year with a grand ceremony at Notre Dame de Paris, staged with all the pathos that the fifteenth century knew so well how to command. Joan's mother was brought out of retirement to present the papal rescript personally to the pope's own commissioners, and 'with great sighs and groanings' she told her story:

> By my legal marriage, I brought into the world a daughter whom I duly caused to receive the honour of the sacraments of baptism and confirmation, whom I brought up in the fear of God, respectful and faithful towards the Church insofar as her age and the simplicity of her estate allowed . . . Then, although she had not thought, or plotted or done anything not according to the faith . . . envious persons wishing her evil . . . embroiled her in an ecclesiastical trial . . . wickedly condemning her at the last . . . and burning her.

The words were not her own. Only a lawyer could have put such sentences together. But the emotion was real, and as the well-coached crowd filling the cathedral echoed her appeal for Joan's rehabilitation, Isabelle collapsed under the tension of it, and had to be helped by the inquisitor Bréhal into the sacristy to recover.

The enquiry thus dramatically instituted lasted eight months. Altogether, a hundred and fourteen witnesses were heard, speaking on every aspect of Joan's life and condemnation. Most of them probably thought they were speaking nothing but the truth: it is difficult to go all the way with a modern French historian, Gérard Pesme, who finds the commission's report *un document incomplet, mensonge, et tuffé de faux temoinages*, 'an incomplete document, lying and stuffed with false witness'. D'Estouteville's commission was obviously as biased against Cauchon as Cauchon himself had been against Joan. Unfortunately Cauchon could not be called to answer the case made against him. He had died suddenly in his see-city of Lisieux on 14 December 1442. Listening to only one side of the story, by mid-1456 the commission reached the inevitable conclusion that Joan had been corruptly tried and wrongly condemned, and on 7 July of that year she was solemnly rehabilitated and the sentence of excommunication against her annulled in Rouen. Two weeks later the public cult of 'Jeanne la Pucelle', part nationalist heroine and part saint, began in France with a celebration at Orléans presided over by the Bishop of Coutances and Inquisitor Bréhal. The city accounts note the expenses: '. . . ten quarts and a half of wine . . . for Monseigneur the Bishop of Coutances and the Inquisitor of the Faith . . . 8 *sous*, 9 *deniers* of Paris.

'. . . to the six men who, on 21 July, carried the six torches . . . for the achievement(s) of Jeanne la Pucelle . . . 4 *sous* of Paris.'

Public celebrations on a minor scale like this, however, were all the official recognition that Joan was afforded in her own century. Charles VII did not commemorate her upon any of the many medals he struck to mark his victories, and in official and authoritative French histories till the seventeenth century she appeared only as the creature of Charles VII or Robert de Baudricourt.[6] To the English, she was always 'the pievishe, painted Puzell . . . more to be marvayled at as a false prophetisse and seducer of the people than to be honoured or worshipped as a Saint sent from God into the realme of France',[7] La Pucelle of *Henry VI part* 1, who sold herself 'body, soul and all' to hell in exchange for a French victory, and whom York was right to condemn as 'foul accursèd minister of hell'.[8]

It was in art and literature, reflecting popular opinion and religion in France, that Joan was first openly proclaimed a heroine and a saint. To François Villon, in her own century, she was already one of the great women of times gone by: *Jeanne, la bonne Lorraine/Qu'Anglais brûlèrent à Rouen* and in Martin le Franc's *Champion des Dames,* illuminated at Arras in 1451—five years *before* her rehabilitation—she is shown as a national heroine-saint, the contemporary French parallel to the Old Testament Judith. By the sixteenth century, she was well established in France—outside official circles—as one of the 'virtuous women' of the world. She was becoming, in the words of Shakespeare, 'France's saint',[9] although no move had been made to canonize her. That came only centuries later, when France was threatened by rationalism and secularism, at the end of the nineteenth century. Official France awakened to her very slowly. Richelieu put her statue in the gallery of famous women at the Palais-Royal, but it was a century later before Chapelain, the court poet of the day, made her the subject of an heroic epic, and a century after that before there appeared the first work in praise of her to be published away from Orléans, the Abbé Lengket-Dufresnoy's *Histoire de Jeanne d'Arc* 'Virgin, Heroine and Martyr for the State raised up by Providence to re-establish the French Monarchy', which appeared in 1753, forty years before the Revolution. Voltaire wrote a life of Joan, a book full of errors and insults, but it was fittingly the Emperor Napoleon who opened the door to the public cult of Joan in French official life, when in 1803 he wrote in a letter approving the erection of a statue to her at Orléans to replace one smashed in the Revolution, in which he linked her name with the ability of the French people to unite in times of trouble 'when national independence is threatened. United, the French nation,' he said, 'has never been conquered, but our neighbours, abusing the openness and loyalty of our character, continually sow among us dissensions from which spring such calamities as those of the epoch when this French heroine lived, and all the disasters characterising our history'. Whether Joan would have liked it or not, she was becoming 'the Virgin from Chesnu Woods' who did miracles and saved France. Her brother Pierre du Lis's great-grandson, Etienne Hordal, stood at the beginning of a long tradition when in the mid-sixteenth century he built a chapel in Chesnu Woods and put in it the statue of Joan which is now to be seen in Domrémy, outside the house which is supposed to have been her home.[10]

Joan the Heroine really flowered in the nineteenth century as one by one all French revolutionary and counter-revolutionary parties both in politics and religion sought to claim her as their herald. It has been estimated that by 1910—immediately after her beatification but a decade before her

canonization—there were 20,000 statues of her in churches and
public places in France.

The nineteenth century also saw the first real attempt to
unravel the historical truth about Joan in the work of Jules
Quicherat who, between 1841 and 1849, published in five
volumes entitled *Procès de condemnation et rehabilitation de Jeanne
d'Arc dite la Pucelle* . . . all the Latin records of her trial and
rehabilitation, together with extracts from all the chronicles he
could find referring to her. Strangely enough, however, his
careful historical study was preceded forty years earlier by
another which rejects almost everything said about Joan (and
most that was said by her) in her own century, putting forward
publicly for the first time the 'Bastardy Theory' of Joan's
origins which has recently been receiving so much attention.
This work was *La verité sur l'histoire de Jeanne d'Arc* by Pierre
Caze who, when his book appeared in 1819, was sub-prefect
of Bergerac.

The bastardy theory makes Joan a half-sister to both
Charles VII and Charles the Duke of Orléans by suggesting
that it was she—and not Charles the Dauphin—who was born
of the notorious affair between Queen Isabella of Bavaria and
Louis the Duke of Orléans. Its appeal, of course, lies in the
explanation it appears to offer of Joan's unpeasantlike abilities
in leadership, grasp of affairs, quickwittedness and even the
arts of war. Its main weakness is that, itself resting on the
flimsiest evidence, it has to presuppose a vast conspiracy of
silence, lasting throughout French history till the Revolution
and (in the modern version of the story) persisting at the
Vatican even today.

The feeling that Joan was more than she pretended appears
very early among chroniclers, annalists and story-tellers.
Grafton's English chronicle, with its story of Joan having
been 'a chamberlein in a common hostrey' seems to have been
quoting the fifteenth-century Burgundian chronicler who
claimed that 'Joan dwelled for a long time at a hostellery, and
was very bold at exercising horses and taking them to water,
and doing other things which it is not customary for young
women to do.'[11] Already then, in her own day there were
doubts about the utter simplicity of Joan's origins—though
they are not supported by anything substantial said about her

either at her trial, or in the documents relating to her rehabilitation. When she made the great leap forward from the
stable-yard to the front parlour of things is not known.
Probably it was in the imagination of some French storyteller.
It had obviously been made before *King Henry VI: Part* 1 was
written, for there Joan is represented not only as a witch, but
also—when denying her own father, and lying to the English—
as claiming royal blood: 'Peasant avaunt!—(to York) You
have suborn'd this man, Of purpose to obscure my noble
birth,' and

> First, let me tell you whom you have condemn'd
> Not me begotten of a shepherd swain,
> But issued from the progeny of kings . . .' (Act V, scene 4).

In its modern form, the story is briefly this:
Joan was lying when she said—or let it be understood
—that she was about seventeen when her voices drove her to
seek out Robert de Baudricourt. She was in fact about twenty-
three or -four, and had been born in 1407, very shortly before
Louis, the Duke of Orléans, had been stabbed to death in a
narrow Parisian alley. In fact, Queen Isabella's last child was
not the still-born Philippe, but Joan: 'Philippe' may have been
a dead child smuggled into the Hôtel Barbette when Joan was
smuggled out, or perhaps no more than a couple of stones
weighting a baby's coffin. When Louis of Orléans was
murdered, it became urgently necessary to conceal the baby,
because John the Fearless had sworn to wipe out the whole
race of Orléans. She was given into the custody of a noble-
woman herself named Jeanne d'Arc, the widow of Sir Eudes
de Recey and a lady of honour to the queen, now married to
one Nicolas, the brother of Jacques d'Arc of Domrémy, and
it was to her husband's brother and his wife Isabelle Roumée
that she turned for help in this emergency. Jacques d'Arc was
not the poor man of the accepted story but a prosperous
country gentleman, whose family had borne arms for centuries.[12] The d'Arcs brought her up as a sister to their own
children. Among them she naturally learned the skills of country
gentry—the peasant-neighbours lied to preserve the secret
when they told the cardinal's men in 1456 that she was a

peasant girl 'like the rest'—learning the rudiments of riding
and sword-play from her foster-brothers, needlework and
polite forms of speech from her foster-mother, and the inner
workings of government from secret messengers who reached
her from time to time. The fact that she was half-sister to both
Charles of Orléans and Jean 'the Bastard' accounts for the
deep concern she felt for them.

One of the variants of this tale has an ingenious explanation
for Joan's 'voices'. They were, it claims, members of the third
(lay) order of St Francis who came to instruct her in her
'royal' duties. The first voice that came to her, in her thirteenth-
fourteenth year, was that of the head of the order, Colette de
Courbie (herself later canonized), nurse and mentor also to the
Dauphin Charles during the Burgundian-Armagnac wars, who
in 1420 had refused to surrender him to his mother the queen
with the words, 'A woman in the power of lovers had no need
of children. You might make him mad like his father, or kill
him like his brothers, or sell him to the English as you yourself
have been sold. Come and take him if you dare.' This woman
was Joan's angel 'who taught her how to behave' and gave
her proofs of her parentage, supposedly sufficient to prove to
Charles that she was not and he was legitimate. It was this
evidence that provided 'the sign to her king' which she refused
to disclose to Cauchon's court.[13]

The interrogation at Poitiers in 1429 was essentially an
enquiry into the validity of Joan's claims, and a final polishing
of her story and everyone else's. The record kept of it was
afterwards destroyed, lest it should fall into English hands.
(A modern version of this strange history claims that a copy
of it was sent to the Vatican, where it was discovered some
years ago, but immediately suppressed, as likely to be confusing
to the simple faithful.) In fact, although welcoming the news
his half-sister had brought him, Charles did not welcome her
person. He did nothing to dissuade her risking her life in
battle, nothing to rescue her when she was in prison—except
reassure her through new 'voices' that steps were being taken
on her behalf—and next to nothing for her after she came out.
For, of course, Joan was not burned at Rouen. Although she
dared say nothing openly about her birth, her pointed
references to 'the Book of Poitiers' had alerted Cauchon to the

fact that there was something special about her apart from her
dress and her success in the field, and he entered into secret
negotiations which led ultimately to her being smuggled out
of Rouen while another woman condemned for witchcraft
was burned in her place. The witch was drugged, and her face
was hidden by the mitre—made specially loose-fitting so that
it came down over her face—which prisoners condemned by
the inquisition wore. For the next five years, till the Duke of
Bedford died and Burgundy and France were reconciled, she
lived in obscurity, probably at the Castle of Crotoy in Picardy.
Her brother Pierre was freed from a Burgundian prison under
an amnesty in that year, and she contacted him at the beginning
of the next, planning a return to public life. She reappeared as
'Claude' at Metz on 20 May 1436, was 'identified' by her
brothers, and afterwards lived with the Duchess of Luxemburg
at Arlon Castle: the duchess was, of course, aunt to her half-
brother Jean 'the Bastard', and they had been friends during
her imprisonment at Beaurevoir. At Arlon, in September of
that year, she married Robert de Baudricourt's cousin, Robert
of Armoires, and so became the Claude d'Armoires who
appeared in Orléans at a later date. Between 1437 and 1439 she
fought with Gilles de Rais against the skinners, but in August
1439, when she met Charles and the Bastard of Orléans at the
treasurer's house in the city, he persuaded her that he was now
master of his own affairs and there was nothing further that
she could do to help France. She retired to her husband's
house at Puligny, and died and was buried there in 1449.
Charles deliberately delayed the process of her rehabilitation
until after she was dead, and his agents took great care to make
sure that the truth did not leak out. But no secret can be kept
for ever: hints of it crept into the Metz Chronicle, and into
popular songs and stories that had Joan fighting all over
France, till the last Englishmen were driven out of La Rochelle
and Bordeaux. They are to be found in such popularizations as
Henry VI: Part 1—but not in French royalist histories, because
they reflect on Charles VII and his mother. Caze stumbled on
the truth early in the nineteenth century and it was confirmed
by the discoveries in Rome around 1933, discoveries since
suppressed . . .

As Joan once said to Jean Beaupère, 'Believe me or not, as

you like.' The Bastardy-theory is ingenious, entertaining, un-proven—and unproductive of any significant result even if it could be shown to be true. Joan's influence on history—not only the immediate history of her own times, but also on all western history since—has not depended on who she herself was, but on the image of her in the public mind. Napoleon was right when he suggested that she symbolized the unity and resistance of France. If she was indeed a concocted figure—built by Colette de Courbie or anyone else out of the farmed-out love-child of a worthless queen—she was a work of genius: deliberately to create a new 'Virgin Armed', touching the common spirit of the people of France as profoundly as ever Pallas Athene, the Virgin with the spear who stood upon the Acropolis, touched the people of Athens, or Judith, the Virgin with the sword, touched the oppressed Jews, was a work beyond the imagination or the skill of most moulders of public opinion.

The bastardy-theory might or might not ultimately prove true: in its barest form, leaving aside the question of whether Joan was burned or not, it would account for some of the strange features in her story—though most of them (apart from the question of what persuaded Charles VII and the nobles of his following to accept her) could be explained by the assumption that 'Jacques Tart' was not quite as backward a peasant as he is usually thought to have been. The part of the story which seems to be quite unjustifiable by any normal standards of evidence is the second half of it, the adventures of Joan after she had survived the fire at Rouen. Apart from a handful of late stories linking her, through 'Claude des Armoires' with Gilles de Rais, the original Bluebeard, it rests on a note in a manuscript chronicle in the British Museum reading 'Finally, they had her burned publicly or some other woman like her', another in the Breton Chronicle, 'La Pucelle was burned at Rouen—or condemned to be', and a third in the Metz Chronicle, 'In the town of Rouen in Normandy, she was burned and consumed in a fire, as they would say, but (it) has since proved to the contrary', together with the fact that no one who saw her burned afterwards mentioned having seen her face. The rest is twentieth-century wishful thinking, based on the wishful thinking and dreaming of the fifteenth and sixteenth. Chroniclers—especially those far away from the events they recount—can pick up the echoes of dreams, as well as of facts. Some chroniclers have even dreamed for themselves, like poets. The bailiff of Rouen certified to the regent that he had burned Joan called La Pucelle, and the regent in the king's name certified it to the world: she 'was publicly burned in the sight of all the people'. In 1450, Bouillé confirmed it. By normal standards the fact would seem irrefutable.

However, even if this judgement, that Joan was burned at Rouen, should be proved to be wrong—if the bailiff and the regent were deceived by a bishop who was not clever enough to collect a reward for his deception, either in cash or honour—the value and force of Joan's story would not now be altered. It is the myth that has mattered and still matters: the very fact that people still find the question of her burning significant shows how integral a part she has become of our mythology. There are two Joans: the Joan of history, about whom scholars speculate, and the Joan of mythology after whom streets, schools, libraries and curio shops are named. A change in the portrait of the one would only slowly, if at all, change the appearance of the other. The Roman church canonized Joan in 1920 not because historians and theologians had suddenly proved how holy she was, but because religious and political events in France and elsewhere had shown how necessary she was. This is no criticism of her canonization. To judge her holiness in the technical sense of the word is impossible for any but theologians. At the time of her beatification in 1909, however, Catholic France was tragically divided by the Dreyfus Affair and its aftermath and anti-Catholic France was rejoicing to watch the church pulling itself apart. By the cynical, to offer Joan of Arc to the young as their own heroine, Catholic and French, uniting them above their fathers' heads as it were in proud dedication against seemingly impossible odds, could be interpreted as a despairing gesture. But the need was there—clearly demonstrated in the ever-growing cult of Joan—long before the process of her beatification was officially begun.[14] The universal welcome given in 1920, after the devastating experience of the First World War, to her canonization demonstrated how profound was the need for what she symbolized both in France and the United States, where the spread of her cult was extremely rapid. But the person revered in France in 1920 by giving her chosen feast-day the status of a national holiday was not Joan-from-Domrémy but St Joan, Heroine—not the sharp-tongued, uninformedly pious transvestite ultimately broken by interrogation and betrayed by her limitless faith in her own unstable gifts of precognition and second-sight, but what was left after piety and political expediency had leached out the undesirable elements in her character and filled in the rather thin material remaining with hopes, dreams, religious theorizing, political fantasies and poetic meditations.

To Catholic France, Joan has primarily been the Warrior-Virgin coming to do miracles and ultimately triumphing over her enemies (and France's) if not in Rouen marketplace then more gloriously in heaven. To all the western world (France included) she has also been in this century a good deal more than that, something greater, more tragic and yet more hopeful. George Bernard Shaw was illustrating what she has become when in his *Saint Joan* he made her the greatest of protestants against mediaeval orthodoxy and uniformity; so also was Professor Margaret Murray in drawing Joan as a leader among the oppressed but undespairing community of witches. In our own society, Joan represents the individual human being standing against the dark powers of the world. She is the archetypal victim, ultimately destroyed in the body but victorious in her destruction as she lives on in the minds of all other potential victims, those who in this century may be crushed for their very dreams' sake, let alone—as she was—for attempting to make those dreams come true.

Joan of Arc, the French national symbol—a female embodiment of French national feeling—does not need to be burned. There is indeed a deep-seated longing among the French to prove that she never was burned. In the specifically French vision of her—the vision cast in bronze in her public statues in France—she rides on forever in her white armour, leading the true king to his anointing, or advances for ever, banner in hand, on the enemy-held towers of Les Tourelles, willing them to fall.

Joan the Maid, Joan from Domrémy, the international,

unsectarian Joan, the lonely Joan of Gauguin's imagining—
this Joan has to be burned. It is from her lonely death, the end
of her hopes, that our thinking about her begins. French or
not, Christian or not, we stand with her defying the powers
till we can defy them no longer. Then we surrender and die—
but in dying we triumph, for ideas and ideals live on.

Joan from Domrémy was not a saint, or a witch, or a
princess, or a protestant. Maybe she was not even likeable. But
she was 'I', the 'I' we fear the powers may well kill but hope
they can never annihilate.

Notes

CHAPTER 1: *Joan's France*

1. The abjuration which Joan signed on Thursday, 24 May
    1431, either in the cemetery of St-Ouen at Rouen or in her
    prison a few hours later ends with the words *Tesmoing mon
    seing manuel. Signé Jhenne. Une croix.* 'In testimony whereof
    my sign manual: signed Joan: a cross.' (See chap. 11, n. 2,
    p. 213.)
        She told her judges at the beginning of her formal
    interrogation, on Wednesday, 21 February 1431, that *du
    surnom n'en sçait rien.* She had no surname that she knew,
    her father's name Darc or Tart being personal to himself.
2. The original transcript of the trial record does not survive.
    The manuscripts are early copies made from it. They are
    (a) a copy of a version in Latin made from the original by
    the recorder at the trial, Guillaume Manchon himself, for
    use by the assessors at the process leading to Joan's
    rehabilitation in 1456. This copy was made for the Admiral
    of France, Louis Malet de Graville, at the end of the
    fifteenth century and afterwards deposited in the library
    of the Urfé family from where it finally passed in a
    mutilated condition to the Bibliotheque Nationale in Paris
    (Manuscrit Urfé: Latin 8838).
        (b) Another, made by the order of the same Admiral de
    Graville for Louis XII about the year 1500 and now in the
    Orléans library (Orléans 518). It is of special importance
    because the replies of the accused are given in French;
    although the language is that of 1500 rather than 1431,
    P. Doncoeur has recently established beyond all reasonable

doubt that Orléans 518 does contain the original answers Joan made at her trial in only slightly 'modernized' form. See his *La minute Française des Interrogations de Jeanne la Pucelle*, Melun, 1952. It is this version which has largely been followed in this book.

(c) The 'official' transcript of the trial, in Latin throughout, prepared by Manchon under the direction of the Parisian lawyer and noted Latinist Thomas de Courcelles who at the trial itself had revealed to Joan the sixty-seven articles of the *libellus* against her. Five copies were originally made and authenticated. Three still survive, bearing the signatures of the notaries (*Bibliotheque de l'Assemblée Nationale* 1119; *Bibliotheque Nationale* Latin 5965 and 5966).

3. Orléans 518: minute of the interrogation on Wednesday, 21 February. The details were for the most part confirmed by witnesses from Domrémy at the process of rehabilitation in 1456. Witnesses said that Joan was considered to be over-pious by her contemporaries (cf. the evidence of Menguette and Hauviette in Doncoeur and Lanhers, *Documents et recherches relatifs à Jeanne la Pucelle*, Melun, 1952–61). Hauviette, aged 'forty-five or thereabouts', in 1456 claimed that Joan was 'three or four years older' than she—possibly a mistake, but if not, the only support from Domrémy for the theory that Joan was not who she claimed to be and might possibly have been the daughter of Queen Isabelle of France—which requires her to have been born in 1407 (cf. pp. 187ff.).

4. Orléans 518: minute of the interrogation for Thursday, 22 February. The persistent references to cattle-herding are intriguing. Herdsmen and women were considered suspect of both sexual promiscuity and witchcraft. Joan was anxious to deny both shortcomings. At the rehabilitation her godfather Jean Moreau and godmother Beatrice Estellin gave somewhat more balanced pictures: 'She sometimes followed the plough, and warded the animals in the fields, and did women's tasks, spinning and so on' (Moreau). 'She busied herself with various jobs about her parental home and sometimes span goathair or sheep's wool' (Estellin). When 'not doing womanly things' was

made a charge against Joan, her answer to it was, 'There are enough women to do them' (Orléans 518, Tuesday, 27 March).

5. Orléans 518: Saturday, 24 February. 'The Island' has sometimes been identified with the Castle of Vaucouleurs but may have been a lesser strongpoint. This Burgundian attack may have been that of 1428—after Joan's two unsuccessful attempts to persuade Robert de Baudricourt to send her to Chinon and shortly before he agreed to help her.

6. Orléans 518: Thursday, 22 February. The Lady of Beaurevoir offered Joan, when prisoner, stuff to make herself a dress but she refused it, and seems to have taken no part in sewing the standard of which she was so proud.

7. Orléans 518: Saturday, 24 February. Her reply to the next question—had her voices told her to hate Burgundians in her childhood?—was much more circumspect and restrained: 'Since she had learned that the voices were for the king of France she had not liked Burgundians.'

8. Robert Blondell, *De reductione Normanniae*, 12. Blondell's family had lived in Normandy since at least the twelfth century. They were early French nationalists in that they refused to submit to the rule of Henry V, preferring to exile themselves to Brittany. Robert Blondell was born about 1390 and so was Joan's slightly older contemporary. To him, the greatest of all English crimes was the sacking of the monastery of Our Lady at Cléry; Joan was 'the Maid with the spirit and dress of a man' inspired by 'neither a military nor any other human being' but 'by a divine commission', under whose onslaught the English were driven to death 'like swine to the butcher's' and who led Charles 'the then dauphin to be consecrated with the sacred oil at Rheims'. See, Stephenson, *Narratives of the Expulsion of the English from Normandy*, Longmans, Green, London 1863.

9. Volume 5 of Jules Quicherat's *Procès de condemnation et de réhabilitation de Jeanne d'Arc dite la Pucelle*, Paris 1841–9, contains chronicle references to Joan herself. The 'official' history of the reign is contained in the *Vigiles de Charles VII*, an MS illuminated in 1484. The most readily available

introductions to the period in English are the relevant
chapters in the *Cambridge Mediaeval History*, vol. 8 (1959
edition) and E. F. Jacobs, *The Fifteenth Century*, Oxford
1961. Cf. also Lavisse, *Histoire de France*, vol. 4, Paris 1902,
Le Marquis du Fresne de Beaucourt, *L'histoire de Charles VII*,
Stephenson, *Letters and Papers illustrative of the Wars of the
English in France*, vol. 2, Longmans, Green, London 1864.

10. *Journal d'un Bourgeois de Paris* (ed. A. Twetey, Paris 1881):
the *Bourgeois*, a Burgundian sympathizer, believed Joan to
have been inspired by the devil—yet could give her a
Franciscan childhood: 'When she was very small, and
looked after the sheep, the birds of the woods and fields
would come to her when she called, to eat bread from her
lap'.

11. In his *Histoire de Charles VII*, de Beaucourt has tried
(successfully in the opinion of some) to demonstrate that
there was nothing homosexual about Charles's relation-
ships with his favourites. There may, indeed, have been no
overt vice of any kind (except murder) at his court but
there can be no doubt that the whole atmosphere there was
very peculiar indeed.

CHAPTER 2: *Voices*

1. In the indirect third-person form of the trial documents
'. . . and taught her *se gubernandum, se gouverner*': in which
direction to go, how to comport herself, how to behave,
or simply what to do. The point is that the voices made
themselves Joan's mentors and she surrendered to them
completely—minute of the interrogation on Thursday, 22
February.

2. Orléans 518: minute of the interrogation on Tuesday, 27
February.

3. The text of the minutes of the earlier part of the fifth
session of interrogation, on Thursday, 1 March, is preserved only in the official Latin version of the trial record:
it was largely devoted to proving that Joan was a witch,
using mandrake and her rings as charms, and to demonstrating that her attitude to her voices was one of perverted

sexuality, such as was ascribed to the practitioners of witchcraft.

4. On Tuesday, 27 February, in the hall of the prison at the castle, Jean Beaupère asked if since her interrogation on the previous Saturday Joan had heard her voices. She replied: Yes, many times. He then asked her if she had heard them in that room on Saturday and after some prevarication she replied: Yes. His next question was what had they said on Saturday? To this she replied, 'I did not hear them clearly and did not hear anything I can repeat to you until I returned to my room.' Several times she refused to answer questions on the day they were asked, but promised to answer them later—presumably after she had consulted her voices on what answers she should give.

5. Interrogation on the afternoon of Monday, 12 March, in the prison at the castle.

6. Interrogation in the morning of Monday, 12 March, in the prison at the castle: 'Asked if she had promised our Lord to keep her virginity: replied, It should be enough to have promised those sent by him, that is to say St Catherine and St Margaret' . . . 'The first time she had heard her voices she had vowed her virginity to God in so far as it was pleasing to God. And she was about thirteen years old.' But she did not believe herself fanatical on the subject: in the prison on Saturday, 17 March, in the afternoon, she was asked if it had ever been revealed to her that if she lost her virginity she would lose 'her armament' and her voices would not come to her again, and replied 'That has not been revealed to me.' Asked if her voices would come when she married, she replied, 'I do not know. I bow to our Lord'.

7. She had just claimed—answering a question from Beaupère —to be an angel, a messenger, direct from God, and not long previously had refused to swear to tell the truth. The bishop's exasperation is understandable. Her reply to his question was another indirect warning that she would not tell the truth: 'The voices have told me things for my king, and not for you'.

8. On Tuesday, 27 February, she spoke both of 'the salvation' and 'the comfort' brought to her by her saints, and on

Thursday, 1 March, said that her voices had 'promised to lead her to paradise'. Her faith in this promise was one of the chief charges on which she was found guilty: (9) 'You said that St Catherine and St Margaret promised to lead you to paradise . . . You have made a temerarious and pre-sumptuous assertion, a pernicious lie'.

9. The interrogation in prison on the morning of Monday, 12 March.

10. The interrogation in prison on the morning of Saturday, 17 March: it was 'a white suit of armour, complete, for a soldier' which she had 'won before Paris'. The church of St Denis was the traditional burial place of France's kings. This suit of armour was not Joan's own, but the spoils of war, taken from a soldier who had surrendered to her. It may be seen in France's military museum, *Le Musée de l'Armée*.

11. The minute of her interrogation on Thursday, 1 March. In her challenge to the king of England written from Poitiers in 1429, she said, 'King of England—wherever I find your people in France, I shall make them leave . . .I have been sent here by God the king of heaven to thrust you out of all France, body for body. And if they (*your soldiers*) will obey, I will have mercy. And you cannot have any other opinion because you do not hold the kingdom of France from God, the king of heaven, the son of Saint Mary; but it will be held by King Charles, the true heir: for so the king of heaven wills.'

Later in the same letter she claimed that 'The French are doing the finest thing that has ever been done for Christendom'.

12. The minute of her interrogation on Saturday, 17 March. This assertion duly appeared *verbatim* in the final bill of indictment and was condemned as it was bound to be.

13. In the prison on Wednesday, 14 March in the afternoon, when she was given a list of four 'sins' to ponder upon, this being the last of them.

14. Laxart's evidence to the tribunal for Joan's rehabilitation: see, Doncoeur and Lanhers, *La réhabilitation de Jeanne la Pucelle, in loc.* Laxart told the tribunal that among the arguments Joan used to persuade him to accompany her

to Vaucouleurs was a prophecy then current in the countryside to the effect that 'France had been lost by a woman and would have to be recovered by a virgin'. Joan identified the woman with 'Queen Venus' and the virgin with herself.

15. Grafton's *Chronicle* for the seventh year of Henry VI; London, 1809, p. 580.

CHAPTER 3: *Knight of France*

1. The military situation at Orléans and its significance is brilliantly described in Fuller, *Decisive Battles of the Western World*: *The Relief of Orléans*, Eyre & Spottiswoode, 1954. For a contemporary account from the French angle see the *Journal du Siege d'Orléans 1428-9*, ed. Charpentier and Chissaud, Paris, 1896.

For the theory that Joan was a half-sister to Jean the Bastard of Orléans, see chapter 12 and the references in the notes there. During Joan's lifetime, Jean signed himself 'the bastard': Charles VII made him Count of Dunois (by which name he is often called) only in 1436.

2. Doncoeur and Lanhers, *Réhabilitation, in loc.*

3. The minute of the interrogation on Thursday, 22 February.

4. The story was told in the 1520s, during the reign of Francis I, by one Pierre Sala in his panegyric *Hardiesses de grands rois et empereurs*. He claimed to have had it directly from Guillaume Gouffier of whose friendship with Charles VII the historian Charles Rolant says that the king would rather have 'no other gentleman in his bed before him': *nul gentilhomme en son lit fors luy*.

The *Recapitulation* with which MS Orléans 518 (*c.* 1500) begins relates a slightly different version of the same story: 'Testing Joan, the king asked how he could be sure that she came from God. She said, "If I tell you things so secret that only God and you know them, will you believe that I have been sent from God?"

'The king said yes, and the Pucelle asked him, "Sire: do you not recall that on last All Saints Day you were in the chapel of the Castle of Loches, quite alone in your oratory (and) you asked God for three things?"

'The king admitted that it was so.

'Joan asked him if he had ever told them to anyone, even in confession. He said no, and she told him, "The first request which you made to God was that if you were the true heir of France he would give you the courage to persevere . . . the second thing you begged of him was that if the great adversities and tribulations which the poor people of France were suffering and had suffered so long sprang from your sin and were caused by it, it would be his pleasure to relieve the people of it and that you alone should be punished for it . . . and the third thing was that if the sin of the people was the cause of these adversities, it would please him to pardon the people and still his anger, taking away from the kingdom the tribulations it had and had had twelve years and more".'

5. Some say that it has been: cf. pp. 189ff.

6. Joan herself talked only about the first two of these promises at her trial. The four were given to the tribunal of rehabilitation in 1456 by the sole survivor of the hearing at Poitiers, the Dominican Brother Seguin Seguin.

7. The challenge, dated 22 March 1429, is printed in full in a modern French version in R. Pernoud, *Jeanne d'Arc,* Editions du Seuil, Paris, 1959: the original text is in Quicherat, Procès, vol. 5, p. 196.

8. The minute of the interrogation in prison on Saturday, 10 March: it is with these arms that Joan is depicted in the *Champion des Dames,* 1451, though the sword transfixes a crown (Illustration 13).

9. The minute of the interrogation on Tuesday, 27 February.

10. The minute of the interrogation on Saturday, 17 March: the English were certainly afraid of her standard and the French encouraged by the sight of it—but this did not make the standard itself magical.

CHAPTER 4: *Orléans*

1. *Le Journal du Siège d'Orléans* graphically describes the straits to which the besieged were reduced.

2. Minute of the interrogation for Thursday, 1 March.
3. The *Recapitulation*, Orléans 518, folio 19.
4. The story was told by the Bastard of Orléans himself in his evidence to the commission for Joan's rehabilitation.
5. Joan is said to have told Charles at Chinon that 'Saint Louis and Charlemagne'—both forerunners of his as kings of France—'are on their knees making petition for you'— Cousiet de Montreuil, *Chronique de la Pucelle*, ed. Vallet et Virirelle, Paris, p. 274.
6. *Journal of the Siege*, p. 77. The enthusiastic *Journal* describes her as 'in full armour, mounted upon a white horse, having carried before her her standard, also white with on it two angels each holding a fleur-de-lis while on the pennon was depicted the Annunciation'. The banner the chronicler remembered was not precisely that which Joan herself described.
7. Contes told this story at Joan's rehabilitation. It was also on this day, according to Joan's chaplain Pasquerel, that she made one of her terrifyingly accurate predictions, this time to the effect that the siege would be raised within five
8. days. One wishes one could always believe Pasquerel. Was this the truth? One of the charges against Joan was that she had second sight and used it.
9. The lead taken by Joan throughout this campaign is confirmed by evidence as varied as the Bastard's, Pasquerel's and that of the contemporary Burgundian chronicler Wavrin.
10. J. H. Ramsay, *Lancaster and York*, vol. 1, p. 398, quotes this letter in full. The English collapse was caused by Joan's 'false enchantements and sourcerie'. Some excuse had to be found for the failure of morale at Orléans and after.
11. *Journal of the Siege*, p. 86. Joan's page, Louis de Contes, says that Joan told the soldiers that Les Tourelles would fall not when her flagpole touched it but when the wind changed and blew her pennon towards it. The picture is almost as terrifying.
12. Wavrin, *Chronicle*, in *Recueil des Chroniques . . . de la Grant Bretaigne . . .* ed. W. Hardy, Rolls Series, 1879, vol. 5, bk. 4, p. 275.

13. Wavrin, *op. cit.*, p. 281. Interrogated on Thursday, 1 March, Joan herself denied that she was ever told state secrets.

CHAPTER 5: '*And now we must go to Rheims*'

1. Perceval de Cagny, *Chronicle,* in Quicherat, *op. cit.,* vol. 4. Joan accepted the leadership. Wavrin says that throughout the summer 'Joan la Pucelle was at the front with her standard before all' (p. 287). Thibaut d'Armagnac, a comrade-in-arms, claimed that 'all the men-at-arms admired her valour'.

2. So the Duke of Alençon, giving evidence in support of Joan's rehabilitation. Many stories were told about her bloodthirsty courage during those days. Unhorsed at Jargeau, for instance, she is said to have picked herself up and shouted, 'Friends—friends—onwards! Onwards! Our Lord has damned the English: now they are ours!'

3. Wavrin, *op. cit.,* p. 305. Wavrin had himself fought—on the English side—at the Battle of Patay.

4. Wavrin, *op. cit.,* p. 305. At her trial Joan denied knowing state secrets: the truth is probably that she was accepted as a war-leader only. The *Recapitulation* opening Orléans 518 says 'She became a leader of all his enterprises', though the reason given there is not perhaps the fundamental one for which men like La Hire were ready to accept her as their equal: 'because of the holy and straight life which she led. They saw that she went to confession very often and received the body of our Lord every week: but on the other hand they never saw her doing any women's work whatsoever'. ('Women's work' in the thinking of the fifteenth-century clergy tended to include not only housekeeping and so on, but also the seduction of men.)

5. Perceval de Cagny, *Chronicle.* The whole sentence reads, 'Although the king had no money whatsoever wherewith to pay its charges, no one—none of the knights, squires, men-at-arms or footsoldiers—refused to go and serve the king in his travels with the Pucelle, saying that they would go wherever she wanted to go'.

Charles himself, in his only known acknowledgement of his debt to Joan, speaks in a postscript to a letter (now preserved at Narbonne) describing the 'miracle' of the capture of these places of 'la Pucelle, who has always been personally present at the accomplishment of all these things'.

6. Joan described Brother Richard's 'trial of the spirits' at her interrogation on 3 March and was told of his appropriation of her standard later on the same day.

7. According to Joan, there was only one king in France, God himself. It was his right to choose who would rule as his regent there. She is said to have told Charles at Chinon, 'I am come with a mission from God to bring help to you and to the kingdom, and the king of heaven orders you through me to be anointed and crowned at Rheims, and to be the lieutenant of the king of heaven who is the king of France' (Quicherat, *op. cit.,* vol. 3, p. 103).

8. She may have lost heart, but she had lost none of her arrogant certitude: the letter, dated 17 July, read in part, '*La Pucelle* requires of you in the name of the King of Heaven . . . that you and the king of France should make a good and stable peace which will last a long time. Forgive one another wholeheartedly, as brave Christians should do.'

9. Du Fresne de Beaucourt, *Histoire de Charles VII*, vol. 2, p. 230.

CHAPTER 6: '*I want to see Paris from closer to*'

1. Questioned by Magistri, during the interrogation in prison on Tuesday, 13 March.

2. The Duke of Alençon's evidence to the commission for Joan's rehabilitation. He was certainly her very warm admirer. 'Everyone marvelled,' he told the commission, 'that she acted in so prudent and informed a way where war was concerned'. He also said that she was very skilled in the placement of guns—a new art in which he himself excelled.

3. Stephenson, *Letters and Papers*, under 1 September 1429.

Special precautions had to be taken that summer to prevent deserters from fleeing to England.

4. Wavrin, *op. cit.,* pp. 339 ff.
5. Grafton, *op. cit.,* p. 586.
6. The interrogation on Thursday, 22 February—the second session. The passage is difficult but suggests that in attacking Paris she had deliberately disobeyed her voices and they had permitted her wounding almost as a punishment. 'She said her voices told her she should stay at St Denis, where in fact she did not want to stay . . .'
7. The minute of the interrogation in prison on Tuesday, 13 March. Having attacked Paris on a feast day was included among the short list of sins presented to Joan for her consideration the following day: the thought of having done so obviously oppressed her.
8. The minute of the interrogation on Saturday, 17 March.
9. Perceval de Cagny, *Chronicle,* in Quicherat, *op. cit.,* vol. 4, p. 29.

CHAPTER 7: *The Living Legend*

1. The minute of the interrogation on Tuesday, 13 March, answering the vice-inquisitor.
2. Perceval de Cagny, *op. cit.*—to whom we are indebted for the clearest account of the intrigues at Charles's court that winter. At her trial Joan was accused of having tried to capture the town by magic with holy water, but hotly denied that she had 'thrown water or caused it to be thrown in the manner of an aspersion' to dissolve the town's defences.
3. 'Asked if midwives had not touched their rings to those she wore: replied, many women have touched my hands and rings, but I do not know their hearts and minds'. She owned at least two rings, perhaps more. One was given her by her parents: of it she said (on 1 March) 'I think it was inscribed Jesus-Maria. I do not know who did the writing. There was no stone in it, as I recall. They gave it to me at Domrémy' . . . 'if it was gold, it was not fine gold. I do not know if it was gold or electrum. I believe

it had three crosses, and no other sign except Jesus-Maria'
(17 March, afternoon). The other was the gift of her
brother. Her judges would no doubt have liked to believe
that the inscription on the ring was a magical formula and
that midwives touched their rings to it so that power might
pass from it to them, but at the fifth session of interrogation she had already said that 'her rings had not healed
anyone'.

4. The minute of the interrogation on the afternoon of
Wednesday, 14 March.

CHAPTER 8: *Prisoner of the French*

1. The minute of the interrogation in prison on Saturday,
10 March.

2. The minute of the interrogation in prison on Tuesday, 13
March.

3. The minutes of the interrogations in prison on Saturday,
10 March and Tuesday, 13 March.

4. Wavrin, *Chronicle*, chap. 24: '*Comment Jehanne la Pucelle fut
prinse*'. *op. cit.*

5. The minute of the interrogation in prison on Thursday,
15 March.

6. The minute of the interrogation in the chapel royal of the
castle at Rouen, Wednesday, 21 February.

7. The work Gerson dedicated to Charles VII in 1429 was his
Trilogy of Astrology Theologized. On Gerson's treaty de-
fending Joan, see D. G. Wayman, *The Chancellor and
Jeanne d'Arc* in *Franciscan Studies*, 17, no. 2–3 (June-
September 1957), St Bonaventure Press, New York.

8. Preserved in the *Recapitulation* opening Orléans 518,
folios 32–33.

9. *Ibid.*, folios 34–35.

10. The minute of the interrogation in prison on Wednesday,
14 March.

11. The minute of the interrogation at the archbishop's house
on Saturday, 3 March—found only in the French of
Orléans 518, folio 98.

On both occasions when Joan was closely questioned

about this escape attempt the questioning was directed towards making her admit the sins of both suicidal despair and blasphemy. At the sixth interrogation session—that on 3 March—the questions and answers ran: 'Asked what happened when she jumped: replied, some said that she was dead: as soon as the Burgundians saw that she was alive they asked her why she had jumped.'

'Asked if she had not said that she would rather die than be in the hands of the English: replied, she would rather give her soul to God than be in the hands of the English.'

'Asked if she was not angry, and had not blasphemed the name of God: replied, that she had never cursed a saint (male or female) and that it was not her habit to swear.'

Similarly, interrogated in the prison of the castle on 14 March, after being asked about her fall, she was asked, 'if when she could speak again she had not denied and damned God and his saints because she had been given away by an informant, or so her questioner had been told: replied, that she had no memory of that as far as she could recall, of ever having denied or damned God and his saints, there or elsewhere. There was nothing for her to confess because she had no memory of having said or done so.'

Nevertheless, blasphemy as well as suicidal despair appeared among the final charges against her.

12. M. A. Murray, *The Witch Cult in Western Europe* (Clarendon Press, Oxford, 1921), lays the foundation of this school of thought. Professor Murray drew a distinction between 'operative' and 'ritual' witchcraft, operative witchcraft being the use of spells, charms and the like to achieve some practical end, ritual witchcraft the pursuit of the witchcult. Joan denied most vehemently that she was an operative witch in her answers about her rings and so on. If she was a ritual witch, a worshipping witch—as Professor Murray believed that she was—she concealed her connection with the cult too successfully for me to pierce her disguise as an operative and ritual Christian.

13. The mediaeval *Indiculus Superstitionem*, and canons of councils and synods from Ancyra onwards forbade such

practices as making offerings at trees, stones, fountains and crossroads, lighting fires or candles in honour of them, or addressing vows to them. Also forbidden was the worship of graves, stones, wells and rivers. In addition, the *Indiculus* forbids anyone to give the title 'Lord' to the sun or moon, and bans wizardry, tempest-raising, divination, sorcery, the use of charms and attendance at orgies. See H. C. Lear, *A History of the Inquisition in the Middle Ages* (1911); H. C. Lear, *Material towards a History of Witchcraft* (1939). Pennethorne Hughes, *Witchcraft*, Longmans, Green, London, 1952.

14. The minute of the interrogation at the archbishop's house on Saturday, 24 February.

15. The same session: at the fifth session (1 March) Joan admitted to having heard her voices at the nearby spring, but not at the tree. What they said at the spring 'she did not recall'.

16. A fairy wood—a fairy tree—a fairy spring—and the Virgin who should come as a prophecy well known in the countryside . . . it is not surprising, perhaps, that Cauchon and the others tried to make something out of it all. Joan herself felt free to use others' belief in it—she reminded her Uncle Laxart of the local prophecies about the Virgin coming to save France.

The *Tournai Chronicle* maintains that Charles VII had always expected 'divine' (or magical) help and when Joan presented herself to him promptly thought of saving women such as Judith: 'always hoping to have help from the grace of God, and remembering that certain women have done wonders, like Judith and others' he decided to receive Joan. Joan's choice of title for herself laid her open to charges of either witchcraft or blasphemy against 'the Virgin Mother of God'. There had been a *Pucelette* in France before, a certain Marguerite, a young shepherdess who overcame devils and forced them to beg for grace—see Lavisse, *Histoire de France* (1902), vol. 4, 2, part 1, cap. 3.

17. The minute of the interrogation in prison on Saturday, 17 March. Cultic witchcraft was believed to run in families, the rituals being handed down from mother to daughter,

aunt to niece or as here—as Joan's judges hoped to suggest—from godmother to godchild.

18. The question recalls a whole cycle of stories like that told in the *Ballad of Thomas the Rhymer*. Those who went away with the fairies returned after a year-and-a-day, or after seven years, no older than they had left—if they could avoid eating the whole time they were in fairyland. For Joan to have admitted going away—or astray—with the fairies either in this way or sexually would indeed have been a confession of sorcery. The legend was probably in origin a parable of the *esbat* or of an even earlier initiation-rite. (The Psalmist says: one day in thy courts is better than a thousand . . .)

CHAPTER 9: *Prisoner of the English*

1. Pierre Cauchon had been a doctor of the University of Paris and a faithful follower of Duke John the Fearless of Burgundy. He was one of the delegates for the University at the conversations which led up to the marriage of Henry V and Catherine of Valois, and the disinheritance of the 'so-called Dauphin of Viennois' in the Treaty of Troyes. Shortly afterwards, the University petitioned that he be made a bishop and on 27 August 1420 Philip the Good presented him with the see of Beauvais.

2. The affidavit—preserved in folios 49–50 of Orléans 518—reads in part:

'In the Year of Grace 1430, the sixteenth day of July . . . at the fortress of the most illustrious prince my Lord the Duke of Burgundy, established in siege before Compiègne, in the presence of those noble men, my lords . . . the bailiff of Vermandois and Jehan de Pressy, knights, with many other nobles . . . there was presented to the said illustrious prince my lord the Duke of Burgundy by the reverend father in God Pierre, bishop and count of Beauvais, a paper citation containing word for word what is written above [the bishop's own letter and that from the university]. Of the existence of which citation the lord Duke advised in act and fact that noble man Nicolle Raoullin, his

chancellor, who was there present, and commanded him to
convey it to the noble and mighty lord Jehan of Luxemburg, the Lord of Beaurevoir, the which citation the said
chancellor did in fact convey to the said Luxemburg, he
being present, and the which he received, as was apparent
to me. These things written here were done in my
presence: thus signs Triquelot, Notary and Tabellion
Apostolic and Imperial.'

3. The letter is preserved in the *Recapitulation* to Orléans 518,
folios 38–39.

4. Naturally there is room for debate on this question and
different authorities on mediaeval law have adopted a
variety of attitudes on it. See the discussions in P. Tisset,
Les procès de condemnation de Jeanne d'Arc, art. in *Mémorial
du Ve centenaire de la réhabilitation de Jeanne d'Arc 1456–1956*
(Paris 1956); E. Perroy, *The Hundred Years War*, Eyre &
Spottiswoode, 1951, pp. 287 ff. W. P. Barrett, *The Trial
of Jeanne d'Arc* (1931).

5. *Recapitulation*, Orléans 518, folios 51–52.

6. The names are preserved in Orléans 518, folio 55. The
treasurer of the cathedral, Raoul Roussell, a doctor of civil
law, later became archbishop of Rouen—a position
Cauchon is said to have coveted for himself.

7. Orléans 518, folios 55–56.

8. Orléans 518, folio 57.

9. Orléans 518, folio 58. Joan was not completely repulsive
sexually—or such, at any rate, was the evidence of the
soldiers who slept in the same tent with her on campaign
as reported to the commission for her rehabilitation by
the Duke of Alençon. One of the soldiers had told him, 'I
have heard it said by several of those familiar with Joan
that they never felt desire for her—that is to say, they felt
physical lust sometimes but they never dared to let it
loose'. Her squire Jean de Metz admitted to being 'on fire
with love for her—I believe, a divine love' because he was
'so afraid of her that I would never have dared to solicit
her'. If her body could arouse lust and she had taken a
vow of virginity, she was right to bear it in mind that not
every man she met would necessarily reverence and fear
her: article 54 of the *libellus* against her (disclosed to her

on 27 March) accused her of having lived loosely with the soldiers; to this accusation she replied, 'When in lodging I most often had a woman with me, and when I was in the field, I went armed and armoured when I could not find a woman'.

10. The evidence is collected and assessed in A. Harmand, *Jeanne d'Arc, ses costumes, ses armures*, Paris 1929.

11. Quicherat, *op. cit.*, vol. 3, p. 325.

12. Orléans 518, folio 63.

13. Beaupère's attitude towards Joan never softened. In 1456 he said, 'She was very subtle, with the subtlty of the female.' By this time, Beaupère had slipped formally into heresy and out of it again, by attaching himself to the Council of Basel and serving its anti-pope Felix V, formerly Amadeus VIII, Count of Savoy. Since his return to France he had become the loyal follower of Charles VII.

14. Orléans 518, folio 68.

15. As early as the *Recapitulation* to Orléans 518, folio 8— which, as has been said, can scarcely be later than 1500, even if Manchon did not write it when preparing the story of Joan's trial for the commission of rehabilitation—the fleur-de-lis have already appeared: 'And she begged the king that he would send one of his armourers to St Catherine de Fierbois and that he would bring her the sword which he would find in the church in the place she would tell him of. On that sword—on each side of it— there would be five engraved fleurs-de-lis . . . And she told the king that with that sword—and with the help of God and his own gallant captains and soldiers—she would raise the siege of Orléans and bring him to his anointing and crowning at Rheims as his predecessors, the kings of France, had been at that place before him.'

16. G. Pesme, *Jeanne d'Arc n'a pas brulée*, Editions Balzac, Paris 1960, believes that a copy of the record of Poitiers still exists at the Vatican. It was, he claims, found in 1933 by one Edward Schneider (now deceased) but caused to vanish again by Cardinal Tisserant before it could be published.

CHAPTER 10: *The breaking-point*

1. Orléans 518, folios 126 ff.
2. The Savoyard Pope Felix V named Thomas Courcelles a cardinal, for services rendered to him at Basle and elsewhere. He afterwards became a fiery partisan of Charles VII.
3. For summaries of the cases against these arch-heretics, on the precedent provided by whose stories so much of the case against Joan depended, see my *The Great Schism*, Hamish Hamilton, London, 1970, pp. 130 ff., 183 ff.

CHAPTER 11: *Death at Rouen*

1. In theory, anyone condemned by the local bishop's court or the inquisitor's court could appeal to the pope. The Bishop of Avranches, one of Joan's judges, claimed afterwards that he had argued for her right to do so. 'In doubtful matters,' he had said, 'recourse should always be had to the pope or a general council', but Cauchon had overruled him, refusing to allow the recorder to enter his opinion in the minutes of the trial. Isembart de la Pierre told the king's notary Bouillé on 4 March 1450 that Joan had said she would be happy to submit her case to the pope 'but not the persons present conducting her trial because—as she had often said—they were her enemies'. He claimed that he had suggested to her that she should appeal to the Council of Basle, which was already in session but had not yet shown the schismatic tendencies it later exhibited. She had asked him what a General Council was and he had told her 'a universal assembly of the whole church' and that 'it had people of her own party in it as well as those on the English side'. When Joan heard that, she had said, 'Oh—are there people on our side?' He had confirmed that there were, and Joan had said that she would 'happily' submit to such a council. 'Immediately, the Bishop of Beauvais, full of spite and anger, shouted, "Silence—for the devil's sake!" and told the notary not to

record that she submitted to a General Council'. De la Pierre also claimed that Cauchon had threatened to have him thrown into the Seine if he ever told this story to anyone.

2. In the French of Orléans 518 this abjuration reads:
'Je, Jhenne, appellee la Pucelle, miserable pecheresse, apprez ce que j'ay congneu le las d'erreur auquel je estoys tenue et que par la grace de Dieu suis retournee a nostre mere Saincte Eglise; affin que on veoye que, non pas fainctement mais de bon coeur et de bonne volunté suis retournee a icelle, je confesse que j'ay griefment peché en faignant mensoigneusement avoir eu revelacions et apparicions de par Dieu et ses anges, sainte Katherine et Margueritte. Et tous mes dictes et fais qui sont contre l'Eglise je me revocque et vueuil demourer en union de l'eglise sans jamais en departyr. Tesmoing mon seing manuel.'

3. Isembart de la Pierre's statement to the commission for her rehabilitation.

4. Orléans 518, folios 195 ff.

5. Guillaume Manchon refused to sign the pages of the official transcripts relating to this part of the case—folios 112–120 of MS. *Bib. Ass. Nat.* 1119—because they make Joan deny her voices for the last time at the moment of her execution and he claimed that the evidence on this point had been falsified by Cauchon. Perhaps, nonetheless, Joan did cry for mercy and offer to promise anything if only she could be spared—and who could blame her for such a panic reaction?

6. Either de la Pierre's imagination was unbounded or the executioner was inexperienced and muffed his job. De la Pierre told the king's notary in 1450 'Immediately after the execution, the executioner came to me and my companion Brother Martin Ladvenu struck and shaken by wonderful repentence and terrible contrition, like a man quite desperate, fearing that he would never be able to beg pardon and indulgence from God for what he had done to this holy woman. And the executioner said and declared that notwithstanding the oil, the brimstone and the charcoal he had pulled up against Joan's intestines and

heart, he had not been able to burn or reduce her intestines and heart to ashes in the least—by which, quite obviously, he was as astonished as by a miracle.'

7. Wavrin, *Chronicle*, cap. 34, *op. cit.*, p. 403.

8. Luxemburg had been given to Burgundy by Elizabeth the Lady of Luxemburg in 1417 on the death of her husband Antoine, the Duke of Brabant and brother of John the Fearless: she had inherited it in 1396 from her father John of Luxemburg, Duke of Görlitz, there being no direct male heir.

9. For this period of French history, see de Beaucourt, *Histoire de Charles VII*, vol. 4; Lavisse, *Histoire de France*, vol. 4, 2, cap. 4.

10. Doncoeur and Lanhers, Paris, 1956: *La réhabilitation de Jeanne la Pucelle: l'enquête ordonnée par Charles VII en 1450 et le codicille de Guillaume Bouillé.*

CHAPTER 12: *Afterwards*

1. The minute of the interrogation on Saturday, 3 March.

2. Orléans 518, folio 93, minute of the interrogation for Saturday, 3 March.

3. The reference cannot fail to recall Robin Hood's companion 'Little John'—the Basque Jannicot, a late form of the two-faced Janus, one of the gods of the witches.

4. For the legends of Joan's survival and also of her 'royal' breeding—the bastardy-theory—see M. David-Darnac, *L'histoire véridique et merveilleuse de la Pucelle d'Orléans*, La Table Ronde, Paris, 1965; G. Pesme, *Jeanne d'Arc n'a pas brulée*, Editions Balzac, Paris, 1960; C. Saramen, *Pour la défense de Jeanne d'Arc*, art. in *Annuaire-Bulletin de la Société d'Histoire de France*, vol. 85, 1952–3.

5. Volumes 2 and 3 of Quicherat's monumental work are devoted to the documents of Joan's rehabilitation. See also Doncoeur and Lanhers: *La réhabilitation de Jeanne la Pucelle, l'enquête de Cardinal d'Estouville en 1456.*

6. The story of Joan's gradual recognition in official France is told in P. Marot, *De la réhabilitation à la glorification de*

Jeanne d'Arc: *Essai sur l'historiographie et le culte de l'heroine en France pendant cinq siècles* in the *Mémorial du Vème centenaire de la réhabilitation*, etc., Paris 1956.

7. Grafton, *op. cit.*, p. 589.
8. *Henry VI*, part 1, act V, scene 4.
9. *Henry VI*, part 1, act I, scene 6: 'No longer on Saint Dennis will we cry, But Joan la Pucelle shall be France's saint'.
10. One of the earliest accounts of Joan was a dissertation written by Etienne Hordal's son Jean and published at Pont-à-Mousson in 1612.
11. Wavrin, *op. cit.*, cap. 34, p. 403.
12. According to Pesme, the arms of d'Arc were 'd'azur . . . a un arc posé en fasce, chargé de 3 flèches entre-croisées, les peintes ferrues, deux d'or ferrées et plumetée d'argent, le troisième d'argent ferré et plumetée d'or: en chef d'argent chargé un lion gueules'.
13. Pesme, *op. cit.*, discusses this theory in detail. It is unconvincing.
14. Fittingly enough, it was a Bishop of Orléans—Mgr Dupanloup—who, in 1869, first petitioned for Joan's canonization. But Bishop Dupanloup was a notorious 'liberal' in church affairs, strongly opposed to any definition of papal or ecclesiastical infallibility, and may well have been rather twisting the pope's tail than making a proposal he expected to see seriously entertained. Official sanction for the process leading to canonization came only in 1894, from Pope Leo XIII; the three miracles required for beatification were attested among nuns by 1891, but, even so, political considerations delayed Joan's beatification until 1909.

Chronology of Events Surrounding the Life of Joan of Arc

1328—Death of Charles IV of France: succession of Philip of Valois and exclusion of Edward III of England.

1346—Battle of Crécy. (*1349-50—The Black Death*)

1356—Battle of Poitiers.

1360—Peace of Brétigny.

1364-80—Charles V King of France: renewal of war with England.

1376—Death of the Black Prince.

1377—Death of Edward III: accession of Richard II. (*1377—Gregory XI's return to Rome from Avignon*) (*1378—death of Gregory XI: election of Urban VI: counter-election of 'Clement VII': beginning of the Great Schism*)

1380—Death of Charles V: accession of Charles VI.

1381—The Peasants' Revolt in England.

1384—Death of John Wyclif.

1385—Marriage of Charles VI and Isabella of Bavaria-Ingolstadt.

1389—'Feasts of Queen Venus' at Paris. (*1389—Death of 'Clement VII': election of 'Benedict XIII'*)

1396—Marriage of Richard II and Isabella, d. of Charles VI. (*1396—Battle of Nicopolis: Bulgaria a Turkish province*)

1397—Richard cedes Brest to France.

1399—Deposition of Richard II: usurpation of Henry IV. Arthur of Brittany created Duke of Richmond.

1401—Birth of Catherine of Valois. Murder of Richard II: return of Isabella of Valois to France.

1403—Birth of Charles of Viennois (Joan's *gentil Dauphin*).

1404—Death of Philip the Bold of Burgundy.
Accession of John the Fearless.
Henry Beaufort nominated as Bishop of Winchester
(*1404—death of Boniface IX: election of Innocent VII*
(*1406—death of Innocent VII: election of Gregory XII*)

1407—Murder of Louis Duke of Orléans: accession o
Charles Duke of Orléans.
(*1408—the Council of Pisa: election of 'Pope' Alexande
V 1409–10 and 'John XXII', 1410–15*)

1409—'Peace of Melun' between Isabella of Bavaria an
John the Fearless.
(*1410—election of Sigismund as Holy Roman Emperor*

1411—Civil war of Armagnacs and Burgundians begin
with a challenge from Orléans to Burgundy.

1412—Birth of Joan of Arc at Domrémy.

1413—Death of Henry IV of England: accession of Henr
V.

1415—Siege of Harfleur: battle of Agincourt. (*1415–
Council of Constance: John Huss executed: John Wycli
condemned: John XXII condemned: Gregory XII forced t
resign*)

1416—Treaty of Calais: Anglo-Burgundian alliance.

1417—Death of Jean le Dauphin: proclamation of Charle
as heir-apparent. (*1417—election of Martin V*)

1418—Seizure of Paris by John the Fearless: triumph o
John and Queen Isabella: siege and capture o
Rouen by the English.

1419—Murder of John the Fearless: accession of Philip th
Good: flight of Charles of Viennois. (*1419–36–
Hussite Wars in Bohemia*)

1420—Treaty of Troyes: marriage of Henry V an
Catherine of Valois and of Philip the Good an
Michelle of Valois.
Pierre Cauchon nominated Bishop of Beauvai
(*1420—à Kempis*, The Imitation of Christ *published*

1421—Birth of Henry VI.

1422—Death of Henry V and Charles VI: Henry VI pro
claimed in London and Paris—John of Bedfor
made Regent in France.
Charles VII proclaimed at Méhun-sur-Yèvre.

Henry of Gloucester, protector of England, allied with Jacqueline of Hainault.

1423—Treaty of Amiens between Bedford, Brittany and Burgundy: marriage of John V of Brittany to Marguerite of Burgundy and John of Bedford to Anne of Burgundy. (*Death of 'Benedict XIII': election 'Clement VIII'*)

1424—Battle of Verneuil: fall of Vitry: elimination of Scots contingents in the Valois army.

1425—Arthur of Richmond made Constable of France.
Georges de la Trémouille invited to Bourges.
Treaty of Saumur between John V and Charles VII.

1426—January: Bedford declares war on Brittany.
6 March: Battle of St Jacques: defeat of Arthur of Richmond.
3 July: Reaffirmation of the Triple Alliance.
Fall of Laval in Maine to the English: siege of Montargis.
First exile of Georges de la Trémouille.

1427—Murder of de Giac.
(?) First visit of Joan to Vaucouleurs.

1428—(? First and) second visit of Joan to Vaucouleurs.
Siege of Vaucouleurs.
12 October: Beginning of the siege of Orléans.
Cardinal Beaufort's crusade preached in England.

1429—January: Third visit of Joan to Vaucouleurs.
12 February: Battle of the Herrings.
(?) 23 February: Joan's arrival at Chinon.
25 February: Joan's first interview with Charles VII.
March 1–21: Joan interrogated at Poitiers.
22 March: Joan's first challenge to the English.
28 April: March on Orléans begun from Blois.
29 April: Joan enters Orléans.
7 May: fall of Les Tourelles: death of Glasdale.
8 May: siege of Orléans raised.
9 May: Joan and Jean the Bastard at Loches with Charles VII.
12 June: Capture of Jargeau.
15 June: Capture of Meung.
17 June: Capture of Beaugency.

18 June: Battle of Patay.

29 June: March on Rheims begun.

30 June: At Auxerre.

4 July: Before Troyes.

10 July: Capture of Troyes.

14 July: Fall of Chalons.

16 July: Fall of Rheims.

17 July: Coronation of Charles VII at Rheims.

August: Philip the Good appointed governor o
Paris: measures against English deserters.

8 September: Attack on Paris.

31 September: Army disbanded at Gien.

24 November: Siege of La Charité.

24 December: Letters patent of nobility granted t
Jean and Pierre 'du Lys' or Lis.

1430—8 January: Marriage of Philip the Good to Isabell
of Portugal.

April: Joan at Melun, Senlis, Lagny, Compiègne
Soissons.

23 April: Cardinal Beaufort's crusaders disembarke
at Calais.

22 May: Siege of Compiègne begun.

23 May: Joan captured at Compiègne.

25 May: University of Paris calls for Joan's con
demnation.

14 July: Pierre Cauchon delivers letters calling fo
Joan's surrender to himself. Joan at Beaulieu an
Beaurevoir.

25 October: Siege of Compiègne raised.

13 November: Death of the Lady of Beaurevoir.

December: Joan at Arras: surrendered to Pierr
Cauchon.

1431—3 January: Joan at Rouen.

9 January: Court assembled for Joan's trial.

21 February: First session of interrogation. (Feb
*ruary: death of Pope Martin V: accession of Eugene IV
ending of Cardinal Beaufort's legatine powers*)

10 March: 'Closed sessions' of interrogation i
prison begun.

17 March: Interrogations completed.

27 March: Reading of the *libellus* against Joan begun.

18 April: The charitable admonitions. (*8 May: executions of plotters against de la Trémouille*)

19 May: Letter of condemnation from University of Paris read.

23 May: Final admonitions.

24 May: Joan's abjuration at St-Ouen cemetery.

27 May: Joan resumes male dress.

28 May: Joan condemned as a relapsed heretic.

30 May: Joan's execution.

16 December: Coronation of Henry VI at Paris.

(*1 December: opening of Council of Basle*)

1432—Cardinal Beaufort cleared of treason charges (February).

Rouen attacked: execution of the attackers.

Georges de la Trémouille made Constable of France.

Death of Anne, wife of John of Bedford.

1433—Fall of Georges de la Trémouille: restoration to favour of Arthur of Richmond.

John of Bedford marries Jacquetta of Luxemburg.

1435—14 September: Death of John of Bedford.

21 September: Treaty of Arras between Burgundy and Charles VII.

1436—Surrender of Paris to Constable Richmond.

1436-9—Activities of Claude 'des Armoires'.

1436—Bastard of Orléans named Count of Dunois. ✓

Reorganization of the French army to combat the skinners.

1437—December: Charles VII enters Paris.

1442—Death of Pierre Cauchon at Lisieux.

(*1443—death of Felix V, antipope of the Council of Basle*)

1445—Marriage of Henry VI of England to Margaret of Anjou.

(*1447—death of Eugene IV: election of Nicholas V*)

1446—Death of Philip the Good; accession of Francis I as Duke of Burgundy.

Death of Georges de la Trémouille.

1448—Rouen falls to the French. (*1449—end of the Council of Basle*)

1450—Collapse of English resistance in Normandy.
      Bouillé's enquiry into Joan's death.
1452—Cardinal Estouteville's preliminary enquiry.
1453—Collapse of English resistance in Gienne. (*1453—
      Fall of Constantinople*)
1455-6—The process of rehabilitation. (*1455—death of
      Nicholas V: election of Calixtus III*)

Table Illustrating the Bastardy Theory of the Descent of Joan 'of Orléans'

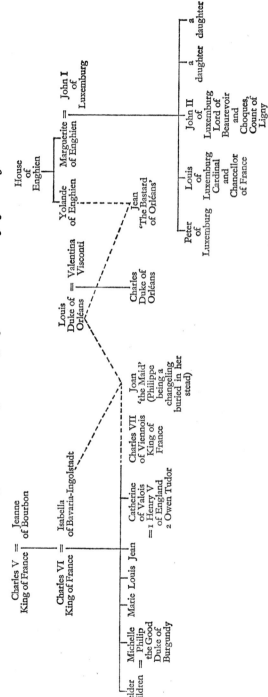

So that Charles VII, Joan 'the Maid (of Orléans)', Charles 'the Duke of Orléans' and Jean 'the Bastard of Orléans' were all half-siblings with a variety of mothers. Catherine of Valois was probably legitimate and Joan persuaded Charles that he was also.

King Ph
King of

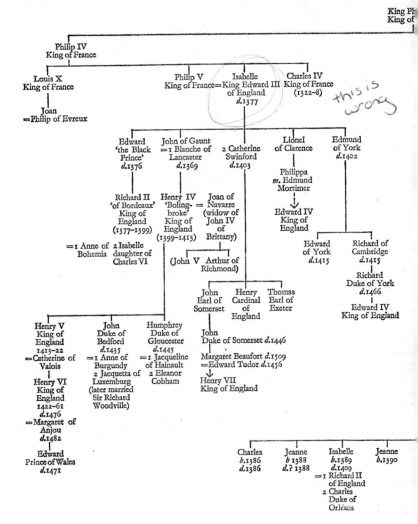

Philip IV
King of France

Louis X
King of France

Joan
=Philip of Evreux

Philip V
King of France

Isabelle
=King Edward III
of England
*d.*1377

Charles IV
King of France
(1322–8)

this is wrong

Edward
'the Black
Prince'
*d.*1376

John of Gaunt
=1 Blanche of
Lancaster
*d.*1369

2 Catherine
Swinford
*d.*1403

Lionel
of Clarence

Edmund
of York
*d.*1402

Richard II
'of Bordeaux'
King of
England
(1377–1399)

Henry IV
'Boling-
broke'
King of
England
(1399–1413)

=

Joan of
Navarre
(widow of
John IV
of
Brittany)

Philippa
m. Edmund
Mortimer

Edward IV
King of
England

=1 Anne of
Bohemia

2 Isabelle
daughter of
Charles VI

(John V Arthur of
Richmond)

Edward
of York
*d.*1415

Richard of
Cambridge
*d.*1415

Richard
Duke of York
*d.*1466

John
Earl of
Somerset

Henry
Cardinal
of
England

Thomas
Earl of
Exeter

Edward IV
King of England

Henry V
King of
England
1413–22
=Catherine of
Valois

John
Duke of
Bedford
*d.*1435
=1 Anne of
Burgundy
2 Jacquetta of
Luxemburg
(later married
Sir Richard
Woodville)

Humphrey
Duke of
Gloucester
*d.*1445
=1 Jacqueline
of Hainault
2 Eleanor
Cobham

John
Duke of Somerset *d.*1446

Margaret Beaufort *d.*1509
=Edward Tudor *d.*1456

Henry VII
King of England

Henry VI
King of
England
1422–61
*d.*1476
=Margaret of
Anjou
*d.*1482

Edward
Prince of Wales
*d.*1471

Charles
*b.*1386
*d.*1386

Jeanne
b 1388
d.? 1388

Isabelle
*b.*1389
*d.*1409
=1 Richard II
of England
2 Charles
Duke of
Orléans

Jeanne
*b.*1390

g Philip III of France

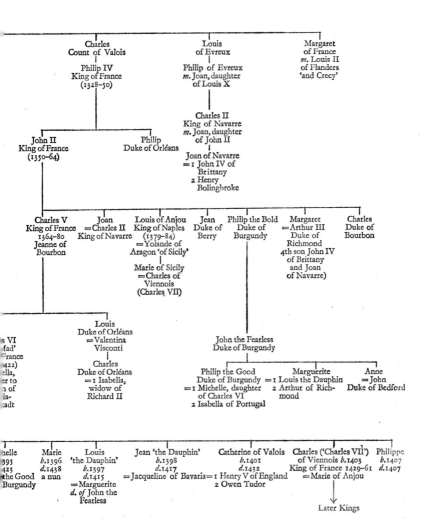

Index